Goodbye

Goodbye
In Search of
GORDON JENKINS

Bruce Jenkins

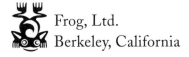

Frog, Ltd.
Berkeley, California

Published by Frog, Ltd.

Frog, Ltd. books are distributed by
North Atlantic Books
P.O. Box 12327
Berkeley, California 94712

Cover and book design by Paula Morrison
Printed in the United States of America
Distributed to the book trade by Publishers Group West

Library of Congress Cataloging-in-Publication Data

Jenkins, Bruce, 1948–
    Goodbye : in search of Gordon Jenkins / by Bruce Jenkins.
        p. cm.
    "Biography of famous composer, arranger, conducter, and performer Gordon Jenkins, by his son, who draws on his own intimate memories and reflections, as well as on interviews with celebrities who worked with his father"—Provided by the publisher.
        Discography: p. .
        ISBN 1-58394-126-6 (pbk.)
    1. Jenkins, Gordon. 2. Composers—United States—Biography. I. Title.
    ML410.J443J46 2005
    780'.92—dc22

                                    2005016430

        1 2 3 4 5 6 7 8 9 DATA 10 09 08 07 06 05

For Beverly

Other books by Bruce Jenkins
North Shore Chronicles: Big-Wave Surfing in Hawaii
A Good Man: The Pete Newell Story

Contents

Introduction

FRANK SINATRA ONCE TOLD ME that he and my father were the two saddest men. I only knew the half of it. But then, everyone knew about Sinatra.

My father always spoke of his life as beyond any sane man's expectations. He dated gorgeous women with rhythm and soul. He was a dominant musical figure in New York City for many years. With his quadruple-threat talent as composer, arranger, conductor and performer, he cut eight albums with Sinatra and worked intimately with Judy Garland, Louis Armstrong and Nat Cole. He had generous friends who laughed a lot, and he married a dream. In the thirty-six years our family had together, I never heard my parents even raise their voices to each other.

Sadness? Some would tell you that his music defined the word. Gordon Jenkins's string arrangements were a swirling backdrop to broken romance. He wrote more than his share of joyous material, but he is best remembered as a purveyor of deep regret. "Gordy, man, he was one sad cat," Sinatra said. "Beautifully so."

I knew what he meant, but vaguely. There was so much I didn't know, for Gordon Jenkins came from a generation of successful men who spoke little of their life. They didn't walk through the door high-fiving people or doing a celebratory dance. They worked like madmen and with great humility, because they were taught that way, and the self-promoters be damned.

At a time when he should have been savoring that wonderful life, easing into his seventies, Gordon Jenkins's whole world went to hell. Our beach house in Malibu burned straight to the ground. My parents had a searing, head-on car crash that left my uncle dead on the pavement. My father came down with ALS, Lou Gehrig's disease, and watched his body deteriorate without recourse for two hopeless years.

Even as a journalist, I never thought to activate his memory bank. I guess I felt it would cheapen the relationship somehow. It had always been true and pure, mostly unspoken, conveyed through smiles or glances. But I yearned for the details after his death, at the age of seventy-three, in 1984. I discovered a number of radio interviews he'd done over the years—tapes I never knew existed—and began researching his life through hundreds of interviews over a fifteen-year period. And that's what led me to Martha Tilton's house in fashionable West Los Angeles on a summer day in 1991.

They called her "Liltin' Martha Tilton" in her day, and she was a peach—sweet, pretty, and right on time. She sang with the Benny Goodman band for years, worked with just about everyone who mattered, and sang extensively with my father's orchestra in the early 1940s. They were called "Sweet and Serious" on one NBC radio show, and word came down they'd had a little affair. But mostly I wanted to ask her about "Goodbye," Goodman's longtime theme song, published in 1935 and played unfailingly at the end of every Goodman concert. We were about a half-hour into a delightful interview when I steered it that way.

"Well," she said, her bright smile fading, "there's a story behind that."

"Why don't you tell me, then."

"No."

"No?"

"If you don't know it, I'm not gonna tell ya," she said, and things pretty much stopped dead right there.

I did know a few things about the song. Gor, as I always called my dad, had written it during his stint with the famed Isham Jones band in the early Thirties. Jones had thrown it right back at him, saying it was too sad. In the meantime, Gor had become quite friendly with Goodman, socializing and playing tennis with him regularly in New York. "We used to hang around my Tudor City apartment, playing records and whatever, and he told me he was gonna get his own band together for the 'Let's Dance' radio program [1934]," Gor said in a radio interview years later. "I helped him get some guys, and he asked me if I had anything he could use for a theme song. So we're sitting there having a drink, fooling around with stuff, and I started playing 'Goodbye.' I played a couple bars and it was like the movies: Benny said, 'That's it, that's the one!'"

A number of critics, including Leonard Feather and Alec Wilder *(The American Popular Song)*, have rated it among their all-time favorites. "As sad a song as I know," wrote Wilder. "As beautifully as Goodman played it, Jenkins's afterthought phrases became so integral a part of the Goodman arrangement." Feather, writing in the *Los Angeles Times,* put it in his top ten among "songs that would be the hardest to tire of hearing."

"It was perfect for radio," said Los Angeles disc jockey/collector Chuck Cecil, "because the stations could fade out at any time. If you have only a few seconds, you need only three bars and if you're any kind of a Goodman fan, you know the show's over. Really a fantastic closing tune."

As the late Herb Caen wrote so passionately in the *San Francisco Chronicle* upon Goodman's death in 1986, the concerts were "bedlam. Gene Krupa riding his high hat like a dervish. Harry James puffing out his cheeks till surely they must burst, the rhythm always burning and churning and driving you out of your mind, and then, just when you thought nothing could get hotter, Benny's clarinet rising like a burnished bird out of the tightly controlled maelstrom and soaring to the heavens, outscreaming even the crowd. Orgasmic, yes. And then, after all the hours that went too fast, the plaintive melody of 'Goodbye,' and the audience, spent, filing out reluctantly in a sort of post-coital depression."

The song was recorded by many artists, from Sinatra (a rare use of the lyrics) to Marshall Royal, the lead saxophonist from Count Basie's band, but nothing ever touched a Goodman version, and from 1937 through 1939, Martha Tilton was right there on stage. It was killing me, what she said—or didn't say—in her living room so many years later.

After a long pause, she told me, "He didn't write it for Benny, you know. It was nothing that had to do with me, but … uh … I think this was before Gordon was married, a very long time ago. I think Gordon told me himself about it. But it's nothing that has to be.…"

"You sure got my curiosity up," I said.

"Well, I'm sorry I mentioned it."

About this time, Martha's husband, Jim Brooks, walked in and caught the drift. "He's a grown man, honey, it's all right."

"No, Jim, I just can't do it."

Three or four months went by. I asked around, friends and musicians, but nobody seemed to know that story. Finally I decided to call the Tilton home, praying that Jim Brooks would answer. He did. He seemed grateful that I was pressing the issue.

What happened, Jim told me, was that a very long time ago, my father had fallen deeply in love with someone, and before they really knew what was happening, she was pregnant. "In those days," said Jim, "if you got a girl in trouble, it was pretty much understood that you'd marry her."

On the day of birth, both mother and child died.

I'll never forget you
I'll never forget you
I'll never forget how we promised one day
To love one another forever that way
We said we'd never say
Goodbye
But that was long ago
Now you've forgotten, I know
No use to wonder why
Let's say farewell with a sigh
Let love die
But we'll go on living
Our own way of living
So you take the high road
And I'll take the low
It's time that we parted
It's much better so
But kiss me as you go
Goodbye

Chapter 1

Well Past Hollywood

THE BEACHES OF NORTH MALIBU were so quiet back then, my parents would slip off their clothes and make love in the dunes. This was years before we saw Katherine Hepburn standing gallantly out front, face to the wind. Before the likes of Steve McQueen, Robert Redford and Dustin Hoffman moved in. Before Ronald Reagan lived on one side of us and Beach Boys drummer Dennis Wilson—with special guest Charles Manson—on the other.

There wasn't much to see on Broad Beach Road in 1947, just a few scattered houses and the crashing surf. Gordon Jenkins, meanwhile, had lost his mind. The feeling around Hollywood was that he'd gone right off the edge. "Did you hear he moved to cow country?" they'd say. "And he doesn't even have a phone."

Gor had fled to the beach, a solid ten miles past the storied Malibu Colony, to get away from songpluggers, "idea" guys and assorted pains in the ass. If you had any thought of reaching him, you'd have to pray that he use the pay phone down the road. The rugged, two-hour drive didn't seem worth the trouble to see him in person, and it would probably take longer to get back. That's just how he wanted it. He became one of the few people, then or now, to live *exactly* on his terms.

He was a pretty big name by then, having written such standards as "P.S. I Love You" (pre-Beatles by a couple of generations),

"San Fernando Valley" (Bing Crosby vocal), "Blue Prelude" (Woody Herman's longtime theme song) and "Goodbye." His loving tribute to New York City, "Manhattan Tower," was the first concept album ever written, essentially a Broadway play on record and a huge success around the country. He was an established star on NBC radio, particularly with singer Dick Haymes and the "Auto-Lite" show. And I knew all that—sort of.

The thing was, we didn't live rich. There wasn't a hint of celebrity in the way he acted or the company he kept. For every rare visit by the likes of Jonathan Winters or Nat Cole, there was a constant flow of trumpet players, saxophonists, fishermen, lifeguards and just-plain neighbors. The style and conversation felt more country, in a sophisticated way, than upscale L.A.

The money would pour in, and he'd turn right around and spend it—on vacations, lavish meals, top-of-the-line recording equipment, the gambling tables of Las Vegas and particularly his hobbies. I got the occasional taste of his career, the chance to sit in on a Frank Sinatra recording session or watch Gor conduct a huge orchestra at the Hollywood Bowl. He even snuck me into a Vegas show, bare breasts and all, when I was *way* under age. But I knew him more as a carpenter, a man who built a huge workshop, filled it with the very best equipment and produced nearly half of the furniture in our house. I was astounded at his photography: state-of-the-art, black-and-white stills and meticulously edited 16-millimeter home movies, complete with special effects. Since he played golf virtually every day, he could have passed for a man of leisure, striking a pleasant balance between his seven-iron and a hip flask.

As all of this took place, in the early 1950s, he was entering his prime. He kicked off a magnificent relationship with Sinatra with the album "Where Are You?" He commuted constantly to New York, where he was Decca's top-selling talent and recorded with the likes of Ella Fitzgerald, Peggy Lee, Billie Holiday and the

McGuire Sisters. He had a memorable series of concerts in London with Judy Garland. He quite innocently launched the popularization of American folk music by bringing the Weavers into the recording studio at a time when nobody else would touch them. He reached his peak with the Grammy-winning album "September of My Years" with Sinatra in 1965, which included his signature arrangement ("It Was a Very Good Year") and the song that he considered his finest composition, "This Is All I Ask." And he was elected to the Songwriters Hall of Fame in 1982—as it happened, right along with Bob Dylan.

None of this made him as famous as, say, Nelson Riddle, Sinatra's most prominent arranger and a longtime hero of mine. I'd mention Gor's name around my high-school friends and get no reaction at all. Which was wonderful. I never felt like a special kid, nor was there any such mood around the house from my father or mother, Beverly, a nationally known singing star on radio before I came along (1948) and forced a shift in priorities.

The biggest thing I remember about Gor is the silence. He was always heavily preoccupied—and hell, if he was under the gun to orchestrate a forty-piece band for a Sinatra session by Tuesday, you wouldn't be real keen on barging in. He could be ardently stern and demanding, and he had no appreciable manners or social graces unless such behavior was absolutely necessary. People called him an eccentric, or worse, and only his close friends knew the truth, how he cried so openly at a beautiful piece of music, how he had one of the great laughs of all time, how a very simple thing—an act of kindness, or a baby's face—could melt him right down.

It wasn't until I heard from Lyle Spencer, an old friend, that I even considered bringing my dad's story to life. I knew Lyle from Santa Monica High, where we played basketball and worked on the school newspaper together. He was wise and soulful, a kid who grew up in the black part of town, understood the deep-down angles of sports and had exquisite taste in music. Lyle was a Motown/Stax guy, which connected us for life, but to my great surprise, his favorite record was "But I Loved Her," a Jenkins song made famous by Sinatra *("She was Boston/I was Vegas")*. He'd met my dad a couple of times and liked his style. A sportswriter himself, Lyle approached me with the book idea in the press box of the Oakland Coliseum about a year after Gor's death, and he reinforced the notion in a subsequent letter.

"I'd say it first hit me in Denver, the winter of 1981–1982 as I watched a Sinatra TV special," he wrote. "And there was that one tune, still the best song I've ever heard. Listening to the magic of that Jenkins music made me wish I'd known more about the man. I guess I'd been carrying that thought around all that time. For a giant in the field, he was a gentle, compassionate man. I think you're blessed in so many ways to have a legacy like that to give to the world."

The book project became sort of a running joke around my household, because it seldom left the back burner. I began the research in 1987 and didn't start writing until the spring of 2001. "You know what a shrink would say," observed my friend Bonnie DeSimone, of the *Chicago Tribune*. "That the project somehow keeps him alive." Without a doubt. I wrote two other books, got a newspaper column, had three lovely daughters and did extensive magazine work during those fifteen years, but it was true; I didn't want the research to end. As late as 2000, I got interviews with Billy May and Johnny Mandel that gave the story a bit more flavor. The whole process went that way. I just kept learning more about a man who had spoken only vaguely of his life, seldom offering specifics of any kind.

Martha Tilton's "Goodbye" story was a stunner, to say the least. So was my interview with Gor's first wife, Nancy, who was in her seventies and had not fully recovered from their breakup some forty years before. She spoke of his carousing and philandering and left me feeling devastated as I left her apartment. I discovered that my dad's blunt nature—a lack of finesse, shall we say—cost him a friendship and working relationship with Bing Crosby, who held the grudge for the rest of his life. And then there was Jonathan Schwartz, the prominent New York disc jockey who has loudly pronounced his disgust with Jenkins's music over the years. Once he was certain I hadn't arrived to throw punches, he explained his reasoning in harrowing detail.

Most of the interviews, though, revealed my father's nature as a true romantic. Maria Cole told me that Nat proposed to her with "Manhattan Tower" playing in the background. Director Nora Ephron, who has used his music extensively in her films, said she was "obsessed" with him as a teenager. I invariably played it straight with my notepad and tape recorder, not trying to elicit any particular response, but some two dozen people were in tears by the end of the interview, overcome by the power of his string arrangements and the fact that he was gone.

Early on, right around the summer of 1987, I made a run at Sinatra. My mother had the private line for his A-1 secretary, Dorothy, who seemed to think it might work. "The way he loved your dad," she said, "I'm sure he'd love to talk to you." So I waited. And waited some more. There's a fine line somewhere between persistence and annoyance, so I'd check in every few months. "Oh, he definitely wants to see you," she'd say. "It's just that he's so busy right now."

The Sinatras had purchased a house on Broad Beach Road, less than a half-mile from ours, and while they weren't out there much, I did try to make contact with his wife, Barbara. One afternoon I strolled down there, like a neighbor borrowing sugar, and left a little note in their mailbox. She got my hopes up with a phone call ("Friday sounds good"), but then made herself unavailable until that Sunday ("It's just too frantic"). She didn't really get the whole Sinatra-Jenkins thing, and I never heard from her again. I was blown off like an encyclopedia salesman with gas.

Most everyone else was trying to stifle laughter. They couldn't believe I even had the notion of interviewing Sinatra. "I've always said I'll give $100,000 reward to anyone who can answer three simple questions," the great lyricist Sammy Cahn told me. "How's Frank, where's Frank, and when will he be here. So don't feel alone."

I told Ronnie Gilbert, of the Weavers, that I'd get Sinatra if I had to climb his massive security gate. "You may have to climb over the Pope, is what I hear," she said. And Johnny Green nailed it solid: "It's just ridiculous. Can you imagine being that unattainable? You'll have more trouble getting to Sinatra than Columbus had getting here from Ferdinand and Isabella."

Right on cue, I floundered on the Sinatra front for months. But there were many destinations in the search to bring my sad and silent father to life. I had to go back to the very start, in a little suburb of St. Louis called Webster Groves, the place where he was born and "spent twenty-one humid summers," as he once said, "all of them horrible." I chose the month of August for my visit. So much more sultry that way.

Chapter 2

The Prodigy

THE TOWNSFOLK WERE APPALLED. Family members hid their eyes. Gordon Jenkins, president of the junior class, had abandoned high school to work in a St. Louis speakeasy.

The kid who looked so promising—ace of the Poetry Club, heartthrob of the female set, son of a distinguished church organist—had gone across town to play piano for a bunch of drunks. Surely there was no hope for him now. Gracious, could you get any more tawdry?

If you could, he wanted to find out how.

Webster Groves is a delightful little suburb if you like convention, small-town obedience and a life without surprises. My father couldn't wait to get out of there. He wanted to get the hell surprised out of him. There was a kind of destiny to it all, a fantasy of bright lights, uptown jazz, champagne toasts and the infectious chatter of horn-honking traffic. Gordon Jenkins was a New Yorker when he was four. He just happened to be nineteen when he showed up for real.

I had seen it all so clearly on the two or three visits my family made to Webster Groves in the 1950s. I'd already been to New York, spent many months there, had it in my blood. We invariably hit Missouri in summertime, with an oppressive brand of heat that slowed everything to a standstill. There seemed to be no movement in the town, not a single thing happening of consequence. And there, on the porch of the Jenkins house at 41 Plant Avenue, was his aging mother, Angelica, gently rocking away.

I wish I could have met his father, who had died many years before. We're all "Jenks," as it turns out. William Marshall Jenkins went by that nickname, my dad sort of inherited it, and I came upon it independently among my closest friends in California. The details of the Jenkins family history aren't terribly exciting—clean and simple living, accentuated by the distance my father crafted from his brother and sisters—but I like the Jenks angle. It lends a little jolt of recognition. People described my grandfather as a thin, reserved fellow who didn't say much, so when I learned that he liked to make people laugh by playing tortured, off-key versions of popular songs, it was a gem of information.

He played a mighty organ, old Will. Newspaper accounts spoke of his soul-stirring renditions of religious and classical material— and the occasional bouncy, let's-dance material at social functions. He had been playing church organs since he was ten years old. Invariably the house was filled with music, emanating from an elegant Smith-American parlor organ with five octaves, and there were times when it proved to be a most worthy tonic.

I had never heard of George Rowan Jenkins, the second of Will's five children. My father never spoke of him and, in fact, never knew him. Born in 1894, little George seemed to have inherited all of his dad's musical talent, with a few bars to spare. The two of them used to sit down and play the piano together, and even at the age of four, George could carry a melody and change keys with his one-fingered stabs. And then he vanished. Struck down by the kind of lightning-bolt disease that characterized the times, he was taken without warning on Christmas Day 1898. They say Will was a teetotaler of the highest order, but come the holidays, he felt an overwhelming sense of melancholy. Every Christmas—and that day only—he reached for a shot of brandy.

Nearly a dozen years passed before Gordon came along, on the 12th of May 1910. His sisters, Anne and Evelyn, and brother Marshal all played the piano quite capably, but they were soon dwarfed by Gordon's prowess. This was like seeing little Rowan again, a true prodigy, a talent that seemed bestowed by a higher power.

"One thing I distinctly remember is that he learned to read at the age of two," said Jean Shirley, Anne's daughter. "Nobody believed this, but it was true. Some woman dared my grandmother to prove it, so she brought out the Bible and Gordon read from it—of course, having no idea what any of it meant." One night when he was three, Anne recalled, "He sang the hymn 'Holy, Holy, Holy' in his sleep at the top of his voice. The whole family was standing around the crib, entranced."

The signature moment came when he was four, said Evelyn, "the day papa and I took him to see a stage presentation of 'The Wizard of Oz.' He spent the whole show just staring at the conductor, and when it was over, he pointed up there and said, 'I want to be like him.' When we got home, he went to the piano, and with one finger played the music he had caught by ear."

By this time Will had become dean of the Missouri Guild of Organists, and he had taken a side job at a music store to help support the family. With such convenient access, he decided that Gordon was ready for his own piano at the age of six. Rather than have it delivered, Will borrowed a horse and wagon, got the thing sturdily mounted and asked a friend to take the reins. What an image: Little Gordon was playing outside the house when his father came around the corner, clippity-clop, merrily playing the shining new gift.

"Things just kind of took off from there," said Allan Clark, one of Gordon's friends from early childhood. "One day the two of us took the afternoon off from school and bravely went into downtown St. Louis just to look around. Somehow we wound up in

Famous & Barr, the big department store. I guess we were seven or eight years old. Gordon went unerringly to the piano department and sat right down to play a flawless 'Sweet Lorraine.' The sales staff was astounded."

Angelica Jenkins—a name that carries on through my middle daughter—lived to be ninety years old, finally passing away in 1959. By that time, Gordon was a full-fledged celebrity, having worked with just about every big name in the business. It's a shame that Will never got to enjoy his son's good fortune. They shared a love of music, photography and baseball, which was quite a gold mine in St. Louis during my dad's upbringing (the Browns had the great George Sisler, among others, in the 1920s; the Cardinals had some of their best-ever teams, featuring Grover Cleveland Alexander, Sunny Jim Bottomley, Rogers Hornsby and my dad's personal favorite on name alone, Wee Willie Sherdel). But Gordon was just twenty-two when his dad died in 1932, at the age of sixty-five, and the family connection suffered badly from that point on. Gordon adored his mother, wrote her at every opportunity, stopped into the house from time to time. But he was so completely different from his brother and sisters, a veritable bohemian in a house full of squares, that he maintained only a token relationship with them. They seemed filled with remorse, particularly Evelyn, who devoted her life to collecting snapshots, newspaper clippings and memorabilia of Gordon's career. He essentially turned his back on them—just as he had done on Webster Groves High in 1927.

I was astounded to learn that he had been president of the junior class. I guess it was typical of a man who cast aside most of his awards and never could find the Grammy he'd won; if any golden words came forth about his career, they were spoken by others. But when I asked him where he went to college, he replied, "I only got through the eleventh grade," and the subject was quickly dropped. He wasn't embarrassed that he'd gone to work in a nightclub, but it wasn't necessarily the lifestyle he endorsed—especially to his own son.

He was just on a different path, period, from the very start. He bypassed the high-school band and orchestra altogether, feeling he was way past that noise. He took exactly three months of music lessons in his life, at fourteen, from a strait-laced, classically trained piano teacher named Mrs. Stevenson. "I can't teach you anything," she concluded, and there went his formal training. All of his ability, from conducting to arranging to playing virtually any instrument with a degree of professionalism, was entirely self-taught.

Years later, an interviewer marveled at the stories about Gordon, how he could instinctively arrange a complicated number for a sixty-piece orchestra in a matter of minutes. "It didn't look hard to me," Gor answered. "I remember how it all started: I was about thirteen or fourteen, sittin' at the piano with some sheet music, and I thought, hell, *somebody* wrote that down. I never heard of him; why can't I do that? I couldn't read music, but I could figure out the notes in an hour or so. So I took a song I'd heard around the house, 'Song of India,' and tried to write it down. Eventually I figured out what the chords were, and it all worked out pretty good. I showed it to somebody, and they said, 'Yeah, that's Song of India.' It just wasn't too hard."

Gordon and some talented friends already had some experience playing shanty taverns around town at $3 a night. The idea of hooking up with a speakeasy seemed perfectly natural—"wheeling his battered piano from table to table," wrote *Time* magazine years later, "collecting $40 to $60 in tips from enthusiastic bootleg-whisky drinkers." He actually tried joining his brother in a band for a while —Gordon on banjo, Marshal on piano—"but Marshal just quit after a while," Gor recalled. "He didn't like the life: the hours, the drinking, the musicians. I stuck with it. I liked all of those things."

Jean Shirley: "Do you know that he was only three months away from graduation when he left school? People were shocked, told him quite sternly that he'd live to regret it. I remember one of our cousins once said to grandmother in a very somber tone, 'Just how long is your son going to play in bars?' She said, 'Just as long as your sons go to drink in them.' And my goodness, the girlfriends. There was always some girl in love with him, knocking on the door."

Someone took a liking to Gordon at KMOX, to this day the biggest radio station in St. Louis, and hired him to entertain. He grabbed that ball and ran like the wind: "I'd open the station at 9 a.m. and play the piano for fifteen minutes. Then I'd use another name and play the organ for fifteen minutes. At 9:30, I would go on the air as 'Abe Snake, the piano-accordion virtuoso.' At 9:45 I was someone else, playing the ukulele, and at 10 o'clock, if no one else had shown up yet, I would take it from the top and do the whole thing over again. I'd been playing the banjo since I was four, so I threw that in there, too. I was about sixteen, and I could read notes and play six instruments at that time. If nothing else, it gave me a sense of my own worth—that I was somebody who could do something."

Meanwhile, he had landed a summer job at Wildwood Springs, a resort hotel in the Ozarks, playing sprightly music for the dinnertime crowd. "My first band," he said. "All of three pieces." The sax player, Wally Simmons, had known Gordon since they were tiny kids. "We played three summers up there," he said. "Then Gordon got a little ahead of us. We have a pretty solid musical tradition around here [Missouri], the likes of Glenn Miller, Coleman Hawkins, Yank Lawson, Jess Stacy, Pee Wee Russell, Bix Beiderbecke, Frankie Trumbauer—and Miles Davis was from across the river in Brooklyn, Illinois. I always put Gordon in that company. He could play any song, any chord, any key at any time. And he had perfect pitch. You could drop a spoon on the floor and he'd tell you exactly the note. If you've got a big band playing, if somebody hits an E flat instead of E natural, he'll not only hear it, he'll tell you which guy did it."

I asked Wally if Gor had ever played with Beiderbecke, the trumpeting legend, as some reports indicated. "No, and it would have been so easy for him to make that claim," he said. "A lot of guys would have said, 'Oh, sure, lots of times.' Gordon said, 'No, he was a little ahead of me—although I probably sat on the same barstool he did.' He wouldn't lie to better himself."

And he never groveled to get a job—mostly because they fell right in his lap. "My whole life's been like someone planned it for me," Gor once said. "I joined the union on a Thursday, in 1928, and I got my first job on a Saturday with the Joe Gill band [the biggest and best in town, playing out of the Hotel Chase]. That was the first arranging I'd ever done and I made a ton of mistakes, but Joe could see that I had something, and he put up with it all. Then, just before sound films came around, I got a job at the Fox Theater, which in those days had a big orchestra to play numbers between shows. I had a very sympathetic conductor who would let me try any arrangement I wanted, and if it didn't come off, I could try something else. That's the best possible education, when you're 18 and you've got ideas, and you can try things without its costing anybody anything. It beats any school in the world.

"Of course, the sound films put all those little orchestras out of business, but the theater owners got together and came up with one big orchestra. And who should they appoint to conduct this thing but my friend who'd been helping me before. He says, 'Kid, these are the numbers we're going to play. Make me an overture.' I said OK, like I knew everything. I wasn't bright enough to know that people had written books about instrumentation, so I just walked over to the union, went up to the bartender and said, 'Point me a bassoon player.' He says, 'Right over there, playing pinochle.' So I went over and said, 'Excuse me, I want you to tell me the range and the key that the bassoon is in.' He said sure, put his cards down, wrote it out for me. I said thank you very much, are there any oboe players around here [laughter]? That's the only way I can explain it. I ran all of these guys down, wrote down what they told me, put an arrangement together and it sounded great—at least to me. It's a miracle that it came off at all."

Simmons: "You can't imagine what kind of nerve that took, a kid with no experience going around like that, taking jobs he knew almost nothing about. Next thing you know he's down in the pit at the Fox Theater, playing piano and doing beautiful arrangements for a big band—best job in town. That's right about the time he dropped the whole business and went cold turkey to New York. Figured he'd pretty much exhausted the possibilities around here."

He was nineteen years old. Years later, at the mention of St. Louis or Webster Groves, he'd make a hilariously sour face. But he left behind a pretty good chunk of his heart. He never forgot his favorite spots in town, his mother's cooking, the friends and holidays, finding that first girlfriend with rhythm. Such memories made a terrific theme for wartime, just the thing for a lonesome American stationed overseas, and the images all came forth in the 1945 hit that Frank Sinatra recorded for Columbia, "Homesick, That's All":

> *I miss the thrill of grammar-school romances*
> *I miss the junior prom and graduation dances*
> *The gossip in assembly halls*
> *I'm homesick, that's all.*
> *I miss the gang that hangs around at Miller's*
> *Devouring chocolate sodas with the whipped cream fillers*
> *The girl I promised I'd call*
> *I'm homesick, that's all.*
> *I miss the midnight services on Christmas Eve*
> *And the joy when Christmas morning came.*

I miss the scramble for the wishbone every Sunday
And the big Thanksgiving football game.*
I miss the times I had to set the table
I miss the rolls my mother made when she was able
The fragrant bonfires in the fall
I'm homesick, that's all.

Sometime around 1960, when the Jenkins home was sold, a Mr. Tanner moved in at 41 Plant Avenue. I'm not sure if my father actually sent the following letter or composed it for his own amusement, but I found it in a stack of old papers one day:

Dear Mr. Tanner:

I consider myself an authority on this house, having lived in it for 15 very happy years. A few hints that you might find helpful:

Stay out of the bedroom to the right of the bathroom in the wintertime. For some reason that I could never fathom, that room never got any heat, and as I was the youngest, it was assigned to me. I was in my teens before I realized that everyone didn't sleep in a freezing room.

When you get down to the basement, see if there are any baseball cards still on the walls. If you see a Rogers Hornsby or Tris Speaker, they were put there by my older brother, who couldn't understand why Mother wouldn't name me Honus Wagner Jenkins.

If you have a basketball that needs inflating, I highly rec-

---

*In the fall of 2002, *Sports Illustrated* devoted a lengthy piece to the annual showdown between the Webster Groves Statesmen and the Kirkwood Pioneers, describing it as the essence of high-school competition and America's small-town culture. The series dates back to 1907.

ommend the floor heater in the front hall. Just leave it there a few seconds, and it firms up real good. Of course, when it cools, you're worse off than before, but you can't have everything.

Should you feel the desire to pole vault, that bare place in the side yard is the spot for it. I did fine, up to about four feet, and then took a fall that sent me back to tennis immediately.

The front porch was our gathering place, of a summer night. Instead of television, or even radio, we kids caught lightning bugs and put them in jars, while Mother just rocked, rocked and rocked. Soon after I discovered that people would pay me for playing the piano, I had it screened for her, thereby disappointing 231,009 mosquitoes who had our family pegged as their very own.

You may notice a faint smell of tobacco in the bathroom. I naturally had to smoke because the drummer and bass player did, and having promised Mother I wouldn't, I used to go into the bathroom and puff away, positive that I was fooling all concerned.

It's quite possible you may hear music in the living room, without any equipment turned on. I'm sure there must be some left over, as everyone in the family played the piano, all the time. I struck my first chord in that room, two little notes, and I can still remember the excitement, how two were so much nicer than one.

I'll get back to Webster Groves someday, back to the heat and humidity and the profound absence of motion. Since my last visit in 1988, I have felt an undeniable urge to return. I don't expect to see much, meet anyone or do a single thing worth mentioning. I do hope to hear things.

Chapter 3

A Seat Up Front

"It was raining the first time I saw my tower ... my heart beat faster than the raindrops as I looked up and saw it painted against the sky."
—*From the opening passage of "Manhattan Tower," 1945*

THE GREAT CITY WAS RUNNING OUT OF TIME. Not a soul could know. I jumped in a cab at 42nd and Lexington and headed for the airport, memories of a wonderful assignment (the U.S. Open tennis tournament) still fresh in my mind. It was a beautiful, clear morning, September 10, 2001, the last innocent day in New York.

Back home the following day, I watched the horrifying images on television while my two-year-old daughter demanded puzzles and Cheerios. Manhattan's two greatest towers were tumbling to the ground. I had flown on United Airlines from Newark to San Francisco, a death flight just twenty-four hours later, and my wife clung to me, hard.

There is no shaking the images of American jetliners slamming into the World Trade Center. No geographical distance, nor the passage of time, can lessen the impact. The event is forever yesterday, with all the disturbing implications of a family catastrophe. My blind-luck story was insignificant against the barren Ground Zero landscape, but I felt an overwhelming sense of loss. If there's one thing I inherited from my father, it was a raging love affair with New York City.

I grew up playing an only-child's games in the back yard while my parents and their friends sat in the studio, deeply immersed in "Manhattan Tower," the story of a young man who comes to the city and meets the woman of his dreams. As shy and humble as Gor seemed at times, he enjoyed playing his own music for people who truly appreciated it. They didn't chat or make small talk; they sat down and *listened,* no distractions allowed.

The whole scene was way too heavy for a grade-school boy; I felt spectacularly uncomfortable on the few occasions I entered that room. At that age, you don't really care how much somebody loves the damn town, or how desperately he fell in love. But it was important, I knew that, and even then I had some vital snapshots in my mind: high-level views of Central Park, a busy midtown street, being wheeled in a stroller to nursery school. Because my dad kept going back to New York—for work, for any old reason—I spent more than two years of my early childhood there.

As I grew older, I found that I kept going back, feeling a greater rush of exhilaration each time. The *Chronicle* sports page became my vehicle—the Open, the NBA playoffs, baseball stops with the Giants or Oakland A's—and for the only times in my life, I felt the riveting sensation of being cut from my father's mold. I loved the town unconditionally and assumed a separate personality there, drinking heavily, socializing at all hours, frequenting nightclubs, walking the streets endlessly at night. I felt I was doing my best work there, that nothing could ever go wrong. Nor did it—until a bunch of terrorists killed thousands of innocent people behind the incomprehensible belief that they would be rewarded with praise and comely virgins in the sweet hereafter.

In the wake of September 11, "Manhattan Tower" is an absurd fantasy—conceivable, one would imagine, but nothing you'd display in public. A lot of people felt that way at the time, finding Gordon Jenkins's New York to be a place they did not recognize, but skeptics formed the minority back then. World War II had just ended; it was a time of pride and great hope in this country. People sang to each other in the movies, and audiences found few things more invigorating than an old-fashioned love story.

Such themes were a staple on the Auto-Lite (sparkplugs) radio show, out of Hollywood, in the early 1940s. As the bandleader and musical director, Jenkins and head writer Tom Adair crafted jaunty mini-operas each week for the marvelous singer Dick Haymes and a huge cast of characters. It was a wildly successful show, first on NBC and then CBS, and it was enjoying a special New York run, in August 1945, when "Manhattan Tower" began to take shape. Gor had been a full-time New Yorker from 1933 through 1937, having the time of his life, before career opportunities took him west. Now he was back, for a month, acting like one of those lucky guys in the movies.

"Showing off, playing the part of the big orchestra leader, I took a suite in the Ritz Tower Hotel at 57th and Park," he said. "Friends, musicians and ad-agency people started coming up there as a gathering place, and we had about a three-week party. Not anything too wild, staying up all night or anything, just everybody having a wonderful time for days on end. I was making a bundle of money, throwing it around like it was going out of style, and I had a lot of nice people around me. New York always knocked me out. I just thought I'd try to write it down."

It came to him in a rush, aboard a train from New York to California. "I had an elaborate scheme cooked up with my manager to intentionally miss the train, assuring us of a few more days in New York," he wrote on the inside cover of the complete "Tower" sheet music for Pickwick Music Corporation in 1946. But he was due back in L.A. for the resumption of the Haymes show, and he was left with his homesick thoughts as the train steamed west. "I began forming it in my mind, and when we got back to L.A., I was worried that the pressure of radio work would prevent me from ever getting it down on paper. Luckily for me, the war came to an end right then, and I had a week off. I wrote the lyrics and narration the first day, and the music and orchestration the next four." Meanwhile, he was already checking the train and airline schedules, obsessed with the idea of getting back to New York as soon as possible.

"I mean, this is how crazy he was about the place," said music publisher Sam Weiss. "He gets back to California and he's got this lovely home in the San Fernando Valley, but there's not a damn thing going on. He says, 'Sam, I got used to the noise back there. It excited me. I can't think of a better background for writing an arrangement than a bunch of garbage trucks going by. It's too quiet out here.'"

As viewed on paper, the "Tower" script doesn't sound like much. A man named Steven visits New York, meets Julie, and falls hard. He takes a fancy hotel suite—his Manhattan tower—and throws terrific parties. It seems that the entire city is celebrating their romance. But when it comes time for him to leave, they must go their separate ways. He tells of his heartbreak, but of a promising future that will see him visit that tower once again. Gordon's trumpet-playing friend Bruce Hudson was certain it would never sell, telling him, "You're the only guy in the world who feels this way about New York. Who's gonna buy it?" Over lunch at the Brown Derby, songwriting icon Johnny Mercer told Gor the script was "too saccharine—not up to your standards, I don't think." But neither man had actually heard it. "I played on the date," said Hudson. "The minute you heard it, you realized it was a masterpiece."

When people speak of "concept" albums, they generally point to Sinatra's 1955 collaboration with Nelson Riddle, "In the Wee

Small Hours," as the ground-breaker. And it was, in terms of all songs connecting to a single theme. But "Manhattan Tower" was a full, uninterrupted story, the first of its kind, originally timed in 17 minutes for release on two 12-inch 78s. "For a while, I couldn't give it away," Gor said. "Columbia, Victor and Capitol all turned it down, before Decca finally took it. You couldn't hear it on the radio, it didn't get any special publicity, and it just kind of sat there for months. The sponsor of the Haymes show wouldn't even let me do it, because he was afraid it would offend people in Detroit. But [Decca president] Jack Kapp was adamant about that record. He'd already pressed far more 78s than anybody thought he could sell."

The recording session was a marvel in itself, with a narrator, sound effects, original songs, a full orchestra and chorus, and two lead singers: Bill Lee and Beverly Mahr (my mother, about to become Mrs. Gordon Jenkins). "We made it in one 17-minute take," said narrator Elliott Lewis, who got a three-hour leave from the Army to make the date in September 1945. "We didn't have any choice, there was no audiotape back then. If somebody made a mistake in the last minute, you'd have to start the whole thing over. Tell the kids today you made a 17-minute take with that many people, and they'd just walk away. Wouldn't believe it."

As Decca producer Milt Gabler recalled, "It took months for people to get wise to how great 'Tower' was, but when they did, it was a revelation. Hell, Gordy wound up playing it on the Ed Sullivan Show [February 1950], everybody just loving it, and that was nearly five years after it was recorded. When the Beatles did 'Sergeant Pepper,' I sent him an album with a note that said, 'Look how the sonofabitches are stealing your stuff.' Everybody said Sergeant Pepper was an innovation, and that's the credit it gets. But the original, the first pop concept album, was 'Manhattan Tower.'"

"People don't realize it," said music publisher Howie Richmond, "the way they don't know that Orson Welles introduced certain film techniques. But that's a valid comparison. This was the most advanced stage in the history of recording, a true performance, the first intelligent use of an LP. It's one of the crowning achievements of modern recorded music."

The 17-minute version is a real gem, with its thrilling introduction—a swirl of horns and strings creating the noisy excitement of a New York street—and the party, with a waiter named Noah and the uplifting song "New York's My Home." The work was later expanded into a two-sided Capitol LP, and the honest truth is that most of the new material was over-the-top corny, especially by today's standards. But there was one big exception: a wordsmith's delight called "Married I Can Always Get," perhaps the most enduring piece from "Manhattan Tower." My mother sang it—few could, with its severe demands of range—and it has held up splendidly over the years:

> I want to dance
> Until the darkest heavens turn gray
> Until the dawn strolls in with the day
> Then I'll say
> Don't let the band get away
> But matrimony? I'm not ready yet
> Married I can always get.
> It's not for me
> With all its smug connubial joys
> That ever constant smashing of toys
> Wrecks your poise
> While hubby is out with the boys
> No wedding gown for this silhouette
> Married I can always get.
> I'll live the life that I'm used to
> I'll get a ring when I choose to

Because by now, I have found
That the nicest rings are on a merry-go-round
I'll be blasé
With any man whose motives are base
I'll keep each wily wolf in his place
'Til the chase
Finally ends in embrace
But as for wedlock, unlock me, my pet
Married I can always get.

"I always felt that 'Manhattan Tower' was a powerful thing," said Steve Allen, the beloved comic who died not long after our interview. "I was working radio in L.A. at the time, and it was a very big seller in town. The people with good taste all seemed to have that album. Arrangers, musicians, just hip people in general. It was so fresh and different. They were in awe of Gordon's work."

It must have felt strange to him, all that adulation, because he spent the better part of the Great Depression in resolute awe of New York's finest musicians. When I spoke with Weiss, a giant in the publishing business back then, his most vivid memory was of a Sunday evening in May 1936 at the Imperial Theater—by most accounts the greatest jazz festival ever held. It seemed that a musical era faded into history that night, and another one began.

Gordon Jenkins was relatively new on the New York scene, just twenty-six years old and coming on fast. All the big-orchestra guys knew his name, from his arrangements for the Isham Jones band, and he was a full-time habitué of 52nd Street, internationally famous for its sensational row of jazz clubs. "Gordon was a regular at the Onyx," Weiss said. "He lived to come in that club. Art Tatum, Jack Teagarden, Red Norvo—Gordon just flipped over those guys, and it became a very popular place. Then the owners got this idea to do a big concert at the Imperial, one of the finest concert halls in the city. Gordy knew I was handling the tickets, and he told me to get him as close to the stage as humanly possible. Well, I got him in the very first row.

"The show was incredible: Benny Goodman, Artie Shaw, Paul Whiteman, the Casa Loma orchestra, Bunny Berigan, a bunch of small combos—maybe fifty acts altogether. It started at eight and lasted way into the morning hours, and Gordy never left his spot. I think his favorite guy, Louis Armstrong, came on last, and I can still remember looking down and seeing Gordy falling all over his seat, just *living*."

The event came to be characterized as New York's first "swing music" concert, a pulsating evolution out of the Dixieland years. As described in *The Street That Never Slept*, Arnold Shaw's reminiscence on 52nd Street, "It was historic and new and different, and the place was absolutely packed. Jamming the aisles, crowding the orchestra pit, standing in the back." The book quotes Gor as saying, "It was an evening when you felt that things were happening   and the swing era did begin about that time."

And there he was, front row, his feet up on the rail of the orchestra pit, going crazy. Some musical historians should take note of that scene. Portrayed in a number of books and articles as sullen, standoffish and lacking any semblance of personality, my father was hardly that. Not when it counted. He was hell at a dullards' convention, but toss him into the heart of a musical treasure, and nobody swung harder.

He was nineteen when he first saw New York, and he would never view his native St. Louis in quite the same way. It became merely a place to visit, to say hi to the folks, on his way back to the big time. "It's funny, even when he was broke, he always acted like he belonged in New York," said his childhood friend Wally Simmons. "He'd just gotten married [to Nancy Harkey, a high-school sweetheart], and he had a ton of confidence in himself. Didn't know a soul, but he started selling his talents around town. There was this one band whose arranger had gone out to the coast temporarily, and Gordon marched right in there and announced, 'I can arrange as good as he can.' They gave him a tryout, and of course he made it."

Another hometown friend, Allan Clark, told me that Gor would go without two meals a day "just so he could save up for a window table at fancy places like Sardi's. This let the other guys know that Gordon Hill Jenkins was doing plenty OK, even though he was hungry most of the time and looked like he weighed about 120 pounds."

He happened to be back in St. Louis, in January 1932, when the Chicago-based Isham Jones band came to town. Jenkins was the hottest local name, and when Jones's piano player disappeared for a couple of days, drunk on his ass, Gor got an audition. "It was so cold when they brought me in, I couldn't move my hands," he said years later on "The Swing Thing" radio show with Fred Hall. "Jones was wearing an overcoat, indoors, as he was listening to me. But somehow I got the job. He told me to show up in Cincinnati and pick up the band there, which I did. By that time the piano player had sobered up and come back, so they kept me on as an arranger."

The Jones band, still regarded as one of the finest ever assembled, was a soothing remedy for Depression times. Although he hardly looked the part, Jones was a lyrical dreamer of the highest order, having written "It Had To Be You," "I'll See You in My Dreams," "Swingin' Down the Lane," and many other hit songs. It was Jones and his most prominent violinist, Victor Young, who first targeted the potential of "Stardust," a Hoagy Carmichael tune lying dormant at the time, and their 1930 arrangement gave the song its first significant popularity.

In *The Big Bands*, by George T. Simon, Jones was described as "a somber, long-faced gent who looked more like a strict manual arts teacher than a leader of one of the most romantic-sounding bands of all times. He had a way of getting his men to phrase in long, flowing lines, so they sounded as if they never inhaled, and it was a sound that other bandleaders didn't forget. Often I'd hear one of them, having second thoughts about going too far out as a swing band, say such things as 'What we really should do is sound like the old Isham Jones band.' Gene Krupa was emphatic about trying. So was Lionel Hampton. Neither could bring it off, however."

Ziggy Elman, the mercurial trumpet ace of the Goodman band, told writer Dave Dexter Jr. that Jones "had the greatest sound of the dance orchestras. No one else came close." As Gor once told an interviewer, "It wasn't a jazz band by any stretch of the imagination, but we had some great jazz players [including Woody Herman, Red Ballard and Jack Jenney]. It was the greatest sweet ensemble of that time or any other time."

I caught up with Dexter for an interview in the San Fernando Valley years ago, and he drifted pleasantly back in time, to the days of his youth in Kansas City. "I was a nut on big bands," he said. "I knew every name from *Metronome* [magazine]; that was my only interest in life. Oh, that was a good man, Jones. A strange man, no personality at all, but a first-class musician. They could play hot, but mostly it was just good ballads, nicely orchestrated. It all changed in '35 when Goodman hit it big. The orchestras with strings all died out. But I liked that your father was from Missouri; so many great ones were. Back in those days, that was important."

There is a touching family story from 1933, when Gor's mother, Angelica, came east from St. Louis and had a big night watching the Jones band at the Ambassador Hotel in Atlantic City. Gor had it all planned out: As he and his mother entered the dining room, the band struck up her favorite song, "Slumber Boat," right on cue. While Gor put his arms around her, she broke into tears as they walked in together: "... *Only don't forget to sail back again to me....*"

By 1934, while still arranging for Jones, Gor had branched out all over New York, making stock arrangements for Paul Whiteman, Andre Kostelanetz, Bob Crosby, Jimmy Dorsey, Lennie Hayton, and his tennis-playing partner Goodman, then just twenty-four years old. "I was quite friendly with Benny," Gor said in a lengthy 1978 interview with Chuck Cecil. "We'd meet at my place in Tudor City or out at Mildred Bailey's house in Forest Hills, when she was married to Red Norvo. That was quite a gathering place for musicians. Teddy Wilson on piano, Benny, Willie 'the Lion' Smith, Johnny Mercer would sing, Red would play xylophone. Those were great days. I wasn't in their class as a player, I'd just listen. My whole thing was helping Benny get his new band together, which I did, with three or four guys."

So much of the writing and arranging came naturally to my father, in ways that seemed almost magical, but he got a major assist from one of the giants of the business. Gor was being interviewed by Wink Martindale, of KMPC Los Angeles, nearly forty years after the fact, when he became instantly sentimental over the mention of Victor Young. Aside from his accomplishments with the Jones band, Young was a giant of songwriting: "My Foolish Heart," "I Don't Stand a Ghost of a Chance," "Sweet Sue," "Stella By Starlight" and my personal favorite, "You Made the Pants Too Long." As Gor remembered it, "I grew up in an era where the arrangers weren't trying to get rich. We were trying to write well. Big difference. I don't find anything wrong with money, but we were trying to write like Jerome Kern and Cole Porter, and arrange like Victor Young. We were trying to do it just as good as we could, and if it didn't sell, that's the way it goes. I was fortunate to meet Victor when I was twenty-two, with the Jones band. We went into a studio in Chicago, he was in the booth, and I was barely starting out, but Victor heard something that attracted him, and after the date [voice quavering] . . . I don't think I can get through this story. I've never been able to tell it, it's such a great thing.

"He asked me if I would take a walk with him. We walked for three hours in Lincoln Park and he talked to me about music, some of the things I'd done wrong on the record date, and the things I'd done right. Three hours, he took; never seen me before. Back home, I was ten feet off the ground. I learned more about practical writing that afternoon than I could ever learn in college. When to let the singer sing, when to fill in, things you don't know when you're twenty-two. If I did nothing for the rest of my life but arrange Victor Young songs, I still couldn't repay him."

Jones, meanwhile, was doing Gordon a favor by moving his operation from Chicago to Manhattan. Now Jenkins was getting offers from one big-time band after another, without having to move an inch. "I came up to see Jenks one time," Simmons told me. "We'd go out to some New York diner and musicians would come right up to him, saying they wanted something. 'OK, I'll have it for you tomorrow,' he'd say. People told me he was the fastest writer anyone had seen. Back at his apartment [in Jackson Heights], there would be all sorts of noise and commotion, making it impossible to concentrate, but there he goes, like lightning. Every so often I'd strike up a conversation and he'd keep it going, all the while just furiously scribbling away."

Remarkably, the first song Gor ever had published was "Blue Prelude," in 1933, a longtime standard and Woody Herman's first theme song. The melody came from Joe Bishop, a horn player in the Jones band, and my father wrote the words.

"When Bishop played the melody for Jones, he didn't like it," Gor said. "Felt it sounded too mournful for the band's style. So Joe took it down to some friends in the Casa Loma band, and Walter Winchell [the syndicated New York columnist and radio personality] happened to hear their version of it one night. In those days, Walter Winchell was God. There's nobody like him now; his word was just *it*. And he wrote that Joe Bishop had a new hit with Casa Loma, even though Joe was playing in the Jones band, and when Isham read that, he flipped. 'We've gotta put this thing out right away,' he said. But we didn't have any words. Just by sheer luck, I was sitting there at the table. 'Let me write a lyric,' I said. He reminded me that I wasn't a lyricist, but I asked if he'd just let me try. OK, he said, if you can have it by tomorrow.

"We put the thing out and it was a big hit," Gor said. "So the first song I had out was a lyric, not a melody. The publisher went south with the money and we never did get paid, but it has done extremely well over the years."

In case anyone doubted that Jenkins was a profoundly melancholy individual beyond those lively forays to 52nd Street, he put it out there with "Blue Prelude," a theme that strayed only slightly from "Goodbye" and its tale of love and death. I hear Judy Garland's version, surely one of the best, as the lyrics come forth:

> *Let me sigh*
> *Let me cry*
> *When I'm blue*
> *Let me go*
> *Away from the lone-ly town*
> *Won't be long*
> *'Til my song*
> *Will be through*
> *'Cause I know*
> *I'm on my last go-round*
> *All the love I could steal, beg or borrow*
> *Wouldn't heal all this pain in my soul*
> *What is love but a prelude to sorrow*
> *With a heartbreak ahead for your goal*
> *Here I go*

Now you know
Why I'm leaving
Got the blues
What can I lose
Goodbye

There were times during my research when I doubted the "Goodbye" story, about the girlfriend and infant who died in childbirth. It happened before he turned twenty-three (when he wrote the song), and he was twenty-one when he married Nancy. Could it have happened so early in life? Why doesn't anyone else tell that story?

Then I see that one line: "What is love but a prelude to sorrow." That's beyond sadness. Only an excruciatingly painful development could foster that kind of outlook on life. And it seems altogether fitting that my father embraced classical symphonic pieces from an early age, often borrowing distinct moods and phrasings to use in his own work, with especially forlorn samplings of the oboe and French horn. (As I perused my father's audio tape collection—Sibelius's Second Symphony, the Walton Concerto, Schoenberg's *Transfigured Night*, a dash of Ravel, or Stravinsky's *Le Sacre du Printemps*—I felt as if I were exploring the interiors of an electrical storm, or the plight of a castaway barge on hundred-foot seas at midnight. Occasionally the musical skies cleared for a hint of respite, and then *right* back to the gloom.)

The Jones band broke up in 1936. As the story goes, Jenkins was asked to take over, with many of the group's big talents intact, but he didn't want to give up his status as all-comers arranger for a life on the road (nor did Nancy take to the idea). "So I asked Woody Herman if he'd like to do it," Gor said. "He was out in Seattle, but he came right back and took over. Worked out pretty well for everybody." Especially Woody and his "Herd," who thrilled audiences for decades thereafter.

Musicians told me that Gor tended to be heavily nostalgic over the Jones band, and it was a process that began almost immediately. Just a year after the breakup, in September 1937, Gor wrote a now-famous article in *Metronome*, remembering how it was:

"The other night I spent a few hours at the radio, listening to dance bands. I heard 458 chromatic runs on accordions, 911 'telegraph ticker' brass figures, 78 sliding trombones, 4 sliding violas, 45 burps into a straw, 91 bands that played the same arrangement on every tune, and 11,000 imitations of Benny Goodman. Slightly nauseated, I finally went to bed, and lay for some time thinking about the Old Jones Band. There, gents, was a band. It may seem incredible nowadays, but the Jones band of 1931, 1932 and 1933 seemed to get along without any of the above-named tricks.

"Jones employed no flourishes—none of the 20-odd guys were comics, none danced or entertained—but when they hit the last chorus of a tune like 'I Can't Believe It's True,' it really sounded like something. Isham Jones doesn't just beat time—he *conducts*. The picture of that big farmer standing up there molding 17 boys (half of whom probably weren't speaking to him at the time) into one gorgeous unit, was something I'll never forget.

"What a brass team we had in those days! Johnny Carlson, George Thow and Clarence Willard, trumpets; Red Ballard and Jack Jenney, trombones. Jack is so well known and universally respected, no further comment is necessary from me. And if I tried to tell you what I think of Red Ballard, you wouldn't believe me anyway. I would simply say that Red was the finest all-around dance musician on any instrument that I've ever known. Put up 10 new arrangements and I'll pay off on every mistake he makes, first time through. I'm sure Benny Goodman is proud to have Red with him."

After mentioning many others, Gor got around to Bishop, who played tuba with Jones and flugelhorn with Herman. "With all respect to Berigan and the boys," he wrote, "give me Bishop, the blues, Scotch and water and I'll settle."

There must have been a shortage of available conductors in New York around the fall of 1936, because Gor was asked to handle that role on Broadway for "The Show Is On," starring Bea Lillie and Bert Lahr. A lot of today's musicians remember Jenkins best as a conductor, but at the time he had never done it—for anyone. "They called me up for this job and I thought they were kidding," he said. But something about his work had impressed the Shuberts, who were producing the show, and director Vincente Minnelli, who was trying to avoid what *Variety* called the "conventional, hackneyed" theater orchestrations of the time.

"I always had my eye on conducting," Gor said. "I used to go down early for the Jones rehearsals and stand up in front of the band, waving the stick around. It didn't do much for anything except my own morale; the guys played the way they wanted to, anyway. But it made me feel like a conductor. I shouldn't have taken the Broadway job, because I was walking right into the big time without any preparation or experience."

So how was it?

"Awful," he said. "The Shuberts fired me every night and Minnelli hired me back the next day. Once the show became a hit, people sort of forgot how horrible the conducting had been."

A first-class production featuring the music of Carmichael, Harold Arlen, Richard Rodgers and George Gershwin, "The Show Is On" opened in Boston in November 1936, started a New York run on Christmas night and staged 237 performances around the Northeast. Gor might have looked like a rookie in the orchestra pit, but he was onto something quite historic. "Minnelli has introduced an innovation that will make musicians sit up," wrote *Variety* after a show in Boston. "As a result of Jenkins's handling, the fiddles do not play the melody with the vocalist and drown out her voice in the process. Jenkins's idea is to accompany the singer, letting her song carry easily and naturally through the music. The formula works, and it does wonders for the performance of Grace Barrie, whose voice does not project as far as her personality."

"What Gordon did," said Howie Richmond, "was come in and say, 'Bands don't play verses any more; we do the chorus and counter-melodies and improvise around that.' It sounds like nothing now, but at the time it was extremely bold. Put simply, he was the first arranger to let a singer carry the melody alone. People thought it was crazy until it caught on. Then everybody started doing it."

There was one thing about my father that no one could imi-tate—his permanently bent finger. It seems that at some point dur-ing "The Show Is On," he took a header trying to climb out of the pit, broke the fall with his right hand and cut it on a wayward Coke bottle, severing a tendon in the middle finger. Through a combi-nation of neglect and slipshod treatment, the top half of the finger never healed. It remained bent, at a ninety-degree angle, for life. This would have been hell on a football receiver, or a yoga instruc-tor, but it didn't seem to hamper Gor in any way. He was left-handed to begin with, it didn't affect his piano playing or golf game, and it became a constant source of amusement. I can still see him com-ing out of his studio, holding up the tortured hand, muttering "Peace" and heading into the main house.

A lot of people believed that his one-fingered piano style, some-thing of a trademark over the years, was due to the injury. It was actually a gimmick he developed, almost by accident, dragging slightly behind the beat on low-register piano solos in his own recordings. It was hardly a testament to virtuosity, but it gained him considerable popularity and gave his arrangements—already instantly recognizable to fans—an even more singular touch.

"It wasn't anything new," he once said. "Claude Thornhill, Ray Noble and particularly Eddie Duchin [with lush backgrounds in the 1930s] had all done the low-register, one-note-at-a-time stuff.

It wasn't even my idea. When I was musical director at NBC [Hollywood, early Forties], one of the really sharp engineers, Bob Moss, was trying to get a different sound out of the orchestra. He put a microphone about a half-inch from the bass strings inside the piano and told me to play the melody one note at a time. I said, 'You're out of your mind.' He said, 'No, that's what we're gonna do. Just try it.' We did, and people kind of liked it. When I started recording outside of the studio, I kept doing it."

One of his favorite background singers, Mack MacLean, said Gor "made a classic" out of that simple style. "He got a beautiful sound, the way it was miked, and when you heard that, you knew it was Gordon Jenkins. It doesn't have to be good [laughter]. Hell, the Lombardos were instantly identifiable with that creamy, pukey little saxophone sound. But you knew it was him. That's something most people never gain."

"He'd have all those strings going, and the voices in the background," said Joe Graydon, who sang the hit record "Again" with the Jenkins band, "and suddenly there's a break, and for maybe eight bars there's that one-finger piano. He got as much feeling out of that one finger as most guys do with ten."

The big thing about Gor's piano playing is that he knew who the real giants were—Wilson, Art Tatum, Erroll Garner, Nat Cole—and soaked up their genius without a hint of jealousy or insecurity. "Except for my own records, I never played professionally after 1932," he said. "I used to play jazz piano down at Nick's in the Village, and I'd sit in with Yank Lawson and the guys down at Eddie Condon's sometimes. Mostly two-beat, Dixieland stuff; I know all those tunes and all the keys. I'm not what you'd call a real hotshot soloist, more of an ensemble player."

(My dad's general humility had led me to believe he that was just another hack on the piano—you couldn't tell a thing from the one-fingered stuff—until I heard a private cassette he made entitled

"Sport Plays for Red." Those were the nicknames he and my auburn-haired mother had for each other. One day in the mid-Seventies, without her knowledge, he sat down at our home Steinway and played her a non-stop, half-hour love letter, with nothing mapped out, just flowing from one romantic melody to the next at the highest level of competence. I'm sure it brought tears to her eyes.)

Those nights in the early Thirties, down on 52nd Street, shaped Jenkins's lifestyle and the way he judged music from then on. He moved along with the times, but just barely. He despised rock music, hated junk composers and didn't much care for frantic, modern jazz. For every new talent he embraced—Barbra Streisand, Jack Jones, Steve Lawrence—there were a thousand acts that were revered by the masses and reviled by him. After all, he'd been to Mecca: The Onyx, The Famous Door, Kelly's Stable, Jimmy Ryan's, all the terrific jazz clubs on 52nd between 5th and 7th, in the prime years between 1934 and 1945. Within those two blocks, you had it all: Count Basie, Dizzy Gillespie, Bessie Smith, Maxine Sullivan, Art Tatum, Sarah Vaughan, Louis Prima, Bunny Berigan, top-notch Dixieland. Those weren't the most enlightened social times in our nation's history, but thanks to the diligence of producers like Gabler and John Hammond, people found that they could hear the great black performers in New York without having to go up to Harlem.

If someone said, "See you on the street," that was all you needed to know. And such *flavor*. The Mafia was a constant, looming presence, lending a bit of intrigue to the atmosphere. The two-block stretch was teeming with converted speakeasies, marijuana smoke and illicit gambling joints, and it was known to have a cathouse or two. Musicians would regularly drop into the tiny, intimate clubs, haul out their instruments and sit in. You were liable to see anyone in the audience, from Judy Garland to Fred Astaire to John Steinbeck. Frank Sinatra said he was never the same after hearing Billie Holiday there in the 1930s ("the greatest single musical influence I ever had"), and as *The Street That Never Slept* quotes jazz trumpeter Max Kaminsky, "Hot jazz music was the thing, and when a musician was building a solo, you never heard a sound from the audience. You could *feel* them listening."

That book devotes a short passage to my father and his devotion to an all-black jazz group known as the Spirits of Rhythm, whose lead singer, Leo Watson, was known to have inspired Louis Armstrong and Ella Fitzgerald. Watson played the drums and trombone, too; he was the talented, smoking-hot essence of 52nd Street. "An amazing performer and singer," Gor says in the book. "I got such a kick out of them, I went there [the Onyx] night after night. Once, when I was giving a cocktail party, I splurged and hired the group. They arrived an hour or so early and immediately began warming up. I was so excited about having them to myself, I didn't wait for the guests to arrive. I began serving food and keeping their glasses filled. Of course, I was sampling the stuff myself. In fact, I sampled so much that I can't remember a thing about the party."

One of my dad's steady companions at the Onyx was Johnny Mercer, with whom he formed a songwriting partnership that led to "P.S. I Love You," written in 1934 and recorded by countless artists thereafter (not including the Beatles, whose identically titled song was their own original). Mercer remembered Jenkins as "a most gifted musician. He understood more serious music than most of the guys did, and he had a great feeling for jazz. But he was really a country bumpkin about the big city. Champagne and things like that were brand-new experiences. He had one meal that he ate constantly—boiled beef with thick, brown gravy and mashed potatoes, and he'd pour ketchup all over it [that rings true from my upbringing; he had the worst diet known to man]. Later, he began to wear tails and drink cocktails. The city really went to his head. You can hear it in 'Manhattan Tower.'"

The city didn't just go to his head, it became his whole reason for living, a luxurious fantasy that simmered constantly in his mind and often sprung to reality. That Spirits of Rhythm gig—bringing his favorite band right into his apartment—is the way he thought. Not on a whimsical afternoon; always. He wanted the best seats for the best show in town, and the drinks were on him. It would be a terrific evening if he could make fifty other people feel just as delighted as he was, and that was the genesis of "Manhattan Tower." As Art Seidenbaum wrote in the *Los Angeles Times,* "Jenkins convinced a whole generation that sentiment could live in a city."

I spent a delightful New York afternoon with Bea Wain, who sang the hit record "Deep Purple" with the Larry Clinton band, and her husband, Andre Baruch, whose long radio career included a play-by-play stint with the old Brooklyn Dodgers. They remembered "Tower" the way a ballplayer recalls his first home run.

"Schmaltzy? Sure it was," she said. "For its time, it was thrilling."

"Maybe the professional musician says it's schmaltzy," said Baruch. "But the person listening, he's saying [taps his chest], 'This hits me right here.'"

On that same trip to New York, I caught up with Jack Rollins, the most revered manager in show business (start with Woody Allen, Billy Crystal, Robin Williams and David Letterman) and his wife, Jane, who sang in the "Manhattan Tower" chorus. "I'd agree that it's schmaltzy," said Jack, "but he was such a romantic. He was like a wide-eyed kid all his life about this city, and it never left him. The thing about Gordon, he was a generous man in every conceivable way. With money, with displaying his pleasure at a performance. That was the most basic feeling about Gordon. People loved him because he gave. He just gave, constantly, openly. And when a person gave something back to him, he could hardly stand up straight."

"That's what happened on the Sullivan Show [in 1950]," said Jane. "After we performed 'Manhattan Tower,' they brought him up on the stage and Mayor O'Dwyer was there, saying how embarrassed he was that the city didn't recognize the piece when it was written. I think he said something like, 'We offer no key to the city, only its heart.' Well, Gordon sort of mumbled something, and then he started to cry. He really was so moved. He was an out-of-town boy who dreamed of coming here and becoming somebody, and that's what happened, and it moved him tremendously."

I'd heard second-hand reports of Mel Brooks meeting Anne Bancroft over a "Manhattan Tower" tune, and suddenly came the verification in *Seriously Funny*, Gerald Nachman's acclaimed study of comedians in the 1950s and 1960s. Nachman noted that they met in 1961, around the time Brooks's landmark "2000-Year-Old Man" routine was recorded: "He arranged to be at a rehearsal of the Perry Como show, and after she'd sung 'Married I Can Always Get,' he burst into applause, rushed over to her, and, legend has it, cried, 'Hi, I'm Mel Brooks. I would kill for you!' They became instant and constant friends, and married three years later."

Then there was the bizarre anecdote I discovered in *As Thousands Cheer*, Laurence Bergreen's book on the life of Irving Berlin. The year was 1949, and Bergreen described it this way:

"Berlin suffered a blow to his pride when he tried out 'Give me your tired, your poor' on Gordon Jenkins, a respected songwriter and arranger. As Jenkins entered the Berlin office with Helmy (Berlin's assistant) one afternoon, Berlin himself suddenly appeared. 'Listen, you guys,' he ordered. 'Just stand there and listen to this.'

"Berlin suddenly fell to his knees, his arms upraised, in a posture worthy of the vaudeville stage, and began to sing his version of the Emma Lazarus poem: 'Give me your tired, your poor, your huddled masses yearning to breathe free....' He was so moved by his own performance that tears filled his eyes. He was determined to prove that at the age of sixty-one, he still had it in him to write hit songs and hit shows.

"When he finished singing, he said, still on his knees, 'By God,

I'll tell you one thing, no one's ever thought of using those lines in a song, and I can tell you it's going to stop 'em cold. The whole house will just sit there in silence. God, what an idea."

Then Jenkins spoke up: "I hate to tell you this, Mr. Berlin, but those words *have* been used before."

"You're a goddamned liar!" Berlin roared. "No one's ever done it before."

"Mr. Berlin, I used those words in a song three years ago [in 'Manhattan Tower']."

Before Gor could elaborate, Bergreen wrote, "Berlin continued to hurl abuse at him: Jenkins was a goddamned liar, a lying prick. Finally he told Jenkins, 'Get the fuck out,' and went back to his office, slamming the door after him. Surprised but composed, Jenkins quietly said goodbye to Helmy, who could manage nothing more than an embarrassed grunt in reply. It was not the first time he had seen his boss fly into a rage, nor would it be the last. Despite the revelation that Gordon Jenkins had set the same Emma Lazarus poem to music only three years earlier, Berlin kept the song in the [stage musical] *Miss Liberty* score."

The beauty of "Manhattan Tower" is that unlike conventional records, rising and falling on the *Billboard* charts, it gained momentum and reputation as the years went on. By 1949, the year he broke the awful truth to Irving Berlin, Gor could virtually write his own ticket in New York. He was promoted to Musical Director of Decca Records that year, living in Malibu but spending huge chunks of time at Decca's New York offices on 57th Street, just off 6th Avenue. As a conductor, arranger and talent scout, he covered the spectrum, working with Louis Armstrong, Ella Fitzgerald, the Weavers, Peggy Lee and an assortment of lesser acts that enjoyed the blessing of his conviction. But his most long-lasting association was with Milt Gabler, Decca's right-hand man to A&R chief Dave Kapp.

The two first met in the early Thirties, when Gor was arranging for the Jones band and Gabler ran a little music shop on 42nd Street across from the Commodore Hotel. That shop turned into Commodore Records, where Gabler cut historic records with Billie Holiday, Coleman Hawkins, Lester Young, Benny Goodman and Eddie Condon. For the better part of ten years, Gabler simultaneously ran the Commodore label and store, produced Decca's top-flight sessions and booked weekly jam sessions at Jimmy Ryan's jazz club on 52nd Street.

"At Decca, I was supposed to make hits," Gabler told me. "At Commodore, I could do whatever I wanted." It's worth noting that Gabler was Billy Crystal's uncle (an older brother of the comedian's mother), and that Gabler's partner at the record shop was Jack Crystal, Billy's father. You can hear Jack's voice in Billy's hilarious depictions of old Jewish men, and when you hear the line, 'We are closed, ya bastards,' that's Jack Crystal behind the Commodore window with the place locked up.

Gabler was the final answer in record production, a minister of vision. Some have pointed to "Rock Around the Clock," by Bill Haley & the Comets in 1954, as the birth of rock and roll; that was a Gabler date. Holiday cut her famous version of "Strange Fruit" for Commodore. Jazz, gospel, R&B, rock, folk—over time, Gabler did it all. His taste and comportment were impeccable, and it was a rare musician who did not trust his judgment.

"He was a round-faced man with a beautiful smile, a permanent case of good vibes, and a track record in the music business unequaled by anyone," wrote critic Ralph Gleason in 1974. "He was one of those record people who always turned up at the crucial points. Talking to Gabler is like tapping the full history of popular music."

Although my father made big-time records with some famous artists at Decca, his greatest success came with his own name attached. At the very peak of his popularity, in July 1950, he had four of the top six records on the charts of *Billboard*, which referred to him as "America's No. 1 recording star." The July 29 issue reveals:

No. 2: "Tzena, Tzena, Tzena," with the Weavers (then completely unknown) and Gordon Jenkins's orchestra.

No. 4: "I Wanna Be Loved," by the Andrews Sisters, his arrangement and orchestra.

No. 5: "Goodnight Irene."

No. 6: "Bewitched," his arrangement and orchestra.

On June 30, the Jenkins version of "My Foolish Heart" had gone to No. 7, so he had five records in the Top 10—an unprecedented feat—over a three-week span. "Goodnight Irene," which sent the Weavers into the stratosphere, was No. 1 for thirteen weeks from August into November. And for those who preferred the rankings of *Your Hit Parade*, Jenkins had each of the top three records on July 15, 1950: "Bewitched," "I Wanna Be Loved" and "My Foolish Heart."

Wrote *Time* magazine: "On the double-jointed tongues of disc jockeys, the lighted plaques of jukeboxes and the shopping lists of record buyers, one name recurred with monotonous frequency: Gordon Hill Jenkins. All tricked out with sobbing, throbbing violins and choruses of female voices, [the songs] were proving once again that America likes nothing better than big, lush arrangements of its popular tunes."

He and Gabler became a famous combination, a veritable bank vault for Decca, and to say the least, Gabler recalled him quite fondly. "The thing about Gordy is that I admired him so much as a person," Gabler told me in a 1988 interview near his home in Connecticut. "He was a pure-thinking guy who came up with the right answers to everyday problems and didn't mix too much in politics. He could have been an even bigger name if he'd gone out on the road with bands, like all the giants did. But I don't think he wanted to be a leader. He'd prefer to write and mail stuff to the band, rather than go out on a tour of one-nighters. He wanted to be a leader in the studio, not a hotel."

Gabler described Jenkins as "a front-runner, always way ahead of the game. That thing he did, combining the use of background vocals with musicians, that was very new. It had technically been done before, but not to the extent or the method that Gordon did it. See, ordinarily you have licks, riffs, obbligatos that the guys play. He wrote melody lines and put words to them for a chorus. They were clever and meaningful—everybody in town copied him—but in Gordon's hands, they brought out such a soul, such heart. He actually had to stop using that signature because he was sick of people copying it.

"People said he borrowed from Tchaikovsky, like that's some sort of evil," Gabler went on. "Well, he absolutely wrote like Tchaikovsky, with those minor chords and changes, and thank heaven for that. He was a latter-day American Tchaikovsky, very commercial, but also completely original and creative. He had a two-chord signature that really became his trademark: '*Da* –dit . . . *da* –dit.' I used to call it '*Gor* –don . . . *Jenk* –ins.' And people copied the hell out of that. So one time, when we were recording 'Don't Cry Joe' with Betty Brewer, he had thirty musicians—all but the rhythm section—playing the melody. Said he'd learned it from his old boss, Isham Jones. I can still see him walking down 9th Avenue, muttering to himself, 'Let 'em beat *that* one.'"

As the Commodore shop flourished, the Gabler connection became a central part of little Billy Crystal's life. He grew up around jazz musicians, once telling National Public Radio, "The house smelled of brisket and bourbon; that's the music I grew up on." When Uncle Milt died, in 2001, Billy set upon a project to honor his career. The result was "Billy Crystal Presents: The Milt Gabler Story," a 26-track Verve release that includes Peggy Lee's "Lover," Louis Armstrong's "Blueberry Hill," and the Weavers' "Goodnight Irene," all arranged and conducted by Jenkins.

"We were a hell of a team in the studio," Gabler told me. "He called me Champ, because he trusted my decisions. Talk about 'direct to disc'—that's really what we did in those days. There was no editing. You got it in one take, and if there was a goof, you did it over from the top. Not only that, when quarter-inch tape came in, you could play it back, but when you were cutting direct to a master, you couldn't play it back without destroying the record. So they had to trust a guy like myself, to either say 'great' or point out something—a mistake in the brass, or maybe the singer could do it better, and we'd go for another one. Usually we'd get our tests back and Gordy would say, 'God damn, Milt's right again,' which I loved, coming from him. Plus, he never over-wrote. Some arrangers wanted to hear their own work, because *they* want to be the champ and they don't care if it overshadows the singer. Hell, I'd get in there and knock out stuff all the time, if it got in the way of the song. I'd say, 'Don't complain, we're makin' it better.' I never had that problem with Gordon. He was my champ. The great ones, they're for real. They can hit a home run every time up."

By this time, my father owned New York. There couldn't have been a better feeling in the world. He had moved from Jackson Heights to a stylish apartment at 68th & 3rd. He was hanging around the 52nd Street clubs and knocking 'em dead with his own recording sessions; he was truly in his element. "If tested," said old St. Louis friend Allan Clark, "I could tell you about the time I went backstage to see him and he held court in his jockey shorts. He sure as hell did. I was with a girl I didn't know very well—she worked for *Life* magazine—and it tested her sophistication level sorely."

They say he practically founded a little bar and steak house called Al & Dick's, on 54th Street. between 6th and 7th. "In the days we worked together," said Gabler, "he'd start writing arrangements around 7 a.m. and put in about five hours, just to be sure he'd be done by noon. He'd go up to Al & Dick's for lunch and a few drinks, then go back there for dinner. And when it came to Gordon's drinking, he could just keep going. I don't know how he did it, but he never really got stoned. But when he'd show up at the bar, all the songwriters and songpluggers would jump on him, because they all wanted him on the air and on record. That's how Al & Dick's was built—guys coming in to see Gordon Jenkins."

One of the sweetest stories came from Joe Thompson, the former NBC radio producer and longtime friend of the family: "I'd been transferred back East, and I sandbagged the network into giving us a half-hour show called 'Gordon Jenkins Comes to New York.' They said we could use any artists we wanted. I guess they didn't know Gordon too well, thought he was a bit of a square, and he told 'em, 'Sure, I'd like to have Billie Holiday and Bobby Hackett.' Well, we did the town that night. We visited the places where Billie and Bobby played, had just a sensational time, and about three in the morning we all wound up at my apartment in the Village. It was one of those steaming New York nights; we threw all the double doors and windows open. And Gordy sat down at the piano and played a medley for about forty-five minutes, the likes of which I have never heard. I was afraid some fishwife voice would cry out, saying, 'Shut up down there!' But instead, rapt silence. And at the end, there were a few beats, and then came the words from a higher floor: 'We who are above you, salute you.' [Pause, and a faraway smile] That is engraved in my soul."

I never knew the city like my father did, but I embraced and understood it all the same. Those *Chronicle* assignments became the highlight of any year, from the summer of 1977 right up to September 2001 and that last innocent day, the last time New Yorkers shared an atmosphere of old-time freedom. I went back for the baseball playoffs within three weeks of the catastrophe, and the experience was shattering. The Ground Zero neighborhood was a lonely ghost town, with many storefronts barricaded and people walking the streets in gas masks. The stench in the air was disturbing, along with a strange, fine mist I could not identify. "The people who live around here notice it gathering on their windshield," a New York friend told me that night. "Yeah, some of it's dust. It's also bodies."

Down in the subways, my customary route to the ballpark, it was impossible to avoid thoughts of germ warfare. The place called "Yankee Stadium" felt distinctly vulnerable and I went numb on entrance, oblivious to the smell of pretzels, the sound of Eddie Layton's cheerful organ music or the public-address voice of Bob Sheppard, who dates back to Joe DiMaggio's time. Two or three innings passed before I got any kind of grasp on the proceedings.

Back in my hotel room, on the 35th floor, the skyline looked empty. It was two Manhattan towers short. I feigned rejuvenation, looking in favorable directions. I tried to hear the echoes of 52nd Street from so many years before. Mostly, I took heart in my father's absence. For the first time in my life, I felt grateful that he was gone.

Chapter 4

Nostalgia Rides Again

I WAS ONCE IN THE PRESENCE OF GOD. I was too young to get the full picture, but I remember Louis Armstrong and the way my father looked at him. After years of confusion, I finally realized why we had a cat named Satchmo.

If there was a single association my father cherished most—more than Sinatra, Judy Garland, Nat Cole, the lot of 'em—it was working with Armstrong in the late Forties and early Fifties. Gor cried as he sat down to dinner after their first recording session together, and it wasn't the first time he lost it that day. He had done so in front of God and some of the best musicians in New York City.

"I'll tell you how Gordy felt about Louis," said Nick Fatool, one of the most versatile and sought-after drummers of all time. "They were on the same bill together at the Paramount Theater in New York [1952]. Afterward, Gordy would go down to Nick's in the Village to hear jazz, and he'd get up every morning with one hell of a hangover. Back at the Paramount, he'd stand in the wings holding Louis's handkerchiefs. And hell, Satch would sweat and spit into those things, you know. But Gordy said just holding those handkerchiefs revived him, like an electric shock. It was his way to get back."

He had revered Armstrong since the mid-1920s, in his early teens, when he got his first taste of the music world outside St. Louis. Nobody was ever the same after hearing Satchmo (an old

Dixieland cat once likened the experience to "looking into the sun"), and while my dad's contributions drifted far away from Deep-South jazz, those were his roots. Quitting school, shocking his family, going to work in those delectably sleazy nightclubs when most kids his age were home studying—he did all that because Armstrong and his followers were out there. The whole idea was to get closer. He looked into the sun and never flinched.

"I think of Gordon as a museum piece," composer Johnny Mandel told me, "and I mean that in the fondest way. He embraced the music of the Twenties and Thirties, and nothing else ever reached him quite the same way. His orchestrations, harmonies, everything dated back to those times, and he never changed his style. So it makes perfect sense that he and Louis were compatible. They came from the same era. Louis never really embraced the swing years—although he could out-swing anyone. He just transcended everybody, ate up the territory. I'm sure he wiped Gordy out; he had to. He wiped everyone out."

I wasn't aware of it until the final years of his life, but Gor assembled a magnificent collection of jazz and blues records from the 1920s and 1930s. Through pure diligence and desire, he sought out tapes and old 78s from every source he could find. On and on it went: Sonny Boy Williamson, Bessie Smith, Mildred Bailey, Bennie Moten, Jelly Roll Morton, Nellie Lutcher, Tampa Red, Bumble Bee Slim and Cousin Joe. Finally satisfied with the project, he put the highlights on a series of cassette tapes he entitled "Nostalgia Rides Again." And I realized that while most critics pinpoint symphonic music as the inspiration for Jenkins's musical style, an equal dose came from early-century America, complete with laughter, the tinkling of glasses and the whiff of sin.

Assembling the pieces of his orchestra years later, he looked hard for kindred spirits. One such man was my godfather, Bruce Hudson, a trumpet player out of Electra, Texas, who became a regular in the Jenkins band. Hudson was smart, funny, a hell of a golfer and the kind of storyteller who could hold his own in any tavern from Cheyenne to Dublin. One day in 1925, Bruce pulled out of Fort Worth with a drummer named Ray McKinley (bound for glory with the Glenn Miller band) en route to Chicago, where they hoped to stir up a gig.

"I was sixteen, Ray was fifteen," Hudson said. "Ray got a job at the Moulin Rouge restaurant, but I ran into some union problems and couldn't work for two weeks. Best thing that ever happened to me. Louis was playing in an orchestra at the Sunset Café on the South Side, and I was there every night. Chicago was really hot then, and Louis was the hottest. He was the Bible. That whole experience just made me. The way that I felt and thought is the way he played. Later on I got to where I could play Louis's solos from several records, and that made a big impression on Gordon. We had a strong connection through Louis's records."

The catalyst of the Jenkins-Armstrong recording sessions was Decca executive Milt Gabler, with his matchless reputation for taste, discovery and record production. "We had Louis under contract from the day Decca started, which was 1934," said Gabler, "and we had him exclusively from 1949 to 1954, which was the peak of Gordon's time with us. Everyone wanted to work with Gordy, and as you look back, he was making history back then. He's the one who brought background vocals into combination with musicians. The Armstrong sessions really typified that."

Just as it's hard to imagine Sandy Koufax getting belted around, or Laurence Olivier fumbling over a simple sentence, it is difficult to fathom Louis Armstrong being in a "slump." His work was pure genius from start to finish. But in September 1949, when he and Jenkins entered the Decca studios for their first recording session, Armstrong's popularity was at an all-time low. Hudson, who devoted his life to the Armstrong sound, remembered it well:

"At some point during the war, Gordon and I had gone down to see Louis at the Firestone Ballroom [Southern California], and maybe twenty or thirty people were there. He'd hit the absolute rock bottom. The last tune they played that night was the 'Star-Spangled Banner.' Louis played the melody and didn't embellish it one bit, but he played it as only Louis could. Being emotional musicians, we stood there and cried. On the way home, Gordon told me, 'I'm gonna do something for him if it's the last thing I ever do.'"

The answer—suggested by Armstrong and approved by Decca chief Dave Kapp—was "Blueberry Hill," the kickoff record on that September 1949 date and the first nationwide hit of Armstrong's career (Fats Domino had a runaway hit with "Blueberry Hill" in 1956, but that's the poor man's version). "Gordon did the same thing for Louis that he did for the Weavers—he brought him into the mainstream," said the respected L.A. disc jockey Chuck Cecil. "It took Louis out of the jazz idiom and gave him a piece of pop music. I've always thought it not only changed his career but prolonged it. Made him more popular than he'd ever been in his life. It gave him the type of boost that 'Hello Dolly' did, years later. As a matter of fact, if it hadn't been for 'Blueberry Hill,' he may never have done 'Hello Dolly.'"

Jenkins: "It just got played so much more than anything he'd had. He was well known around the world, but he'd never appeared with a chorus before, or with strings, that kind of treatment. We made a whole bunch of records, all good. The relationship was . . . oh, perfect. The greatest."

Gabler: "As Gordon put together that special background on 'Blueberry Hill,' there was a place where I felt we could have a trumpet playing an obbligato behind Louis's vocal—like Louis accompanying himself. We had two great trumpet players that just loved him, like all trumpet players did. One was Billy Butterfield, the other was Yank Lawson. Both were dear friends of mine, and I called in Gordon, because the conductor is boss of the session. Gordy said, 'How the hell can I make that choice? We gotta flip a coin.' And it came up for Billy. He played a wonderful muted solo that sounded a hell of a lot like Louis."

Gabler remembered having to change the original lyrics—a common endeavor when it came to traditional works—and Gor approached the task with great enthusiasm. The way he saw it, once you've found your thrill on Blueberry Hill, it's time to get loose:

Come climb the hill with me, baby
We'll see what we shall see
I'll bring my horn with me
I'll be with you where berries are blue
Each afternoon we'll go
Higher than the moon we'll go
Then to a saloon we'll go . . .

"That doesn't sound like much today," said Gabler, "but a woman at NBC, a very strict censor type, told me the saloon bit wasn't acceptable for radio. Gordy was disgusted and told me to put whatever the hell I wanted in there. So I made up a quick rhyme—'To a wedding in June we'll go'—and that's what's on the record. Every time I hear it, I think about the time I loused up Gordon's great lyric."

Not that it mattered in the slightest to Armstrong. "His career just shot out of sight," said Hudson. "The fact is, Louis was very raw. He didn't have much experience dealing with white people, and he didn't know how. He had a white manager [Joe Glaser], a guy from the tough end of Chicago, who guided him everywhere. I mean, he wouldn't go to the bathroom without this guy. He paid very strict attention to everything Glaser said, and in a *New Yorker* article that year, the guy gave Gordon credit for the whole thing. One time years later, when he was performing one of his songs, Louis actually sang, 'Thank you, Gordon Jenkins,' right in the middle of it."

Normally the essence of confidence on a record date, almost to the point of arrogance, Gor was a basket case as he prepared for the Armstrong sessions. "I tried so hard for Louis Armstrong, after worshipping the man all my life, I just about ruined the record date," he said in a 1977 interview. "I over-arranged so bad, you had to open the windows in the place. But at least I knew it. It was just cut, cut, cut until we got it right."

At the moment of truth, Gor said, "I cracked up. I walked into the studio, looked over there, saw Louis and broke down. Cried so hard I couldn't even see him. Later that night I came home, and I was so excited I couldn't eat my dinner. Then I started crying again. I took it pretty big."

"I suspect that deep down," said Nick Perito, Perry Como's longtime arranger and a family friend, "Gordon really wanted to be an old jazz player." And publisher Sam Weiss handed me a touching line in our interview, saying, "When Gordon saw Louis, it was like seeing his own son."

Gabler recalled that first recording session in intimate detail: "We were in Studio A, which was not a large room, and when you threw in thirteen voices, the strings, then a full dance band behind that and a rhythm section, you couldn't move in there. We had a little podium maybe eighteen inches high for Gordon to stand on with his baton, so everyone could see him. So he gets up there, and he makes a speech about how much he loves Louis Armstrong, how this moment was the pinnacle of his life. Louis was lookin' right at him, and Gordon started to cry. It was very touching. He wrote an arrangement and he was gonna conduct for his idol, Louis Armstrong. And it was a bitch!"

A number of critics, especially contemporary types reviewing in retrospect, couldn't tolerate the full chorus or sentimental strings that my father put behind Armstrong. The combination does seem oppressive, at times, if you're looking for that traditional Satchmo sound. But the sessions produced a number of songs—including "When It's Sleepytime Down South," "That Lucky Old Sun," and "Chloe"—that proved a stirring departure. "All the stuff with the strings, I tried to take all of his old licks that he used—and which everybody has used since—and write 'em for strings," Gor said. "Paraphrase 'em a little bit for his personal benefit. It broke him up. Broke a lot of people up."

An especially rare gem, "The Boppenpoof Song," emerged from a record date in 1954. "It was a takeoff on Dizzy Gillespie and all the original Birdland bop writers," Gor said, "and in particular 'The Whiffenpoof Song' [popularized by Bing Crosby in 1947 but dating back to the early 1900s as an adaptation of a Rudyard Kipling poem]. I wrote some parody lyrics and the original publishers just went to pieces, they were so unhappy with it. At the time I was doing real well; otherwise I couldn't have gotten away with it. They insisted on not paying me, which was fine; I just wanted to make the record, get it played, and not get sued. They finally agreed to it. The song was an absolute standout, the kind you hit maybe once in fifty years. Louis wasn't that crazy about the bop scene, nor was I, and we had a little fun with it." [The song appears on the 2001 compilation album, "Satchmo in Style," with its original title.]

I happened to run across a review from my own newspaper, the *San Francisco Chronicle*, by Ralph Gleason in 1954. He put it this way: "There's been too little humor in jazz in recent years. The young musicians have been so busy dedicating their talents to finding new paths and shaking off tradition, they have neglected to laugh. Louis Armstrong, by all odds the greatest individual musician produced by the traditional jazz culture, is a comic too and that's one of his strongest assets. Decca has just released a single disc of Louis singing a parody of 'The Whiffenpoof Song' which I urge everybody who loves jazz and loves Louis and wants a good laugh to buy immediately. If you're bewildered by bebop and frustrated by flatted fifths, this is for you. Gordon Jenkins, whose excellent studio band does the accompaniment, wrote a hysterically funny parody of the famous 'Whiffenpoof' words [We are poor little lambs who have lost our way, etc.] and it is one of the most delightful records ever made. I had intended quoting the lyrics, but the publishers, in a neat bit of public relations, would permit it only if the original lyricists were the only ones credited. Anyway, the Jenkins lyrics will sound funnier than they will read. So go down and buy it and have yourself a ball."

Some other material I came across over the years:

A review from one of the New York papers in 1952, when Gor got equal billing with Louis and his All-Stars at the Paramount Theater in Times Square: "When the Jenkins band joined Louis in the finale, 'When the Saints Go Marchin' In,' the house was in virtual bedlam. Jenkins seems to have such a good time up there, looking at Armstrong and [vocalist] Velma Middleton, he should pay to get in."

Mississippi-born songwriter Floyd Huddleston, who had two of his songs ("I'm Gonna Make It All the Way" and "Satisfy Me One More Time") recorded by Sinatra: "I got to know Gordon pretty well in New York, during his heyday with Louis, and one time they invited me to go up to Harlem for dinner and music. I'm a little Southern boy, never been around that many blacks at one time, and I was nervous as hell. But with Gordon, there was no race. The music was so much bigger than all that nonsense. Being with Louis and Gordy up there, that was one of the great nights of my life."

Huddleston on the Paramount Theater gigs: "Gordon told me

that between shows, he'd go back to Louis's room, and Louis would be back there by himself, playing tapes of his own music. Gordy said, 'Louis, you need some more tapes. That all you got, stuff of yourself?' And Louis said, 'Well, ain't nobody bettah.'"

Bruce Hudson: "On the dates we did with Louis in L.A., it would always be half of us [Jenkins's band] and half of him. During intermission over at Radio Recorders on Santa Monica Boulevard, the big doors would open up and you'd go out in the alley for fresh air and stuff. Guys were smokin' and drinkin' and who knows what. The bass player from Louis's band was a great big guy, about 6-foot-4, and [pianist] Charlie LaVere and I were standing there talking to him. Around came this little black guy, a little gopher who carried the instruments. The big guy pulls a pint of gin out of his pocket, swigs from it hard, then looks down at the little guy and says, 'Boy, you like gin?' Little guy says, 'I *loves* gin.' Big guy says, 'You didn't bring none.' That line was with us from then on."

That's how I remember my father and just about every musician who came around the house, a festival of good times, sweet sounds, laughter and cocktails. More than anything, I love that Nick Fatool story about Gor showing up a bit green-faced from the night before, finding his way backstage and grabbing Louis Armstrong's messy handkerchief. Just to get back.

Chapter 5

Judy

MY FATHER HAD THE DIPLOMATIC SKILLS of a hornet. If a party began to sag, he would abruptly walk out, knowing that Beverly would take care of the goodbyes. Sometimes he'd abandon his own party, right there in our house, and hit the sack at a ridiculously early hour. Admirers or interviewers would come up with long, heartfelt questions about his work, and if he detected the slightest hint of bullshit, he'd give a brutally short answer. We had a dear friend who went a little haywire, bound for a mental institution, and she would call the house in desperation, nearly unintelligible in a strange, raspy voice that sounded like something out of a horror film. Mom would stay on the phone with her for hours, agreeing with everything. Gor would catch maybe five or six syllables and hang up.

Generally, around home, he gave the impression of a man who had just returned from a nine-to-five gig at the hardware store. Grab a cocktail, hit a few chip shots, and let's start dinner. Absolutely zero news to report. One wouldn't have a clue that he just cut "Lonely Town" with Sinatra, or written the "Stardust" arrangement for Nat Cole—or that for a period in the late 1950s, he was among the very few people who could get Judy Garland on stage.

It's so hard for me to picture him that way: patient, comforting, trying to invent a funny line, actually grabbing someone to shake a little sense into her. But that's how it was with Gordon and Judy, night after night, during a memorable string of concerts. My father loved her, unconditionally, in the manner he reserved for the most special talents. I don't believe he fell for her romantically, as he did with many singers over the years. This was a deeper love, rooted in pure emotion over the way her performances made him feel. Someone once asked him if he'd take two Barbra Streisands for one Garland (he adored Streisand's work, although they never worked together), and he answered, "I wouldn't take two of anybody for Judy Garland. She was the greatest female entertainer ever."

She was just twenty-one years old when they first worked together, in March 1943, on a wartime show called the Free World Theater. She sang "The Wings of Freedom" on an episode narrated by the distinguished actor Ronald Colman. They hooked up again in July 1944 on "Everything for the Boys," on the NBC Red Network, when Judy and Dick Haymes teamed up to sing "When Somebody Loves Me," "Long Ago and Far Away" and "There's a Tavern in the Town." Her album "Judy Garland Sings" includes two songs cut with the Jenkins orchestra in 1946, and the collaboration led to two well-circulated albums during his years with Capitol: "Alone" in 1957 and "The Letter" in 1959.

Judy was looking for a real departure on "Alone," something removed from the dreamy little girl ("Over the Rainbow") or the energized woman in charge ("The Trolley Song"). Neither of those themes, regrettably, had much to do with her life at that point. She wanted something along the lines of "Bartender, make that a double," and boy, did she find the right conductor. She sang a couple of mournful Jenkins songs, "Blue Prelude" and "Happy New Year," and several others that fit her evolving mood: "Little Girl Blue," "By Myself," "How About Me," and "I've Got a Right to Sing the Blues." The work reminds me a lot of the Jenkins-Nat Cole album "Love is the Thing": both artists at the top of their game, offsetting each other beautifully. "I feel it's the best record I've ever done,"

Judy said in a 1957 interview. "Somehow, I feel that I have found a new approach to singing in this album, and I consider that my performance is much better with Gordon's arrangements and under his direction than with any other person I have ever sung with."

Judy was particularly moved by "How About Me," the Irving Berlin composition, and the deep, dark places she could discover through a Jenkins arrangement. "It's the saddest song ever written," she once said. "It's just *mean,* it's so sad." The song became a staple of her live performances in the late Fifties, "and you talk about a torch song," said comedian Alan King, her opening act during that time, "I mean, this was total cremation." In John Fricke's liner notes for the Garland 25th Anniversary Perspective CD, King recalls the night when he and Judy "went into a little restaurant, and Irving Berlin was sitting there. He said to her, 'You know, I wrote that song [in 1928]. I've never heard it sung as emotionally, as dramatically as you did it.' And Judy thought it was the greatest compliment she'd ever received. But she did that to all her material." Not long after the recording of "Alone," my father wrote, "The talent of Judy Garland could never be learned, and her electric crescendos are far beyond the scope of any mortal teacher . . . I believe that people cry at Judy for the same reason that they do at sunsets, or symphonies, or cathedrals; when one is confronted with overwhelming greatness, it is impossible not to be touched."

"The Letter" was a concept album, along the lines of "Manhattan Tower," and because my father had essentially invented the genre, there was a buzz of anticipation over this presentation of fully original material. Judy and John Ireland played a couple trying to resurrect a once-beautiful love affair, and according to the liner notes, the orchestra and chorus broke into a standing ovation, quite rare, at the midnight conclusion of the sessions. "The Letter" became the centerpiece of a 1959 U.S. tour through Chicago, San Francisco, Los Angeles and the Metropolitan Opera House in New York, where *Journal-American* critic John McClain wrote, "Only the late Al Jolson, I suspect, had such a magical effect on an audience. Only Jolson and Judy Garland could so completely dominate a congregation that it forgot time, circumstances and the high cost of living. High-bracket clowns and lush prima donnas wept openly. So did I."

Other reviewers, judging strictly on the recorded product, were not so kind. Many of them savaged "The Letter," and while it does include one of the best songs my father wrote, "The Red Balloon," I've always found the piece difficult to defend. The material isn't nearly as fresh or exciting as "Manhattan Tower" and, in a 21st-century context, it comes very close to bombing outright. I tried to give it a fresh listen, in the summer of 2001, and simply hated it. I could hear the critics raging, and the notion of second-rate material was just too hard to take. The first-issue albums (Capitol S/TAO 1188) came with an actual letter inside an envelope, surely a collector's item among Garland fans, and as I stashed the LP onto a darkened shelf, I noticed that it was an original—with the envelope unopened. But I couldn't bring myself to break the seal, as if the act would constitute a violation of some kind. I left it to the memories of Gordon and Judy, both of whom madly loved that album. I consider it a sweet little correspondence between themselves.

The Garland recording sessions certainly had their moments, but it was on stage, during a 1957 engagement at the Dominion Theater in London, where she knocked my father out. They played to capacity houses for four-and-a-half weeks at the stately British establishment and had the honor of a command performance for the Queen and Royal Family at the London Palladium. I don't know how Gor kept it together down in the pit, because the experience overwhelmed him, bringing him to tears *during* the performance at least once nightly. "It's one thing to see her in a film, or hear the records," he said many years later. "But it was nothing like seeing her in the room. I don't know what it was; something about her that just got to me—got to everybody. She'd hit the big note and ... Jesus [trembling voice]. I can hardly talk about it, even now."

For the overture, Gor put together an exciting, this-show's-gonna-blow-your-mind medley that Judy routinely used thereafter as an introduction to her stage shows. Then there was silence as the curtain came up. "On opening night the applause started," Gor said, "and immediately my mind accused her husband [Sid Luft] of embellishing it somehow, like with a sound-effects record. I just didn't think *people* could make that sound."

"That's the thing she had that no one else ever had," Peggy Lee once said. "Remember how they began to applaud and shout before they even saw her? The mere announcement of her name, the news of her approach, filled them with enthusiasm, and she got a welcome as no one else in our profession ever has."

"She won us over before she had sung a note," wrote the *Evening Review*. "Coming onto the stage in a black jersey and white skirt, she heard a voice cry out, 'Welcome back, Judy!' Almost coyly she hung her head and replied, 'Oh, *darling*.'"

And then the show unfolded, a thirty-song sequence of Garland favorites, including "For Me and My Gal," "Rock-A-Bye Your Baby With a Dixie Melody," "A Couple of Swells," "Me and My Shadow," "The Man That Got Away," and the grand finale, "Over the Rainbow," an almost suffocatingly emotional experience for everyone involved—especially Gor, who described the experience as "cold chills and tears, night after night." As critic Kenneth Tynan wrote in *The New Yorker*, "When the voice pours out, as rich and pleading as ever, we know where, and how moved, we are—in the presence of a star, and not embarrassed by tears."

Conducting for Garland required an imaginative, open mind. There was no form or routine; each night she'd launch into renditions radically different from what had come before. "I think the thing I do best is follow singers," Jenkins said. "If they're doing something that isn't in the regular tempo, like Sinatra does, I enjoy that. With Judy, she'd do something different all the time, and I always felt she got better with every performance. She was a joy to work with, because she had exceptional timing. If you looked out the window, you'd be lost."

Judy did not look well during that 1957 London engagement. According to Alan King, this was a time when she weighed 165 pounds and had "dresses lined with steel so she couldn't move." But it was truly amazing how the mood progressed each night. She took the stage overweight, baggy-faced, sort of a walking basket case at the age of thirty-five. By the final strains she was the most beautiful woman on earth.

For my father, following her rollicking on-stage moods was breezy, delightful stuff after the gut-wrenching melodramas that unfolded before the show each night. As her fans well know, Judy was terrified of going on stage, especially at this point of her life. Comparing herself to "a frightened cat," she was certain that she'd "walk onto the stage, open my mouth and nothing would come out." Gor said that was a normal fear among singers, "but Judy's brand was extreme. I had to spend long periods with her, just the two of us, every night, to get her to perform."

The trick was that Gordon, unlike so many people around Judy, did not ridicule or dismiss her anguish. He understood the depth and origins of her sorrow, and for a man deeply in touch with his own shadows, this was familiar territory. But nobody ever knew it quite like Judy. From the very beginning, in her teenage acting years at the MGM studio, she was advised to take pills to ward off her tendency to gain weight. By the age of twenty, according to David Shipman's stunning biography, *The Secret Life of an American Legend*, she was hooked on pills, drinking heavily and suffering from a distinct lack of self-esteem. Her mother, bitter and irresponsible, seldom looked out for her best interests. And from the very beginning, her experiences with men were grotesquely twisted. Her father was eventually revealed to be a homosexual. She routinely fell for men who, behind the cloak of public appearance, were gay. She had three abortions during a series of desultory marriages. There were many occasions when she was either too drunk or drug-sodden to perform, and she not only spoke often of suicide but attempted it several times. That is the extremely condensed version of a tortured life; to digest it all, for anyone who cared about Judy, is almost too much to bear.

Quoted in the biography, Gor said that "Judy, like all great stars, is inclined toward moodiness, which to me is as natural as rain. It would be impossible for Judy to sustain the level of her performances throughout her daily life; it's much too high a pitch, too close to perfection for her not to be allowed an occasional imperfection afterwards. I have always believed that the discords in Judy's life were caused by only one thing—the people around her didn't love her enough to try to understand her. I think all she ever wanted during those troubled days was to have a friendly arm around her."

Backstage at the Dominion Theater, that arm was Gordon's. "Judy was very disturbed then," said King. "But she was on her best behavior—mostly, I think, because of Gordon. She loved Gordy because he was a puppy dog, and because he was someone not wrapped up in his own talent. He was tasteful. She loved it when he sat around and played the piano for everybody. And he could make her laugh."

The ultimate punch line had come just before the London engagement, and while it was quite beyond Gor's control, it was vintage Jenkins. Princess Margaret, an ardent fan of Judy's, had arranged an elegant reception at the Londonderry House for dignitaries, cast and crew. "Everybody turned out for Judy," King recalled. "Hell, everybody in London was there. Your father, I can still see him so vividly. Never combed his hair, the suits never fit too good. In tails, he was the only guy who looked worse than me. Anyway, you didn't just show up at this thing, you were formally introduced. As you reached the top of the stairs, they had one of those toastmasters who would shout out each arrival: 'Lord and Lady Cumberland!' That sort of thing. Then you'd shake hands with Judy and walk in."

Aside from being a bit disheveled, Gor wasn't quite "regular" at the moment of truth. It seems he had to go—really bad. So he pulled aside the toastmaster and asked where he might be able to relieve himself. Which brought about this unforgettable pronouncement to the British elite:

"Mister Men's Room!"

"I swear, Judy almost had a heart attack, she was laughing so hard," said King. "That was the funniest thing she ever heard in her life. She called Gordon 'Mister Men's Room' for years."

All of it mattered when it came to those backstage showdowns, all of the laughter and tears and recording sessions. "She would do anything in the world to keep from going on," Gor recalled in a Fred Hall radio interview. "But she never missed one show when I was with her. I don't think anybody else who worked with her could say that. The thing is, I worked at it. I'd get there early, bring her jokes. I'd go so far as to hang things outside of her dressing-room window and bang on 'em, like a kid on Halloween—anything to get her attention away from herself. And while she's laughing I'm pushing her toward the stage. Literally. I'm maneuvering her out to the wings. If I got her that far, then I could run like hell, get down to the pit and start, and then she'd go on."

"Jeez, what an ordeal," an interviewer once told him.

"Well, I loved Judy," he said, flatly. "I was crazy about her."

There were many nights, in the foul London weather, when several hundred people would be standing outside in the rain after the show. "They didn't bother Judy," Gor said. "They didn't want her autograph. After waiting at least an hour, while she got dressed and all, they just wanted to see her go from the stage door to her car. They'd shout her name and she'd say, 'Hi, everybody!' and then they'd go home. They felt the same way I did, the way we all did, about her on stage. God knows she was successful in movies, but it was nothing like seeing her in the room."

Judy Garland died in June 1969, a complete physical wreck at the age of forty-seven. More than 21,000 people attended her funeral in New York, solemnly filing past an open casket. Mickey Rooney, Lauren Bacall, Ray Bolger, Kay Thompson—so many talented and trusted friends were there. Gor stayed at home, mourning in silence. He didn't speak a word for two days.

Chapter 6

The Sinatra Years

T HERE WAS SOMETHING ABOUT MY FATHER that took the fight out of Frank Sinatra. The dangerous little man became warm and reverential, a tyrant no more. He seemed to view Jenkins as a greater force, musically, than the conductors and arrangers who had come before. The quality of the music will be discussed forever, particularly as it compares to Sinatra's priceless work with Nelson Riddle, but one aspect of their relationship is beyond debate: Sinatra showed more respect for "Lefty," as he called Gor, than for anyone else inside a recording studio.

There's a piece of videotape that brings everything to life, the greatest discovery of my research and something that restores my father's legacy for all time. In 1965, a CBS Television crew made a study of Sinatra, detailing his life and getting him to sit down with Walter Cronkite for an extremely rare one-on-one interview. It could have been any year, with a subject so fascinating. It was my good fortune that they picked 1965, following Sinatra into sessions for the "September of My Years" album—the peak of my father's work and, quite possibly, Sinatra's as well.

The show was called "Sinatra: An American Original," and for a full ten minutes it takes you inside the studio for the recording of "It Was A Very Good Year." There's Frank in his white shirt and black sportcoat, the tie comfortably loosened. Smoke filters tantalizingly from his cigarettes, one after the other. "Good Year" was an oddly upbeat little number when it arrived at Gor's doorstep, and he turned it into a gorgeous ballad that captures the sweet reminiscence of a man easing into middle age. For my money it's his greatest arrangement, unassailably pure. And Sinatra, as the tape so clearly shows, was floored by it.

Seated in a chair during playback, occasionally glancing up at my father like a child seeking approval, Sinatra sheds the many difficult layers of his personality and we reach the core. Marvelous expressions cross his face, flashes of pride and confidence, darkness and regret, perhaps a poignant memory from long ago, all in a half-minute's time; he shakes his head at how beautifully the whole thing is going down. This was a year for the Beatles, the Beach Boys and the Rolling Stones, but "September of My Years" won Grammy awards for Best Album, Best Orchestration, Best Male Vocalist and Best Song, and through that dizzying haze of rock 'n' roll, it stayed on the *Billboard* charts for 69 weeks.

"That was the year Sinatra turned fifty," said Gor, who was fifty-five at the time. "We were exactly the right age to do that album. Talking on the date, Frank and I both felt that way. We both understood those kind of songs. I remember him saying that neither one of us could have made it a day earlier than we did."

In an especially hip set of liner notes, Stan Cornyn set the mood: "Jenkins starts a song, conducting with his arms waist high, sweeping them from side to side. Not leading the orchestra, *being* the orchestra ... Sinatra has lived enough for two lives, and can sing now of September. Of the bruising days. Of the rouged lips and bourbon times. Of chill winds, of forgotten ladies who ride in limousines ... Tonight will not swing. Tonight is for serious."

As the orchestra finished warming up, Cornyn watched Jenkins approach the podium.

"You ready, Gordy?" Sinatra asked.

"I'm ready. I'm always ready. I was ready in 1939."

"I was ready when I was nine."

To watch my father in everyday settings, you wouldn't be particularly struck by his demeanor. He was clearly shy and withdrawn, never demonstrative or confrontational. With the conductor's baton in his hand, he held a fierce and undeniable command over the proceedings. Band members paid the strictest attention, and whoever had the microphone—Jolson, Sinatra, Mussolini—would perform obediently under his rule. There were no arguments, no cries of defiance, because no one dared challenge him. It had nothing to do with physical intimidation; he was a committed pacifist who hadn't thrown a punch since grade school. He ruled on the sheer strength of his knowledge, and his word was final.

"Here's everything you need to know," said drummer Nick Fatool, who worked on many Sinatra dates. "Frank always had an entourage with him—friends, hangers-on, who knew who the hell they were? It was like a little audience, a support group that he had. One time, a bunch of these outsiders were milling around Frank as Gordy warmed up the orchestra, making a heck of a commotion, and Gordy said something like, 'Frank, could you keep it down, we're trying to rehearse over here.'

"Now, normally, that sort of thing could get you killed [laughter]," said Fatool. "But Frank just snapped to it. 'Oh, sure, Gordy,' and he cleared the room like that. You *never* saw that sort of thing. Sinatra was a sarcastic little cat; nobody told him to pipe down. Nobody told him to do anything."

"You bet Sinatra was afraid of Gordon," said conductor-arranger Bud Dant. "That's the only musical director he had that kind of respect for. Of all the talented people I've ever known, Gordon had more self-confidence than any of 'em. Frank never said one derogatory word about his work, and that wasn't the case with anyone else. I've heard Sinatra just tear Nelson Riddle apart. Said the whole thing's wrong, forget it, threw up his hands, just walked right out."

Billy May: "With Nelson, Frank knew that he could do whatever he wanted, and Nelson would be like [hurriedly nervous], 'Oh, sure, I'll change it,' that sort of thing. A little less secure. All too ready to make a change. Don't upset the boss, you know, that kind of crap. I've seen Frank feed off people, and even with a talent like Nelson, he could be a real vitriolic bastard.

"Sweets Edison, a black trumpet player and a good jazz player, was on a date with Frank where if the band stayed too long, it would cost more money, and for some reason Frank was taking advantage of that," said May. "So they're up to take 27, or something, and I happened to drop in. They finished the take. Nelson cut the band off, Frank's lookin' around, and Sweets yells out, 'Shit, daddy, you can't do it no better 'n' that!' Everybody started laughing, including Frank. He said, 'Let's go home.' But Nelson would have stayed there all day."

Alan King, who moved in Sinatra's inner circle, said, "Gordon and Nelson were the all-time opposites. Nelson used to go crazy off the set, he was a wild man. He'd actually get in fights with people. 'I'll have a double Scotch,' somebody says. And he'd say, 'Whaddya mean by that?' Just the complete other side of Gordon. Major, major talent, everybody knows that. But I think Nelson feared Frank, whereas Gordon just respected him. You couldn't threaten or intimidate Gordon Jenkins. He knew what he wanted, and he had the best taste of anybody I ever knew."

In his book *Sinatra: An American Classic,* John Rockwell noted that "Sinatra retains far greater control over his recording sessions than most musicians. Within his own terms, he retains a single-minded dominance over his recordings that he could never achieve with his films." And yet, things were different with my father around.

"Gordon meant class," said arranger Nick Perito. "He meant something with integrity, and that brought him respect. I remember so well in the Fifties, when I was a piano player coming up in

New York, he'd walk into a room and everything would stop. You know those fiddle players, they like to noodle a lot. They're always fooling around with something. But when Gordon stopped the band, they were on their best behavior.

"There was just something about him. I mean, this is a guy who could tell Sinatra to be quiet! And Frank had a reputation for just destroying people. Don Costa in particular. Oh, boy. Like, 'What the hell'd you write that for? Jesus Christ, that's awful.' And of course, Don never wrote an awful arrangement in his life. But Gordon was a man of substance, and Frank knew it. I think Frank got his ounce of class from hanging around Gordon [laughter], I really do."

Singer Loulie Jean Norman, a gifted soprano who was always a must-get for the really high notes in the chorus, described Gor and Sinatra as "like one. Just sheer admiration on both parts. Frank loved everything Gordon did; he could do no wrong. And honey, Frank was terrible. You saw what he did to people, and you just cringed. Like Fred Waring, he was just horrible with him. He found out that Fred could be weak, and of course, Frank always picked on guys like that. Nelson, in his way, was weak. But for some reason he felt totally at ease with Gordon. Listen, whenever Gordon corrected anybody, it was accepted. They knew that musically, he was right."

The Sinatra-Jenkins collaborations dated back to April 1957, with the "Where Are You?" sessions on Capitol Records, and people were certain that the two strong wills would clash. "That first date, about a hundred people showed up to see the fight," Gor said in 1974. "Literally, the studio was jammed. He had a reputation for being very difficult on orchestra leaders, and I was known for not holding back. So everybody showed up to see us go at each other. We disappointed them all. We never did fight. We've never had a cross word, ever."

It's safe to say that Jenkins was treading sacred ground. At that time, Sinatra and Capitol meant Nelson Riddle, period. They had already cut six albums together, including the peerless "Songs For Swingin' Lovers" and "A Swingin' Affair," and you wouldn't go too far wrong saying that this was the greatest singer-arranger partnership in the history of popular music. The core of their elegance was well established with "I've Got You Under My Skin," "Young at Heart," "My Funny Valentine," "I Get a Kick Out of You," "I've Got the World on a String," "You Make Me Feel So Young," and so many others in the bank. It would be another four months before Sinatra had his first association with Billy May in the brassy, up-tempo "Come Fly With Me," and while he had never worked with Jenkins, it seemed they had seen each other coming from miles away.

Admittedly taken with my father's symphonic leanings and romantic bent, Sinatra had cut the Jenkins tune "Homesick, That's All" with Axel Stordahl in 1945 and "P.S. I Love You" with Riddle in 1956. About a year before the "Where Are You?" sessions, he included Gor among a select group of composers (Riddle, Leonard Bernstein, Andre Previn, Victor Young and Alec Wilder among them) asked to write and arrange music for the now-obscure "Tone Poems of Color," a Sinatra album based on the poetic lyrics of Norman Sickel.

"I'd known Gordon many years," Sinatra said in a backstage chat with East Coast disc jockey Sid Mark at the Philadelphia Spectrum in 1984. "I think I was with [Tommy] Dorsey when I first met him. I always dreamed of him doing some work for me, because I'd heard some of the early stuff he did for Judy and Nat Cole, or even going back to 'Manhattan Tower,' which was a beautiful thing."

Looking back, 1957 might have been the defining year of Gor's life. His first albums with Cole ("Love Is the Thing") and Garland ("Alone") were released, he performed his memorable London engagement with Judy, and he was still scorching hot from the

Decca years, where he had hit records with Louis Armstrong ("Blueberry Hill"), Peggy Lee ("Lover"), the Weavers ("Goodnight Irene"), Dick Haymes ("Little White Lies") and the Andrews Sisters ("I Can Dream, Can't I?"), just to scratch the surface.

"I was goin' pretty good before I hooked up with Frank," he said. "But the way Capitol was set up, I couldn't record with any of their people without hearing from a lawyer somewhere. Until I went on the label [for the second time; Gor had been on the original Capitol staff in 1942], and that changed everything. I don't remember how we set it up, exactly, but I assume Frank asked for me."

The common theory among Sinatra fans is that when he wanted a lively, finger-snapping kind of thing, he went with Riddle—and if he was in a downtrodden, set-'em-up-Joe mood, he used Jenkins. That's true, to great extent, but the Sinatra-Riddle association on "In the Wee Small Hours" (1955) set a powerful standard for ballads. As *Time* magazine noted that year, "As Sinatra stands up to the mike, tie loose and blue palmetto hat stuck on awry, his cigarette hung slackly from his lips, a mood curls out into the room like smoke." If Gor had any intent of making this relationship last, he would need a mighty first impression—and "Where Are You?" hit the target dead-on. He came up with two of his all-time best arrangements, on "Laura" and "Lonely Town," and the album was top-to-bottom rich in quality songs.

As it happened, the Fifties were an especially vulnerable time for Sinatra. He had married actress Ava Gardner, for whom his love smoldered past the levels of reason, and the relationship became a raging nightmare. Difficult as it might sound to young fans who knew only the Chairman, aging king of all he surveyed, Sinatra lost nearly everything: his film and recording (Columbia) contracts, his radio shows, even his voice one terrible night at the Copacabana. His fawning, bobbysox fans from the Forties were all grown up, the press was taking potshots at his gaudy lifestyle, and his left-wing political slants weren't too popular in the McCarthy era. He might have hit rock bottom in April 1952, when, according to the *Honolulu Advertiser*, "he was singing in a leaky tent at the Kauai County Fair, a has-been crooner." Capitol had to be talked into giving him a one-year contract, and only if he'd be willing to pay his own studio costs.

Those early Riddle albums seemed sent from the heavens, and the sight of the smiling, winking, swingin' Sinatra left fans feeling the sweet thrill of envy. But deep down, Sinatra wasn't that guy leaning back in a chair, hands clasped self-assuredly behind his head, on the cover of "Nice 'N' Easy." He filed for divorce from Gardner just two months after the "Where Are You?" sessions, and it was tearing him up inside. There was no manufacturing the depth of torment in his voice; it came straight from the heart. (As Riddle once said, "It was Ava who did that, who taught him how to sing a torch song. She was the greatest love of his life, and he lost her.") Successful as he was, Sinatra was also that guy sitting alone at a bar past midnight—and in essence, that explains his universal appeal. He was all things at once: swinger, punk, gentleman, lout, charmer, boor, high roller, two-time loser. Nobody else could pull that off. Johnny Mathis was too effeminate, Perry Como too suburban, Bing Crosby too perfect, Dean Martin too tipsy (or so it seemed). They were all one-dimensional acts next to Sinatra's. It's not really accurate to use that familiar cliché—"you either loved him or hated him, no in between"—because for the people who really plugged in, every known emotion came to the fore.

"He can make any audience feel like he's their kind of guy," Cronkite said on the CBS show. "When he sings, he makes it sound as though it all happened to him ... it probably *did* all happen to him."

Gor was astounded by Sinatra's disdain for rehearsal, but he soon realized that the exercise was irrelevant. Frank knew what he wanted, and he felt it wasteful to send perfectly good phrases into thin air. Johnny Mandel, who arranged and conducted Sinatra's "Ring-A-Ding Ding!" album in 1961, told me, "Frank was just intuitively a good musician. If he heard something once, he knew the arrangement. Buddy Rich was like that. Couldn't read music . . . no, not couldn't. *Wouldn't.* Give him a part, he'd turn it upside down and throw it on the floor. But it didn't matter; he knew it before anyone else, just from the single hearing. And Frank was like that. It went into his head and stayed. He wouldn't rehearse, and on the rare occasion he did, he didn't even sound like Frank. He sounded like somebody who didn't sing very well. Which is why he had sort of a kamikaze approach. He was so used to working before an audience, he had to have those hangers-on around the studio, and he wanted to do everything in one take. But that's where the adrenaline came from. He *made* himself sing. I'm convinced of that. I think when he lost his voice that time, years ago, he didn't really lose it. He had just stopped caring."

One of my dad's strengths was his ability to toss aside the ethics of behavior, when it came to a truly elite artist, and just let the work flow. Temperament and eccentricity didn't bother him if the final product was worthwhile; he cut the great ones all kinds of slack. So if Sinatra didn't want to rehearse, fine; no rehearsal.

"Frank doesn't take kindly to suggestions," Gor said. "If he decides he's done a take that's good enough, that's it. If you ask him to do another one, he won't. He might just go home. But hell, nobody in the world can sing a song like Frank. You try to put as much as you can into it, without getting in the way. That was the trick. The last thing he wants to do is sit down at the piano and run something down with you. He figures we both know what we're gonna do, and if there's some question, he'll say, 'Do that thing you do in here.' And I say, 'OK,' and I go do that thing [laughter].

"Did he know his stuff? Oh, God, more than any of 'em," Gor

said. "I was conducting him at the Sands in Vegas once, and all of a sudden he came storming off the stage. Said, 'The viola player's got it wrong.' And this guy's way the hell over on the other side of the stage. I didn't hear it, and the guys in the band didn't hear it, but Frank did. He hears everything."

It was mentioned that Sinatra worked arduously on his breathing, sometimes holding his breath underwater to build the strength in his lungs. "He swam under too many vodkas," said Gor. "Lots of Jack Daniel's changed hands. I'm no teetotaler, but in my best days, I can't drink with him. He always came to work moderately sober, but there were times, especially in live performances, when he struck me as a complete basket case. I saw it so often with big talents: Judy refusing to go on, Al Jolson ducking into a bathroom to vomit before he went on, and sometimes with Frank, I could see his arm shake. But once all of 'em got out there . . . unbelievable."

As much as Gor had savored his work with Nat Cole, the Sinatra sessions were somehow more exhilarating, a high-wire act, and he loved that kind of challenge. "Nat was a different kind of singer. More contained, more reserved as a person and a singer than most. God knows I'd never find fault with him, but the dates weren't quite as exciting as they were with Sinatra, when you don't know whether he's gonna leave, or throw up, or what the hell he's gonna do. That makes it a little more fun. And you've got a fantastic talent goin' for you."

It confounded Sinatra to see a left-handed conductor. Gor was totally unorthodox to begin with, dramatically swaying and lurching during particularly powerful passages, and you wouldn't exactly compare it with Nureyev's grace. Sometimes he looked downright awkward up there, the Midwestern bumpkin who made it big with a style uniquely his own. (One night while conducting Sinatra at the Sands Hotel in 1965, Gor got a little carried away and banged himself right in the nuts. As he fell to the floor, writhing in agony, the band members broke up.) Once Sinatra got a load of that left hand, "it was very confusing to me," he said. "When you're used to looking at a conductor in front of you on a podium, waving his right hand, and suddenly you're looking for the beat and he's on the other hand . . . it was strange for the first couple of dates. But it worked out in the end."

(An aside on conducting: Like Riddle, May and the other real pros, Gor conducted with downbeats, always ahead of the game, so the tempo would be no mystery. You see these amateur-hour conductors, like the guys leading brassy bands at collegiate sports events, and they're not conducting, just moving in time with the music. For all they're contributing, they could be lying on their backs, smoking a joint and playing air guitar.)

The "Where Are You?" album starts with the title cut, a classy song executed perfectly, and rolls on solidly from there. It was a commercial smash, reaching the #2 slot on *Billboard* and staying on the list for eighteen weeks. In the book *Sinatra: A Celebration*, author Stan Britt was particularly taken by the album, writing, "Year by year, it seems to become more meaningful, more vital. The most memorable track of all is a reading of 'Autumn Leaves' which is like no other. Sinatra's unfolding of Johnny Mercer's English lyric produces an aura of mystery that at times borders on the surrealistic. It is so extraordinary, there is absolutely no chance of anyone else equaling, let alone surpassing it."

My father was always partial to "Laura" and "Lonely Town," and to his dying day, he listed them among his most important work. "I think 'Laura' would be my choice in the best two or three orchestrations I ever made for Frank," he said. "He's probably the only singer in the world who would stand still for an introduction that long. It's quite a while before he sings, maybe 20–25 seconds. But it sets him up beautifully, I think. And he never questioned it. It never came up."

"Lonely Town," from the Leonard Bernstein score of "On the Town," has become famous among Sinatra disciples for its historical significance. Despite the fact that Riddle guided Sinatra back into prominence in the early Fifties, Sinatra described working with Jenkins as "like being back in the womb" and at one point in the studio during the playback of "Lonely Town," he said to an associate, "Gordon Jenkins has just saved my fucking life." It was clear that he still felt some insecurity, about his life and his singing voice, and there was comfort within Gor's sweeping orchestration. If any critics thought that Jenkins over-wrote at times, they couldn't run that opinion past Sinatra. He wouldn't hear of it.

"Of course Nelson Riddle was there when the comeback started," said Ed O'Brien, an upstate New Yorker who has devoted his life to documenting Sinatra's career. "But your father touched something inside Sinatra that brought out a sadness that no one else ever did. It's an astonishing thing to listen to, the two of them."

As far as I know, Sinatra's only lengthy public commentary about my father came in the Sid Mark conversation, and "Lonely Town" was the trigger. "I had a symphonic piece of music [a somewhat obscure work in his collection] that had the beginning of 'New York, New York,' those intonations in it," he told Mark. "Gordy liked it, and it worked out very well. Gordy was a man who was always open to suggestions. He's a good secretary. He sits at a piano with a piece of music, picks out a key, figures out what we should do back of the vocal in the first eight bars, the second eight bars, using the woodwinds or brass, or what have you. But Gordon was one man I felt I could almost leave alone. Just let him work on it himself.

"I think he was the most sensitive man about orchestrations," he went on. "You could hear it in his music. *So* sensitive. Not that the others weren't, Nelson and Billy, but Gordon *displayed* sensitivity. You felt it, you heard it when you spoke to him. I should know, I'm crazy about his orchestrations. I love 'em. Genius is the word for him. He's one of the modern geniuses of the good pop music. He was a genius when he wrote. He still is. I go on a record date and I hear what he's done, and he just puts me away with it. Nobody else has been able to do that."

What a magnificent year, 1957. On May 20, about three weeks after wrapping "Where Are You?" Sinatra cut "Witchcraft" with Riddle. On May 23, he was using Riddle's arrangement on "The Lady Is a Tramp" for the soundtrack of "Pal Joey." And in the July heat of an L.A. summer, he was back in the studio with Jenkins for "A Jolly Christmas from Frank Sinatra" (re-named "The Sinatra Christmas Album"). It was a Capitol rush job, hastily assembled after word came down that Columbia was going to re-issue some old Sinatra cuts for a holiday album, but it hardly sounds that way. Nancy Sinatra called it "simply the best Christmas album ever made—by anyone, anywhere, to this day," and while I'm in no great hurry to quote Nancy, if you like Sinatra at all, she's right. Everything else is a distant second.

Sinatra had Jenkins lined up to do his next album of ballads, "Frank Sinatra Sings For Only the Lonely," in the spring of 1958, but Gor was working on "Tropicana Holiday," a Broadway-style soundtrack for Monte Proser's revue at the Tropicana Hotel in Las Vegas. Nothing ever interrupted my dad's plans, including Sinatra, so the work was turned over to Riddle, with typically spectacular results. The album included a killer Riddle arrangement of "Good-bye" and reached the #1 slot on *Billboard*, but the conflict didn't sway Sinatra's opinion of my father. The next time he wanted a for-lorn excursion into some lonely bar, he dialed GL-72738 (area codes—who knew?) and enlisted Gor for "No One Cares," a 1959 release. In the words of critic Will Friedwald, "Sinatra's plan was to devise the single saddest album ever imagined, and he came up with twelve slices of sublime melancholy, arranged by Gordon Jenkins at his gloomiest. Pure, unvarnished misery set to music. On 'A

Cottage for Sale,' Sinatra sounds as if his best girl cheated him out of house and home."

The album cover couldn't have been more perfect: a busy saloon, people smiling and drinking, and a fur-laden woman sitting right next to Frank. But she's got her back to him, and in the midst of all that merriment, he's moodily pondering his cocktail, left hand on his chin. I found the best moments in "I Don't Stand a Ghost of a Chance" and "Here's That Rainy Day," and nationally syndicated disc jockey Sandy Singer, an invaluable contributor in my Sinatra research, said the album has a special place in his collection. "There's something strange about sadness," he said. "I can sit in a totally dark room, listen to 'No One Cares' and be the most happy person in the world. It's very hard to explain, but it *is* possible to be sadly happy."

The venerable critic Ralph Gleason handled the liner notes on "No One Cares" and wrote this in summation: "For all our gaiety and brass, this is a country with an element of sadness running through its soul. The Italians and the Irish, the Jews and yes, even the English, have a melancholy side to their nature and thus we have a great appetite for the song of unrequited love, the lament of love gone cold or hopeless. This underlying note of tragedy is embedded in most American art, as it is in American life. It is one of the reasons Frank Sinatra can sing the sad songs in this album so well. Those bittersweet, late-night, sad songs of days that used to be require an interpreter who can be sad without being maudlin, who can, in short, be man enough to cry a little and with the tears gain dignity."

Three years passed before Jenkins and Sinatra worked again, on the 1962 Reprise album "All Alone." The title gives you some idea where they were headed: down the path of stark loneliness once again. I found this to be the weakest of their collaborations, although Gor's introductions to "The Song Is Ended" and "Are You Lonesome Tonight?" (better than that song deserves) are the essence of his style, absolutely destroying me every time. Thanks to O'Brien, I got to hear some rejected takes from the session, and Sinatra's voice sounded (for him) noticeably weak. Excessively clearing his throat, he managed to find some humor ("I phrased that like it was my first record date—Holy Christ, you'd think I just got in the business"), but at another stage he halted a take and said, "Once more for me, Gordy. Sorry, I've got a problem here."

"Never was Jenkins more valuable to Frank," O'Brien said. "He covers many of his vocal flaws so apparent around that time. Sinatra responds by singing from the very depths of his emotional being. Overall, this was a noble effort that deserved a better fate [it peaked at No. 25 on *Billboard* and faded quickly]. Among his first ten Reprise albums, this was probably his most effective ballad album. A perfect record for a cold January night."

I spent a good deal of time soliciting Sinatra-with-Jenkins opinions from "The Voice," an Internet society of Sinatra lovers. For jazz critic Vincent Reda, "All Alone" represented the height of torch-song albums. "Sinatra, I believe, loved and felt akin to Jenkins's musical language, particularly with ballads, more than any other arranger's," he said via e-mail. "Frankly, I'm not so sure that without Gordon, we would ever have known how ultimately well Sinatra can sing. And I think the most perfect blend of the two is 'All Alone.' There could have been no better arranger to transport us to a world of Victorian delicacy—which is what those songs demand. I believe it is the most moving album Sinatra ever did.

"When I hear 'Only the Lonely' [with Riddle] I feel as I would in the audience watching 'A Streetcar Named Desire.' I am in awe of the dramatic presentation," said Reda. "But with 'All Alone,' I'm not the fourth wall. I'm within the walls. I'm there in the room with him. The intimacy is that much greater. I never really felt I was *at* the bar with Sinatra during 'One for My Baby.' With 'Alone,' I feel like I'm in a chair on the other side of the telephone, waiting for it to ring and rescue this poor guy."

I was a junior at Santa Monica High School when Gor and Sinatra got together for "September of My Years." Life in 1965 meant trips to Dodger Stadium to watch Sandy Koufax face the Giants; Jerry West going against the titanic Bill Russell and the Boston Celtics at the L.A. Sports Arena; the superbly fit and tanned girls hanging around the volleyball court at the Malibu West Beach Club; and always the afternoon summer breeze coming off the ocean, where we'd bodysurf 'til dusk and try not to be *too* late for dinner (my mom, bless her heart, always felt the waves were a plenty good reason). While Gor ran up and down the scales on his elegant Steinway piano in the studio, or settled deeply into an arranging assignment, I was tucked in my downstairs bedroom with a tiny audio tape recorder, lifting the latest from Marvin Gaye, the Miracles or some esoteric R&B group off the scratchy KGFJ airwaves. I had always been uncomfortable with the notion of hearing my father on the radio, but things changed that summer. I started to get a real appreciation of the Jenkins sound, the fact that Sinatra loved working with him, and that "It Was a Very Good Year" was knocking people dead across the country.

"That album was Frank's idea," Gor once said. "He picked all the songs without interference from the record company, some with a little assist from me. Frank told me it all started with one of my tunes, 'This Is All I Ask,' and the line, 'Beautiful girls, walk a little slower when you walk by me.' He started thinking about songs that fit the idea of growing older, a very personal thing for him. I think it probably was his best album, the best he ever sounded. Those were my best arrangements, too. If I had to pick one album for backing up a singer, that would be it. We had the time, the right guy in the booth [producer Sonny Burke] and the experience—and it sounds like it."

Webster Groves, Missouri, 1914: Even at the age of four, Gordon Jenkins could make sense of a violin. By his teens, he was self-taught on several instruments.

Jenkins at the piano, anchoring the Wildwood Serenaders in the summer of 1926.

At the age of eighteen, Jenkins (third from right) landed a job as arranger for the prestigious Joe Gill band in St. Louis. The famed Pee Wee Russell sits just left of the drums.

On stage with charismatic Charlie LaVere, who sang "Maybe You'll Be There" and played piano in the Jenkins band for years. (Photo courtesy Delta Haze Corporation archives)

December 1941 promotional photo from NBC, where Jenkins had been hired as Hollywood musical director.

The toast of New York: appearing on the Ed Sullivan show in 1950 and sharing the bill with his idol, Louis Armstrong, at the Paramount Theater in 1952.

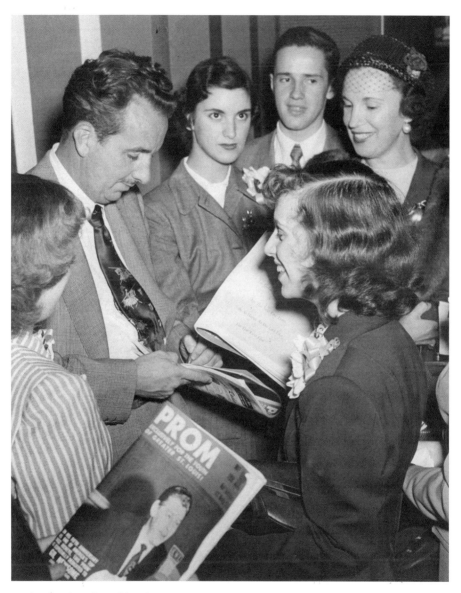

At the height of his hit-making career in the early 1950s, when *Billboard* labeled him "America's No. 1 recording star."

With singers Dick Haymes and Helen Forrest on the Auto-Lite radio show, which had a long and successful run in the 1940s. (Photo by Wayne Rothschild)

Left: Jenkins composed a special piece on the life of Jack Benny (right), who was so impressed, he put it on his NBC radio show, complete with Jenkins's band and chorus.

Below: At home in the San Fernando Valley, 1944. Contemporaries were astounded at how quickly he could produce arrangements and original songs.

Singer Martha Tilton, a mainstay with the Benny Goodman band and source for the inside story behind "Goodbye," which Goodman made his theme song.

Burke, then fifty-one, was a self-taught arranger who worked with Jimmy Dorsey, had many movie credits as an orchestrator and headed up the West Coast office of Decca Records during my dad's time there. As a freelance producer, he became known for his Sinatra collaborations, and Gor trusted him implicitly. "Sonny is an extremely underrated and bright man, particularly for me and Frank, because he knows us so well," Gor said. "He's just about the only person I would trust in the booth. If I'm making an orchestra track, and he says we got it, I'll go to the next one without even hearing it. Because, by God, you can bet he's got it. Through a lot of very shoddy political moves, he was kind of pushed aside in a lot of Frank's stuff, but the best stuff Frank ever did was when Sonny was in there."

Gor was used to cranking out several arrangements within a matter of hours, if necessary, "but on 'September' I had a lot of time. I spent close to a week on every one of those songs. I didn't have to keep looking at my watch, with a copyist waiting. I'd spend an hour on a bar, or even a note. Because if you don't have them right, then the whole thing isn't going to be right. I like all of those songs —except for 'Don't Wait Too Long,' which is kind of a crappy song. It came out all right and fit the idea, but I didn't really have my heart in it."

The song "You Are There" wound up with a stirring and powerful arrangement, but it was in effect saved by Sinatra and his unfailing good taste. "That's one that I did over," Gor said. "It just wasn't the greatest orchestration on the first go-round, and after we recorded it, Frank called me up and said let's take another shot at it. And when he does that, he's not just tossing around an idea; he'll give you the specific hook that he wants to use. He'll say treat it this way, or have this obbligato, give you some direction. I'd always do it for him. And if it came to that, I'd make the second one for nothin'."

One of the album's best songs turned out to be a total shot in the dark, a flash from the distant past. "When I was about fifteen years old, working in the KMOX radio station in St. Louis, there was an announcer named Don Hunt who used to follow me around, humming songs and everything," Gor said. "Years later he sent me a song he'd written, 'When the Wind Was Green.' So I wrote him a letter and asked if he had any more of those. He must have sent me two hundred songs, just suitcases full of 'em, and I mean, the worst stuff imaginable. You never saw such junk in your life. One song, he wrote. Very original and very different."

In the hands of Gor and Sinatra, such tunes as "September Song" and "September of My Years" were bound for glory. But "It Was a Very Good Year" was an all-time sleeper, a song that needed some life-changing revisions. "It was written by a fellow named Ervin Drake, and it was first recorded around 1961 by The Kingston Trio," Gor said. "Frank heard it on the radio and figured it fit the theme of the album, but when they gave it to me it was a rhythm song [snaps fingers to an upbeat tempo]. I did away with that. It was really crummy with that two-four beat and I figured, Frank would hate this. I did it the way I thought it should be."

The song became a singular definition of nostalgia, one man's lifetime in four minutes and twelve seconds. Drake was astounded when he first heard it. "He called me up, and I thought he was gonna break into tears, he was so happy," Gor said. "He didn't know what he had."

Drake told an interviewer that he first heard the song in London, where a British friend played it for him over the telephone. "I made him play it for me twice. As soon as we got home, I ran to the record store. I must have played that cut thirty or forty times the first day, and I've never done that with any other song. The whole album is terrific, but I never get tired of the beautiful way that Gordon Jenkins and Frank Sinatra treated that song."

Even the I'd-rather-hear-Riddle crowd had glowing praise for "September of My Years"; critic Will Friedwald offered, "No Sinatra performance is more movingly bittersweet. Jenkins's gloriously heightened sense of drama helped Sinatra turn a program of predominantly new songs into a perfectly realized concept album. For thirteen tracks, Sinatra reflects nostalgically on the very good years of his youth, when the wind was green and beautiful girls walked a little slower."

Steve Allen, who played a lot of jazz piano during his long career as a comedian, told me, "Sure, we all loved the jazzy stuff, where you're snapping your fingers, ordering another drink, all of that sort of thing. But it doesn't sink into the deep emotional roots, in my mind, the way those beautiful ballads do, and when Gordon worked with Frank, they brought all that beauty out. Sometimes more than the original creator had realized. I think emotion is such an essential ingredient in anything—music, comedy, theater. There have been singers like Andy Williams or Perry Como, wonderful talents, and ninety-eight percent of what they did was share that beautiful noise with the world. But there was more to it with Frank. There was so much thought in his rendition, and how he related to Gordon's arrangements. He didn't just go from G-minor to C-7, for example, or some automatic-pilot thing. He was conscious that he was conveying emotion."

There is a detailed bit of analysis by Richard W. Ackelson in *Frank Sinatra: A Complete Recording History,* a serious effort at explaining exactly how my father operated: "Jenkins's arrangements varied remarkably little in their basic 'feel' during the more than twenty years he wrote for Sinatra. Most of the dominant features were present in the first album, 'Where Are You?'. Jenkins's arrangements were supportive, showcasing and setting Sinatra's voice, rather than competing like Billy May's, or even commingling like Nelson Riddle's. Jenkins's charts were a delicate cloud floating under the singer's voice, lifting it, building to climaxes coincident with the drama presented by the voice, accentuating more than accompanying. Overall, this glowing supportiveness allowed Sinatra to sing with more nuance than ever before. And unlike Axel Stordahl, Jenkins wrote with consciously symphonic elements, less dance-band influence, and with a mournful black-blues underpinning brought from his days with Isham Jones's group.

"Compared to many other Sinatra arrangers, Jenkins wrote longer introductions to set a mood and longer closes to bring the listener out of that mood. Arrangements would usually open with a musical phrase drawn from some part of the song's melody, whether verse, release or chorus, sometimes so altered that the source was nearly unrecognizable. A classic example would be a solo oboe, followed by a solo flute, followed by a section of violins. Another common opening was by French horns, or perhaps strings, then French horn, then woodwinds. After opening, the charts were often dominated by strings, with solo French horn and soft trombones taking on the brass parts. Woodwind sections usually were played without saxophones, but rather with a solo clarinet, flute, oboe or bassoon. String passages might begin with one or two violins, then quickly add more violins, then all the strings (violas, cellos, sometimes a bowed bass fiddle) and build to great volume and richness, a crescendo made not by louder playing but by more musicians.

"There was a general absence of drums; instead, bass and/or guitar kept the beat. This lack of percussion was frequently offset by pizzicato playing of strings, plucked violins and harp, with piano chimes and even flutes emulating the effect of a run of plucked notes. On reflection, it is remarkable how many variations Gordon Jenkins was able to work from a limited number of basic elements, and how appropriately his arrangements serve a wide variety of songs."

I have scant visual evidence of my father's work. There's a BBC video of his London sessions with Harry Nilsson for "A Little Touch of Schmilsson in the Night" in 1973. There are painfully brief flashes of his conducting in a number of television shows. My friend Steve LaVere turned up a Colgate Comedy Hour showing Gor conducting Louis Armstrong at the Hollywood Bowl in 1954, and when the still-thin Jenkins turns around to bow to the audience, it's a personal stunner; I can almost feel the surge of elation inside him. But nothing compares to the CBS video from 1965. A long stretch of the film shows Sinatra singing with my father's active left arm in the foreground. The camera pulls back and you see Gor looking directly at Frank, not the band, to make sure he's in touch with any flights of fancy. At the point of "vintage wine, from fine old kegs," Gor starts swaying and leaning like crazy, not so much a conductor but a character from "Fiddler on the Roof," telling a musical story with his limbs. And it seems that Sinatra finds the very essence of middle age in this song, particularly as he sings "when I was thirty-five" to close that section. The inflection, the passion, the look on his face, the soulful little body movement and the smile ... that's it. The pinnacle. I simply cannot believe that somebody captured it on film.

"There's a magic that takes place at the sessions, between Frank and myself," Gor said. "As close as you're gonna get without being of the opposite sex. It's a hard thing to describe, but it's definitely a mental connection when you're going good. He lets it loose. He's all over the place when he's goin'. He doesn't hold anything back. It's in his personal life that he holds back."

When the two performed live, Gor said, the challenge became even more thrilling. "The excitement is in following him, because he likes to wander around. He doesn't necessarily do a song the way you rehearsed it. So I never take my eyes off him. I wouldn't dare. You can't relax for a minute. If you do, he'll leave you. He'll stop in the middle of a bar and talk to somebody at ringside, then you gotta figure, what—will he start up again right there, or start at the beginning? He generally might give you a little hint, but he might not. He'd just as soon you'd be there, no matter how long you have to stand there with your baton in the air. To me, that's fun. Makes it a lot more interesting than doing a song the same way every night. He can stop and write home if he wants to; I'll catch him somewhere. It comes from experience. Forty years. You use it all. You use every one of those years every night. Because he doesn't make mistakes. Consequently, you don't make any. I have a hell of a time convincing the guys in the orchestra that they can throw that rehearsal version right out the window. They just don't believe me. But once we start, they've all got their eyes on me. They can't afford not to. There's no guarantee what Frank will do, and there shouldn't be. That's why he's Frank Sinatra."

The video rolls on. During the "Good Year" playback, as Sinatra relaxes confidently in a chair, there's Gor standing with both arms stiffly in his pockets and his eyes to the floor—the awkward stance he always struck while listening to music with friends in our home studio (braced to step into the control room and cue up the next number, he rarely sat down; he stood, lost in a private world). Behold two entities as one: the bumpkin, without a whole lot of style, next to Sinatra, who invented it.

Friends often wondered what it must have been like for my dad, hanging out with Sinatra. Typically, he never said a word to me about their relationship, and it was left to my imagination. I had to laugh when I read about Sinatra's all-tightwad team, his personal list of guys who wouldn't pick up a check to save their lives. Rudy Vallee was always the pitcher, and the team generally featured Cary Grant, Bob Hope and Fred MacMurray, among others. Gor couldn't play for that outfit. I knew that he conducted several Vegas dates with Sinatra, and that he was generous to a fault. It wasn't too difficult to imagine them blowing great riches at the tables (old friend George Lee told me, "His big thing was to sit there, drink and play roulette until he lost everything")—or coming up huge, on occasion. But my father kept all of this to himself.

"I don't know Frank at all," he told Wink Martindale in 1974. "I don't know if anybody does. He's the charmer of all time when he feels like it; nobody can come close to him. But when he quits laughing, you're no closer to him than you were before. You talk about high standards, boy, he's the inventor. The things he's gotten into in his life, the scrapes, the bad publicity, in my opinion only because he expected more of people than they ever delivered. If he hires you to do something, he expects it to be the absolute world's best, whether it's cutting the grass or playing the piano. He never questions how much money you want; he pays whatever it is. But he expects it to be perfect, and it depresses him when it isn't. We never had an argument, and I also try to stay away from him as much as I can, when we're not working. It's a real temptation, he has so much to offer, but I figure we've gotten along fine by not being buddies."

"Can you imagine that?" said Nick Perito. "Hell, a lot of guys would give their lives to hang with Frank. I think Gordy knew that familiarity was gonna breed contempt. If Frank was gonna go out and get wasted 'til five in the morning, maybe get in some big brawl, Gordy would just as soon pass. Which is a damn smart thing to do."

Songwriter Floyd Huddleston: "Gordon told me Frank would call him up and ask him out to dinner—except he wouldn't ask, he would *demand* it. Like, we're having dinner tomorrow night at so-and-so. Gordon would say he already had some plans, and that just made Frank mad as hell. But Gordy would say, 'If he wants to invite me, then invite me; don't tell me where I've got to be that night.'"

Sometimes, said Huddleston, the temptation was just too great. "Gordon told me ever since he'd known Frank, he'd made up his mind not to be like Jilly [Rizzo] and all those yes-men just kowtowin' to Frank. But one night in Vegas they had a tremendous opening, all kinds of standing ovations, and afterward Frank had all these people up to his room. So there's Gordon in the hotel lobby in the middle of all this, and he stops and says to himself, 'I'm doing the one thing I said I'd never do.' But he said he knew why: 'He's exciting. Something exciting is always happening around him. And I want to be in the middle of that excitement.' I think he was embarrassed, but he went up there all the same."

Trumpet player Bruce Hudson said the understanding between Gor and Sinatra was so clear, "Gordon never had a contract. Nothing in writing, ever. If they set something up, Gordon would say, 'When do you want me to be there?' and Frank would tell him. There was never any mention of money. In fact, Gordon specifically told his agent to stay out of it. In the end, Frank would pay him double for all the arrangements, get a beautiful suite for him if they were on the road, and pay him a lot more on top of it."

Hudson got some long looks at Sinatra through record dates, and "I wouldn't want to be involved in Frank's personal life one minute. There are two guys there, two Sinatras. I remember when we did 'Tropicana Holiday,' Gordon invited me to come down to the suite one day. He'd arranged to have some food brought in, and in walks Sinatra. That's the reason Gordon wanted me there. It was Frank, Irving Weiss [his music publisher], Nancy and one other guy, and Sinatra was in an incredible mood; just talked his head off. We were all just talking. He wasn't a notch above us, he was right with us. We were just having the best time in there. I still remember some of the stories Frank told us."

One of them centered around an elite gathering in Monte Carlo, where Princess Grace had invited an international cast. Gregory Peck, sitting next to Sinatra, had a dickens of a time trying to identify the couple sitting next to him. As Sinatra told it, Peck finally leaned over to address the man.

"Didn't you work with me on 'Guns of Navarone'?" said Peck.

"No," said the man.

"Maybe it was 'Pork Chop Hill.'"

"No."

"Well, who the hell are you, then?"

"I'm the king of Romania."

Hudson said it went on that way, Sinatra at the top of his game, "and then there was a knock on the door, and here come a couple of his stooges. I heard Nancy whisper, 'Well, there goes father. Here comes Frank Sinatra,' and he changed from day to night. These guys were always around, because Frank's never alone. He's always got people around him, to laugh at the jokes. Just as background."

Weiss, best known as "Sarge," was a good-hearted guy who spent a lot of time at our beach house with his wife, Jill. I thought it might be fun to interview him about the Sinatra-Jenkins sessions, for surely he had some stories. A couple of musicians, marveling at Weiss's sense of humor, told me about the time they were standing outside some hangout in Hollywood, and somehow the conversation got around to actor John Barrymore. "I heard Barrymore was gay," said one of the guys. Irving, without a pause: "Well, I don't know . . . the night he had me, he was."

The interview started well enough. "The first thing I remember about Gordon," Weiss said, "we sat down to play gin one day, I beat him out of a big score, and he paid me in stamps." But when our conversation turned to Sinatra, Weiss clammed up. Talk about paranoia in the Sinatra camp; Weiss seemed terrified by even a casual mention of Frank's name. "I'd just as soon you keep me out of it," he said, looking extremely worried, and hell, I just wanted to talk about the record dates, that magical world where nothing ever seemed to go wrong. But Sinatra was still alive at the time of the interview, and the mere *notion* of an ill-advised comment just scared the daylights out of Weiss.

There was only one real test of my dad's friendship with Sinatra, and while I haven't been able to pinpoint the exact date, it came a few years after the "September of My Years" triumph. A call came in from Milt Krasny, one of Sinatra's business associates, and the conversation went something like this:

Krasny: "Get yourself ready—we're leaving on Tuesday,"

Gor: "What are you talking about?"

"Frank's going out on tour, western states, mostly one-nighters. You're going to conduct."

"I am *not* going to conduct. I'm busy as hell, and I don't do one-nighters any more."

"But this is Frank."

"I don't care who the hell it is. I'm not doing it."

As the story goes, Gor turned to a friend who happened to be in the room and said, "Well, I guess that's the last time I ever work with Sinatra."

It almost worked out that way. Sinatra didn't talk to my father for four years. "It was like a steel curtain that fell," said Gor's business manager, Harold Plant. "No matter what the circumstances might be, Frank wouldn't speak to him. But that was Gordon. If the Pope wanted him to conduct the choir at a Sunday mass, and he didn't like the Pope personally, he'd say, 'Sorry, pops, can't make it.'

"Then one day, out of the blue, Sinatra called Gordon," said Plant. "Says, 'Lefty, how'd you like to do an album?' Like the lapse of time had never occurred."

It might have been a letter (undated, sorry to say) that turned the tide. Sinatra had announced his retirement in March 1971, and even with their little feud in progress, Gor found the news highly disturbing. He sat down at his trusty Royal manual typewriter and hammered away:

"I suppose the reason I'm so late with this letter is that I didn't want to believe that you had really hung up your suit. Like Louis's death, I kept thinking I'd wake up some morning and he'd be swinging again. From my personal, selfish side of the fence, it was a devastating blow, as you were the last of the people I loved to write for. Louis, Nat and Judy were sent for, and then here you go wandering off on your own.

"People are still calling me with, 'Is it really true that Frank has (fill in any infirmity except hangnails or the clap) and that's why he quit?' I say no to everything, although I might venture a private opinion that you simply got sick of the crummy songs the gold-worshippers at Reprise were laying on you.

"I *really* regret that we didn't get to make 'Sunrise, Sunset' together. I had in mind an introduction of some eleven minutes, that would encompass all your children, all of mine, and even a couple of those we weren't quite sure of, through the years. It would have been a real landmark, like the 'September' gem; something for the hackers to shoot at.

"Beverly has always said that the secret of life is to know when you're having fun *at the time,* and not to look back and say, 'Gee, those were great days.' I always knew it at the time, working with you, and it was a ball. Beverly shared my tears over your defection, but we can always play 'Lonely Town' and look down on all those other people from some kind of mountain. I always sign my letters 'Peace' and I never wished it for anyone more. G.H.J."

Sinatra played the cranky guy pretty convincingly, but there was no hiding his fondness for Gor's arrangements. As he prepared his comeback album, "Ol' Blue Eyes Is Back" in 1973, he enlisted Jenkins to arrange and/or conduct nine songs, including "There Used to Be a Ballpark" and one of their signature works together, the Stephen Sondheim song "Send in the Clowns." Gor was blown away by the sheer poetry of that lyric and felt honored to be part of the deal.

"For years, Frank and I both thought 'Lonely Town' was the best record he ever made," Gor said. "He went on record many times saying that. After 'Send in the Clowns,' I think he might have switched over. A couple of critics, for whom I never had much respect, rapped the orchestration as being too fancy and too noisy, but I don't think it is, and Frank doesn't think it is, and the people don't think it is. The people just crack up when Frank does it in a club. They just fall down."

Sinatra thought so much of the song, and the importance of his comeback record, that he asked Gordon if they could rehearse it. "That's about the only time I can remember him doing that," said Gor, who broke his own routine by devoting two full days to the arrangement. "It certainly deserved a little rehearsal. I would have stayed there all night, it's such a song, and I wanted to get it right. I hear it back, and it's the damnedest thing . . . he sings the word 'farce' and your whole life comes up in front of you."

They made a television show out of "Ol' Blue Eyes Is Back," a truly memorable hour for Sinatra's starving fans. Gor conducted a medley of ballads with Sinatra sitting alone in a bar, 'Saloon' forming a blurry, moody image in the background. "Here's that Rainy Day" was a centerpiece, and fans (well, maybe my mother and I) could spot Gor in the shadows, swaying, with the dip of the shoulder and the left-handed beats. Later, Sinatra performed a powerful version of 'Clowns,' at that time still new to many listeners, all done in a closeup of his tanned, saddened face. Sinatra never forgot to introduce his conductors, and as the cameras moved in for a quick shot of the orchestra, Gor took an imaginary, left-handed golf swing and froze at the impact point. He looked at ease, truly like the man in charge—and if you knew his history of television appearances, that was something of a relief.

Most of them went well, over the years, viewers probably not noticing or caring who happened to be conducting. Jenkins had that memorable Colgate Comedy Hour, with Louis Armstrong singing "The Boppenpoof Song"; a lively Kraft Music Hall with

Steve Lawrence and Eydie Gorme; and a series called the U.S. Royal Showcase on NBC, featuring Perry Como, Peggy Lee, Rosemary Clooney, Joel Grey, Bert Lahr and many others. But in the 1950s, with television still feeling its way around, there were some horrendous pratfalls. On a Revlon show out of New York, he couldn't get his headphones to work, and the show opened with Jenkins announcing to the nation, "I still can't hear a goddamn thing." Another NBC show had him separated from the band members, who were supposed to follow him on a monitor, but the screen went out some thirty seconds before air time. As Gor unleashed a dramatic downbeat to kick things off, there wasn't a sound.

In the fall of 1956, NBC enlisted him to perform "Manhattan Tower" with Helen O'Connell, Peter Marshall and Phil Harris. Word came down later that O'Connell was on some kind of medication, and she completely lost track of the tempo—to say nothing of the show's pace within a ninety-minute time frame. "Helen would drag, costing us about forty-five seconds at a time, then she'd go and lock herself in a room backstage," said Gor. "This went on throughout the show. We had to cut two commercials, and with about fifteen minutes left, we were *way* over. We had to cut over two hundred bars out of that thing."

"I don't know what happened backstage afterward," said fellow conductor Bud Dant, "but Gordon went right for the bourbon."

In Sinatra's swingin' years, Jenkins and Riddle shared the conducting on "A Man and His Music," an Emmy-winning NBC show on November 24, 1965, and a sequel with the same title on December 7, 1966. There are only brief glimpses of both men, and at the time, nobody expected much more. Of *course* those are Frank's conductors, no big deal; they'll be around forever. But in retrospect, those are nights for the ages. You really don't have a Riddle or a Jenkins any more, and you'd love to see a quick conversation, a little byplay, *something* to prolong the exposure. (With Gor, who looked a little nervous to be getting any exposure at all, maybe that wouldn't have been such a good idea. Riddle always looked pretty cool.)

There was a six-year gap between "She Shot Me Down," a 1973 album shared with Costa and Riddle, and "Trilogy," my father's last major work with anyone. He was about to turn seventy, and after crafting "The Future," the third and final episode of Sinatra's ambitious undertaking, he was expecting to ease into retirement to the strains of enthusiastic applause. That was hardly the case. "The Future" became a source of great controversy and was blistered in the press, leaving my father devastated and Sinatra quite upset.

I was amazed to learn how long such a project had been on Gor's mind. He usually forgot to date his letters, but I found one he had written to Sinatra on December 3, 1959. It read, in part: "I want to write a legitimate work for orchestra, called 'The Sinatra Story.' It would be around thirty minutes in length, and would try to capture your entire life and times in music. I feel that I can do this better than anyone, due to the fact that I believe that in spite of your fame and all, you are about the most sad of all people, in a neck-and-neck race with me. I don't mean that the work would turn out like a dirge—it couldn't, being about you—but there would be an underlying theme that would be like you, at home, when the people have gone.

"I feel that music can do more to present *your* side of how you are than any story in the world, and I'd like to take a shot at it. If this gets to you, drop me a line and we can go into it more thoroughly."

That was the genesis of "Trilogy," an idea hatched with rock 'n' roll in the furious process of taking over the music business. As we visit a 1980 interview in the L.A. *Herald Examiner,* Sinatra picks up the story: "Over a year ago, Gordon Jenkins and Sonny Burke, may he rest in peace, came to me in Vegas. Sonny said, 'We want to know why you're not recording.' I said, 'What the hell are you guys talking about? You know damn well why. Because there's a lot of garbage out there. I can't record garbage. Nobody's writing songs for me and I don't know what to do about it.' Sonny said, 'Well, we brought you something that Gordon wrote.'

"Gordon had used a synthesizer with six singers, a small version of what the thing was going to be. When they put the tape on, I fell down. I said, 'Holy Christ, how am I going to learn all that stuff?' But it put me away the first time I heard it. Really knocked me out.... See, it's a mythical trip that Gordon takes you on. He and I have known each other for thirty-five years. Either we've talked a great deal about our childhood or he kept notes over the years, but when all the material on the 'Future' side was first presented to me, I realized he knew me pretty well. It was scary."

Once Sinatra got on board, Burke convinced him to make a complete record of old songs with Riddle and a contemporary side with Don Costa (the Riddle angle never materialized, due to a simmering feud with Sinatra that boiled over at the wrong time, and Billy May took over). "The Past" and "The Present" were predictably classy and won largely favorable reviews. Nobody knew quite what to make of "The Future." It was a massive project, with the 105-piece Philharmonic Symphony Orchestra and a mixed chorus of 60, recorded at the L.A. Shrine Auditorium and featuring the dynamite behind-the-scenes combination of Burke (who died suddenly in May 1980) and engineer Lee Hirschberg, an acknowledged genius in his field. They recorded it in vintage style, in single takes, and with the Shrine's ancient bleachers tending to rattle whenever someone stood up, the call for "quiet" was especially urgent.

As Gor explained to KMPC radio personality Pete Smith, the piece is "Frank's way of saying what he wants to do before . . . you hate to say 'die,' that's a tough word . . . before he quits. To thank the different composers who shortened up his nights, to go back to Hoboken, back to Vegas. It's clear that they're gonna come get him, but before that point, this is his farewell. It's hard to stay in the future for thirty-eight minutes. I know Frank pretty well, but I could never do it for money. You need to have the admiration and love for a man to do it."

The Jenkins composition takes Sinatra all over the map and beyond, including a fantasy trip to other planets in "What Time Does the Next Miracle Leave?" It includes a three-minute song, "I've Been There," to stand alone for a quick play on radio. As a piece of reading material, the lyrics get pretty interesting at times. Confronted with the gates of Hades, Sinatra sings, "It's hell when your journey ends there. But you can bet your ass I'll meet a lot of friends there." And the grand conclusion:

And when the music ends, I'd like it to end this way:
I'll ask Chester [Jimmy Van Heusen] *to write one more song*
I'll ask Lefty [Jenkins] *to make me one more chart*
And I'll make one more record with the best musicians in the world.
And when that cat with the scythe comes tugging at my sleeve,
I'll be singing as I leave.

Some of the older critics had been in Jenkins's corner for years, and they weren't about to abandon him now. In the April 15, 1980 *Billboard,* Dave Dexter Jr., wrote, "It's almost like watching Elgin Baylor or Duke Snider at an old-timers game. Frank Sinatra's at the mike again, the tape is rushing through the machines and the most expensive, most artistically ambitious recording project he's ever attempted is completed." Dexter felt that Sinatra hadn't performed so well on an album since the 1960s, and the mood took him far, far back to the Sherman Hotel in Chicago, October 1939, watching "an emaciated kid singer with Harry James's band, wearing an ill-fitting uniform, standing at the mike on a late broadcast plugging his first record." He said Gor's work was reminiscent of "Manhattan Tower," and that it was "by far the most intriguing of the three. It comes off the turntable as an intricate, complex and inordinately difficult suite."

In the *Los Angeles Times,* the esteemed Leonard Feather called it "an extraordinary piece of special material," saying it went off the one-to-ten scale after rating May's side "a major seventh" and Costa's "a flatted fifth." And he went on: "Jenkins is three geniuses. One writes engaging, intricate, amusing and poignant lyrics. Many verses here are so perfectly tailored that it is hard to believe, though true, that Sinatra's hand was not guiding Gordon's. A second Jenkins writes exquisite themes, the kind in which you never know what unexpected note or chord will land in which unpredictable place. The third Jenkins, of course, arranges and conducts the products of the other two." Feather said the piece "calls for a Sinatra in total charge, in confident command, believing in the stories he spins and making us credulous in return. He pulls it off without a hitch."

The most fascinating thumbs-up story came from Sinatra himself, who told the *Times* that he had visited the hospital bedside of author Henry Miller, a close friend, as he lay near death. "Henry was propped up in bed with all the tubes and everything, but he kept a tape going of 'The Future' side. He just kept playing it. The doctor said to me, 'He just sat there in bed and was in tears and kept playing the thing over and over.' Miller told the doctor, 'That's probably the last thing I want to hear.' And sure enough, he died about 12 hours later. I think it's pretty interesting that he was trying to look ahead to where the hell he's gonna go."

For most among the hale and hearty, though, "The Future" did not fly. Chuck Cecil, a huge fan of Gor's music, told me in 1987, "I had a difficult time relating to it, finding something I felt strongly about. I couldn't get into it. I respect Leonard Feather, and his words make me doubt my own ability to analyze it, but I just don't care for it. Everything seemed even to me, without any highs and lows. So much of the older Jenkins-Sinatra stuff got to me, hard, just unforgettable. This didn't have anywhere near the appeal of 'September of My Years,' just to give you one example. I couldn't find one tune in there that really got me."

One of the most valued Sinatra historians, Leonard Mustazza, offered that "'The Future' is too far out, even for Sinatra the experimentalist, and one suspects that most people who own the set have a virtually new copy of this LP since it was likely played only once."

That was exactly how I felt, regrettably, and there were some highly critical reviews all over the country, some real rip jobs. My father sat at home, crestfallen, the discouraging reports coming not long after our Malibu house had burned down. Sinatra, meanwhile, was quoted as saying, "I've been unhappy. Not for myself, because everybody's been kind to me about the album, but the criticism of the Jenkins piece bothers me. A lot of people around the nation didn't understand it. Maybe some smart cookie will come along and do a television show on it, but Gordon . . . I think he was really hurt by the criticism. I spoke to him a few times on the phone and he said, 'Jeez, I don't understand it, Francis. Apparently they don't understand what we were trying to do.' I said, listen, when they get a little older and play it a little more, they're going to catch on to a lot of things. I think the lyrics will wear well. They're too imaginative not to."

I never really talked to Gor about the album, because I couldn't bear to expose my feelings, but Vinny Falcone, Sinatra's touring pianist and a kindred soul to my father, told me, "Gordon never got over that. The feeling was that it came off as too much of an ego thing for Sinatra, but they missed the whole point entirely. It was conceived as being the culmination of a great career. It was saying thank you to all his friends, and reminiscing, even though he hadn't retired yet. Musically, it's terrific. It may not have been classic Sinatra, but it wasn't intended to be. I think that in time, it will be recognized as a major work."

As I heard opinions from "The Voice" critics via the Internet, there was an intriguing entry from one J. Brown, whose e-mail address had closed down by the time I tried to reach him. "I've always liked 'The Future,' and at first, I wasn't sure why," he wrote. "After some 16 years, I'd like to share my thoughts. It is a very personal retrospective that should be listened to when alone. It is not meant as a background for romantic evenings, nor as a showcase of Sinatra talent. It is like reading someone's diary; you sit up in the attic by yourself, reflecting on each page. To share 'The Future' is what can make it embarrassing."

(I had to stop right there, he captured it so perfectly. I grew up in an atmosphere where you bought your favorite records, went crazy over 'em, then had friends over and felt the odd sensation of listening to it through their perception. If you felt they weren't digging it, suddenly it didn't sound all that great to you, either.)

"But to keep it, selfishly, makes it an indulgence," said Mr. Brown. "The lyrics are very clever and very honest. The piece is prophetic, and we get to hear personal things about Frank that might only have been known through an autobiography. To those who might have trouble with this recording, I suggest you lock the doors, turn off the phone, unplug the modem, and play it all to yourself. Listen to the story. It is there simply to enjoy."

Gamely, and with my friend Mr. Tanqueray, I did just that. I wouldn't call it torture, mostly because I strayed radically from my normal listening mode and concentrated intensely on the words. In that sense, there were some pleasant discoveries. But nothing really changed in the big picture. I just never got hooked, and when it comes to my father's music, I'm an easy hook.

It says something about the music business that a seventy-one-year-old man can remain in the big leagues, still in demand, swinging from the heels. Between July and September of 1981, my father's arrangements were used almost exclusively on "She Shot Me Down," and he had plans to conduct most of them. But he was not well. He was experiencing the onset of ALS, Lou Gehrig's disease, and while he didn't fully grasp his condition at the time, he knew that his best work would be limited to well-timed bursts of energy. "Frank told me many times that he wanted this album to be a tribute to Gordon, that he wanted to honor him," said Vinny Falcone. "He was very specific about that, because Gordon was already sick at that time, and Frank figured this would be the last album that Gordon would ever do. Gordon came out to New York, but because he was so sick, I conducted the sessions. He was so wonderful in the studio, so supportive and complimentary, always giving me a wink or putting an arm on my shoulder. He was a man of great generosity. You have no idea what an honor that was for me. The respect I have for him as an artist is as strong as I have for anyone."

"They were some of the best Jenkins charts I ever heard," recalled engineer Frank Laico. "It was just so beautiful. I thought, 'This is going to be a nice time.'"

As a whole, they weren't the most compelling songs ever performed by Sinatra, but there was one notable exception, a song my father had written years before, with Sinatra specifically in mind. It was called "But I Loved Her." In the haunting first three notes of the intro, you're already deep into the Jenkins style. Hear Sinatra, if you please, in the words:

> *She was Boston*
> *I was Vegas*
> *She was crepe suzette*
> *I was pie*
> *She was lectures*
> *I was movies*
> *But I loved her.*
> *She was Mozart*

I was Basie
She was afternoon tea
I was saloon
She was Junior League
I was Dodgers
But I loved her, morning, night and noon.
Opposites attract, the wise men claim
Still I wish we'd been a little more the same
It might have been a shorter war
If we had loved each other more
She was polo
I was racetrack
She was museums
I was T.V.
She knew much more than I did
But there was one thing she didn't know
That I loved her, 'cause I never told her so.

That's how it ended with Sinatra and my father. That's how they
brought down the curtain, with reflection and regret and a love
sadly lost. For years after my father's death, I couldn't listen to their
music without experiencing a sudden departure from reality, a death
grip on my throat and then a complete breakdown. It got easier as
time went on, and I thought I was doing pretty well by the year
2000, when I latched onto a cassette copy of some outtakes from
the "September of My Years" recording session. Cruising a Bay Area
freeway in my car, I heard two hours of real time from 1965. I heard
the two of them joking around, and my father's distinctive laugh.
I heard Sinatra mention that Koufax was pitching that night. I
heard the cadence of the arrangements changing with each take, as
Gor adjusted to Frank, and marveled how they always picked the
right one for the album. My mind drifted back in time, back to old

girlfriends and the winds of a Malibu summer and my father's warm smile. There is such a thing as arrest by violins, and before too long I was charged, booked and jailed. Things got all blurry, and I missed my exit by miles.

Chapter 7

Hits and a Miss

A LITTLE GIRL STRAYED FROM HER MANSION in Bristow, Oklahoma, and sat herself down outside the gospel church, where life made the most sense. She hung around the black maid's quarters so she could hear the real music going down. She came from money, but knew better. She took to the blues in the Roaring Twenties, connecting to folks on the flip side of her world.

She packed up for New York one day, with her sister and another girl who could sing a little, and they all got jobs on the very first day. Before long they were elite backup singers on national radio, lining up alongside stars like Kay Thompson, Paul Whiteman and Andre Kostelanetz. But this one girl, by the name of Beverly, stood out in particular. She found her way to Hollywood and made her name as a soloist. She couldn't help but meet Gordon Jenkins. She couldn't help herself after that, either.

That girl became my mother. If you'd like to know a feeling that is strange as a child, awkward as a teenager and then about the sweetest memory you'll have in your life, it's hearing your mother sing in front of your father's orchestra, for the benefit of millions.

My father fell for so many singers in the late Thirties and early Forties, he should have been arrested. His wife, Nancy, at home with three kids, undoubtedly would have supplied the handcuffs. Most of his affairs were flights of the imagination, a natural carry-over from radio shows or recording sessions. When Gordon met

Beverly, the whole landscape trembled.

There wasn't a thing wrong with Nancy, who had been married to Gordon nearly fifteen years. She was attractive, hard-working and kind. But she never really dug the music scene, and after a thousand starry nights that drained into emptiness—a wife who had not heard the music—he decided to play the field. Scandalous, some said. But what a lovely field.

He had left New York for Hollywood in the fall of 1937 to work for Paramount Pictures, an ill-fated idea that sounded great at the time. Writing to emotions, soaring to a crescendo—who better than Jenkins to score motion pictures? Over the years, he did make two notable forays into film, scoring the first 3-D motion picture, Arch Oboler's "Bwana Devil" in 1952 and "The First Deadly Sin," with Frank Sinatra and Faye Dunaway, in 1980, a work described by *Los Angeles Times* critic Charles Champlin as "the most listenable film music in recent memory." But the Paramount experience was a disaster. He couldn't wait to get out.

"I lasted about a year, and never liked it," he said. "It was too phony and political. In those days you were forced to use Paramount writers, and everybody had a knife in your back all the time. Plus, there's no reality to a piece of film; it's just a bunch of fakers. That's the reason I moved to the beach [a few years later], because I don't like movie stars or that whole scene. I wanted to be as far away as I could from that."

As if he hadn't enjoyed enough lucky breaks already, in 1939, NBC needed someone to replace Meredith Wilson ("The Music Man") as West Coast Musical Director. They turned to Jenkins, who had drawn notice for his writing and orchestration on some freelance radio programs. A gentle soul, he would have been a profoundly inept soldier. Instead, he spent World War II providing spirited entertainment, with a hundred percent artistic freedom and a radio audience that spread both nationally and overseas. It wasn't

New York—nothing could be—but he had a fashionable home in Van Nuys, dined religiously at the renowned Brown Derby, and had the corner of Sunset & Vine as his office.

"I'd do ten or more shows a week, sometimes one right after the other," he said. "They weren't famous shows, just stuff NBC would call 'Night Music' or 'Here's Hollywood,' anything they could make up. I guess after a while I picked up a little following." He soon became the conductor of some front-line programs, featuring the likes of Oboler (a spooky midnight show, with Gor's original music), Dinah Shore, Al Jolson, Bob Burns and Lionel Barrymore, along with the popular "Signal Carnival" starring Jack Carson and Vera Vague (great name; seems she was never quite clear on anything). He was twice commended by the United States Treasury Department for patriotic wartime shows, and it was all very nice. But mostly it was a lead-in to his dream job: working with some of the best musicians in town, preferably heavy drinkers, and fronting hotshot female vocalists who had snappin' rhythm and looked like a million bucks.

You wonder whatever happened in the world of white-girl singers. For every shining light today, there are a thousand vacant-eyed losers who carry an edgy sex appeal (ideal for music videos) but lack even the hint of time, improvisational wit or sight-reading skills. Back then, they were all over the place: Peggy Lee, Jo Stafford, Annie Ross, Kay Thompson, Lee Wiley, Rosemary Clooney. Perhaps because the conditions were so demanding—no video, no over-dubs, and sorry, your only take just raced across the air waves—they *had* to be good, and consistently so. Two of the best, Martha Tilton and Pauline Byrne, found their way in front of my dad's orchestra, and baby, the sparks did fly.

"The thing is, romantically and emotionally, Gordon was kind of like a kid," said his good friend Bud Dant, another top arranger-conductor on the NBC staff. "He fell in love with every girl that ever sang with him—whether she felt that way or not. It just overwhelmed him, the whole wonderful idea of conducting the band with a good-lookin' dame at the microphone. I mean, you're talkin' about a real romantic here."

Forget the torch songs and lost-my-girl ballads that made him famous in the Sinatra-Nat Cole years. Gor played mostly swing music on those radio shows, with clever brass arrangements and delightful charts, openly borrowing from the great Satchmo and some Dixieland idols. "Ahem! Good evening, Mr. and Mrs. America, and all the jitterbugs at sea," I heard him announce on one long-lost audiotape. "Let's go to town!" On came Liltin' Martha Tilton (one of Gor's favorite producers, Mike Dutton, gave her that nickname), and they were on their way, making the first recordings she ever had under her own name.

"Your dad and I had a little romance, sure," Martha told me. "Gordon had a little romance with just about everybody [laughter]. We were quite taken with each other for a while there. We were working together every day, and my goodness—we had a fantastic band, and he knew exactly how to make a singer sound good. Not like so many guys who forget that they're backing you up, and all of a sudden they're the big cheese. Oh, yeah, he could swing. It wasn't his forte, I don't think, but he did it well. He was just ... practically a genius, that's all. You couldn't *not* like Gordon, unless maybe he didn't like you."

Tilton said their affair was strictly "a studio romance. It's not like we were gonna get divorces or anything like that. I actually knew Gordon's wife pretty well. I remember her telling me how Gordon was having these affairs all the time. Says, 'All those pretty girls are down there all dolled up every day, and here I am doing the laundry and ironing with all these kids, and he comes home to that.' I felt so bad for Nan, bless her heart. It's just that she didn't have a lot of musical appreciation. There would be times when Gordon's show would be on two or three times a day, and he'd come home and ask her how she liked it, and she wouldn't have bothered to listen to it. That really hurt him."

On the 1939 NBC show called "Swing Soiree," as sublime as the name suggests, he worked with Pauline Byrne, a somewhat forgotten name but just a *killer* talent who could really sing the blues, and of course, she was beautiful. Ardent collector Steve LaVere, the son of Charlie, my dad's longtime pianist, came up with a scratchy but riveting 78 of "Lord, I Give You My Children," an old Johnny Mercer song designed to introduce the members of the band. That turned out to be a historic night, because Nat Cole—performing only on piano at that time—made his debut on the network. "He was working with his trio across the street, and most of us had never heard of him," Gor said. "But [producer] Joe Thompson was hip to a lot of jazz—which you never heard on the radio in those days—and he had him on as a guest." So Cole takes a solo turn, along with the mainstays of Gor's band, and by the finish—to the sounds of great shouting and applause from a delirious live audience—you just want to reach through the vinyl and hug somebody. Most likely Pauline Byrne.

"One night Gordy and I were having a few drinks," Dant went on, "and he says, 'The worst thing just happened to me.' I guess he was talking on the phone to Pauline when the NBC operator cut in, and it was Nan waiting to talk to him. They put her through, Gordy made some excuse to get her off the phone, and then he went back to Pauline, trying to make a date with her. Except they didn't cut Nan off. She heard the whole thing. Well, that was the beginning of the end. And the hell of it, Gordy set up this big romantic dinner someplace with Pauline, with champagne and catering and his own music playing, and she didn't go for his advances. She just didn't feel that way about him. Oh, he was heartbroken." (Byrne, who made hit records with the Artie Shaw and David Rose bands, later decided that she didn't want to be a professional singer and retired—much too early for her fans' liking.)

George Lee, a music publisher who shared a New York apartment with Gor in the early Fifties, told me, "If he thought a girl singer had potential, he'd go ga-ga over her for a while. It was almost a façade, like a dream, to make him write the way he did. He went head over heels just over the fantasy of being in love with her. I think he needed that. We sure kidded him about it."

"That sounds like a crazy way to go, but I really believe it," said Marguerite Stevens, a close friend of the family whose husband, Bob, sang with the band. "He did do some really dumb things, getting all weepy over girls he had crushes on, but most of the time, it wasn't the girl. It was New York, it was the music, conducting in front of a great big theater, whole bunch of singers . . . he just wanted to be so in *love* with the whole thing. If you have any romantic strains in you at all, you can understand that."

"The thing about Nan, she didn't understand Gordon's music or the life he had," said Dant. "I give him a lot of credit for sticking it out as long as he did, and he was an incredibly impatient person by nature. In that respect he was a good old-fashioned guy. I don't think his *amours* with the singers were the reason for his leaving. That just added fuel to the fire."

Jenkins, Dant and the whole crew would frequent the Key Club, conveniently located directly across from the Vine Street entrance of NBC, or a place called Tropics. The drinking was fun and essential, an outright way of life for people under the stress of live performing, and it was also a way to fill the time between shows. "We'd do one for the East Coast at around 4 p.m., and then another one for the West Coast three hours later," said Dutton. "The second time around was generally a much happier and faster show, if not as sober as the one before. Your dad always got intoxicated with the music, the beat or the girl, and after three hours at the Key Club, with that Wild Turkey and water, he smiled even more."

Allow a little side trip, if you will, into the world of Gor's favorite musicians. It says a lot about the times, the mood, and the kind of lifestyle that led him to my mother.

"The first thing you had to know," said Tilton, "is that Gordon only used guys that he liked. You had to perform, and do it right, and if you didn't, goodbye. But they were all big drinkers. Characters, every one of 'em. The more of a character somebody was, the better Gordon liked him. I think some of the guys drank just to relax, because it was such a nerve-wracking thing: You're live, you've got no chance to do it over, it's now or never. You can't drink and sing, no way. But the guys in the band sure did."

The prototypical Jenkins player was Dent (Dick) Eckels, a crazy man who wailed on reeds. "Gordon got him an alto flute," said Bruce Hudson, "an enormous thing that played a very deep tone. Gordon was known for his one-finger piano solos in the low register, and he'd get behind the beat and just drag there, which bothered the hell out of Eckels sometimes. One time he wrote Dick a solo with him dragging behind it, and about six bars in, Dick said, 'Don't start that shit' [laughter]. Believe me, there was only a handful of guys who could get away with that."

"Dick was always over at the Key Club," said one of the top-notch male singers, Mack MacLean. "He was like Gordy—got pretty lit-up, but never out of line when it was time to play. Well, one time Gordon kind of over-wrote one of Dick's flute parts, and he had to really fight through the East Coast show. Now it's the evening, after a few pops at the Key Club, and here comes Dick's solo. He gets up, starts playing, flubs it a little, and finally he takes the flute and throws it right at Gordon! Of course, they were great friends—and hell, it was radio."

One night they were down at the Tropics, said MacLean, "and Eckels was a real womanizer. I mean, he went after every woman he ever saw. We're sittin' around in our civvies, and a bunch of sailors came up to the bar and started makin' cracks about us, including the woman Dick was hanging out with. About three or four of 'em, young guys. Dick says, 'Come outside with me, won't you?' And he goes out and just buckles 'em, one at a time, just knocked 'em flat. Says, 'There now, laddies, shall we go back inside?' Gordon was sitting right there. Couldn't believe it."

Drummer Nick Fatool: "Dick and I always walked down Vine Street before the dates and he'd announce, 'You know, I'm not gonna have a drink today.' Then we'd walk by the bar, with the smell of booze and beer comin' out, and he'd say, 'Well, let's go in and have just one.' Except it wouldn't be one, it would be four or five. Then we'd go do the show. Sometimes we'd show up a little bit late, people wondering what happened to us, and we'd just been across the street! With Eddie Miller [the matchless tenor-sax player who made his name with the Bobcats] it was different. Ten minutes before the show, he'd grab me to go get a quick one. He'd order a triple, then spit it out on the way across. Wasted three dollars, but it was worth it, just to get that taste."

Another Jenkins regular of that time, sax and clarinet player Archie Rosate, recalled, "Gordy could do tricks with music, man, honest to God. One time on the Dinah Shore show [1942], he came up with a skeleton band: four strings, two reeds, two horns and rhythm. The sound was so full and complete, the way he arranged it, we sounded like a big orchestra—and better, too, than the other bands around. This is where he was a genius: Around the middle of the afternoon, we'd rehearse before Dinah got there. Say it was 'Stardust.' Now, everybody in the world knows that song. But I sit down to play it, and I don't recognize any of the music. The altered chords and harmonic changes he made were so original, set up just for Dinah. Then she comes in to sing, and of course, it's 'Stardust.' But you had to hear the melody to know.

"He was way ahead of his time, that's for sure," said Rosate. "He was a wild man, too. He used to drink up there, man. Oh, my *God*."

How so?

"Well, he was a nipper, as we used to say. Took a little nip when he had to. Around NBC during the day, he was real quiet, a loner. Wouldn't hang around with the guys, you had no idea what he was thinkin' about, and if you passed him in the hallway, you were lucky to get 'hello.' Then we'd get to the dress rehearsal, and he'd take a little nip. Between shows he'd take several nips [laughter]. And when we'd come back for that second show, man, he was *ready!*"

There was nothing Gor enjoyed more than the chance to use the best. Just to say, "I worked with Eddie Miller," your life could end right there, a rousing success. If Eckels was blowing sax, you might find Arthur Gleghorn, a giant in the symphonic world, on flute. Wilbur Schwartz played sax and clarinet with Glenn Miller, Pete Fountain and Benny Goodman. Fatool, a first-choice drummer for decades, was a fixture. On the Louis Armstrong dates he had jazz guitarists George Barnes and Carl Kress, two of the all-time masters. My father loved and got the most out of Bob Stevens, the sterling Irish tenor who could bring an angry blacksmith to tears, and Loulie Jean Norman, the soprano who unquestionably hit the highest, purest notes in Hollywood. And if he wanted to get way down low, he'd find Thurl Ravenscroft (think 'Grrrreat!' from Tony the Tiger). Thurl and Loulie lived about two blocks from each other in the Valley—the entire range of the American singing spectrum within a stone's throw.

"Gordon could be ruthless sometimes, but if he knew you were good, he was the best guy in the world," said Hudson. "We had a bassoonist, Jack Marsh, who was a first-chair man on every recording session in town. One time we'd finished a section and Jack didn't have a part, so he got a book out, and he's very quietly reading, but it turned out that Gordon had changed it to where Jack *did* have a part. We got to that point, and there's silence from Jack. Gordon looked up and said, 'How many under par are you?'

"I remember he wrote a show for the Tropicana in Vegas, some real clever, original music," Hudson said. "I'd been out five years sellin' whiskey, but he asked me to come down. I said, 'Gordon, I can't play a note.' He said, 'You've got three weeks. I'll write you in the low register.' And what I remember most, I was standin' on the side when the rehearsal started and these guys played every tune straight through—music they'd never seen before. I kept listening for something to go wrong, but every time: 'That's a take.' Oh, those guys are phenomenal. They are the equal of neurosurgeons."

Bass player Mike Rubin said he once attended a performance of the L.A. Philharmonic with Gordon, "and it was a fabulous show, just great, but at the intermission I noticed that Gordy was upset. I asked him why, and he said, 'One of the bass players wasn't vibrating.' Like he was taking the night off, in effect. He couldn't stand that. Gordon's talent was just astounding. He could hear a tune on the radio, sit down and copy off the whole arrangement—everybody's part. Just listening to it once."

Wally Simmons, my dad's oldest friend from the Webster Groves days, played the tenor sax for years in local clubs. "I told Gordon once that I was concerned because I didn't have any real technique," he told me in 1987. "He said that isn't important; the thing is to play as few notes as you can get away with, and play 'em as pretty as you can. Those flyin' fingers don't mean much. I was watching the Carson show the other night, and they had a tenor-sax guy on, and I mean, he was *all over* the place. But when he got through, he hadn't played a thing. It was nothin'. Now, take a guy like Eddie Miller. That is *the* prettiest tone I've ever heard. Oh, man."

Fatool: "Gordy had a Dixieland background that really came through on those radio shows. Guys like Eddie and me, that was our whole upbringing, too. People will remember him for his string arrangements, but Gordy could swing, too. Oh hell, yeah. He always had good time, good notes, hell, he knew everything. He *did* everything. Absolutely everything you could do."

When he learned that I was writing the Jenkins book, Wilbur Schwartz took the time to jot down his thoughts. "Whether it was for Sinatra or Nat Cole or any other kind of music, he was in complete control at all times," he wrote, "and it was obvious to everyone in the orchestra. I mean the lyrics, the vocal nuances, every little thing was subject to his keen ear for perfection. He would never settle for a so-so performance if he thought we could do it better, and that included some big stars of the music world. He always insisted on hosting a little party after the date; he really enjoyed the camaraderie, because we were all his good friends. Many of us played golf with him, and he was just as good out there. There was never a lack of integrity in anything he ever addressed."

French horn master Arthur L. Frantz: "I had more pleasure playing for him than any other conductor, and I played for a few: John Philip Sousa in the late Twenties and Otto Klemperer with the L.A. Symphony in 1936. He loved the French horn, and if he liked a particular solo or performance, he'd bow to you, or kinda giggle. The only thing that really upset him was if someone would ask if the notes were 'concert pitch.' He'd say, 'Damn it, those are your notes, don't give me that concert shit.' But he was a pleasure. When it came to backing singers, Sinatra or anyone else, he could not be beat."

Vocalist Ralph Brewster, one of the original Modernaires (1935, later a staple of the Glenn Miller band) and head of the Ralph Brewster Singers: "He was head and shoulders above everybody else I worked with. He had that talent that none of the rest of 'em had. Especially his knowledge of arranging, and how to use the violins to their best advantage. I've got a picture of him in my mind, from a date at the Thunderbird in Vegas. He was sittin' at the piano in the middle of some great number, having such a good time he kicked it with his knees and lifted it about six inches off the floor. He just *loved* it. We had Eddie Miller, Matty Matlock, just a slew of good guys, and every time somebody played a good chorus, or a good solo, Gordon would raise his salary."

"Yeah, and nobody else did that," said Fatool. "Gordy was a beautiful cat. He'd take six or seven guys to dinner and there would be a little gift under each plate, a different one for each guy. I've still got a money clip that he gave me about thirty years ago. I mean, he'd do things that were just unheard of. There were times in rehearsal when instead of paying us scale, which was $10 an hour, he'd pay us recording scale, which was $30. Or he'd pay you $30 out of his own pocket for a good solo, which was a hell of a lot of money for those times. That never happened. No conductor would do that but Gordon."

A bunch of guys in the Jenkins band were dying to compose a joke version of "Manhattan Tower," just to satirize the mud-thick sentiment and play a trick on him. "Bill Seckler, a guy I did a lot of singing with, got the thing started," said Mack MacLean. "Bill Lee [from the original cast] and a lot of real good guys got in on it, and we did a home recording at Seckler's place. We did all the little things in the piece, but we did 'em crazy. It was kind of a touchy deal. Gordy was so hung up on 'Manhattan Tower,' we didn't know if he'd take it right or not. But we sprung it on him one night at a big party at the Brown Derby.

"The tag line was the best: [Dramatically] *And as we were leaving, I turned, took one last look at my tower . . . and it was raining so goddamn hard, I couldn't see the son of a bitch.*"

MacLean nearly fell to the floor as he told the story. "Thank God, Gordy broke up, too," he said. "He thought it was the funniest thing he ever heard. He actually made a record out of it and passed it around to people."

In my line of work, the funniest, most cooperative athletes are usually those on the way up, without the pressures of stardom or celebrity. I found a different scene in Gor's world, a bunch of kick-ass musicians who couldn't wait to share a self-deprecating story or a genuinely funny line. Lloyd Ulyate and Joe Howard were just about the best trombone players on the West Coast. One week they went on a fishing expedition together, practicing duets the entire time, and their lips were in rare form by the time they returned. Back on the Wilmington docks, they heard live music coming from a nearby bar, a little jazz combo of kids who sounded like they were just starting out. Lloyd and Joe had scraggly shirts, week-old beards and easily could have passed for a couple of bums. Which gave them a brilliant idea.

When the band took a break, Joe wandered over to the trombone player and mumbled, "When you come back, play Tommy Dorsey's theme song, would ya? For me?"

"Who's Tommy Dorsey?"

"What? You oughta be ashamed of yourself," said Joe. "Don't kid around with me, anybody can play Tommy Dorsey. Hell, *I* could."

"Then play it your damn self," the kid said, handing Joe the trombone.

Lord, what a setup.

"Well, how do you hold this thing?" asked Joe, who finally picked it up, struggled with it, then unleashed a majestic version of "Gettin' Sentimental Over You."

"Well, shit, you're a trombone player," said the kid, disgusted.

"No, hell, anybody can do this. See that bum over there?" He pointed to Ulyate, looking half-wasted on a nearby bench. "I'll bet even *that* clown could do it. Hey, you! Come over here, would ya?"

Lloyd staggered over and studied the trombone. "Well, whaddya do with it?" he asked, twisting it around with trembling hands. Then he took a deep breath and soared, hitting a bunch of ridiculously high and perfect notes at the end. As the kids sat there, stunned, Joe and Lloyd shrugged and trudged away.

Of the many characters who lit up the music scene in my father's prime, one of them had a special place in his heart: Charlie LaVere, his beloved piano player, one of the most soulful white cats ever to come down the road. A very straight-looking fellow (like Goodman and Dorsey and so many like-minded players back then), Charlie bailed out of Oklahoma University after his freshman year to play jazz full-time. At the tender age of eighteen, he was playing alto sax in Herb Cook's Oklahoma Joy Boys, with the cookin' Charlie Teagarden on trumpet, and he was gravitating toward more esoteric pursuits. According to his son, Steve, "Charlie wrote and arranged the first interracial blues record in history. The record was never issued, probably for that reason; I've got the only known pressing from the original 1935 master.

"It was called 'Boogaboo Blues,' and he sang it with Jabbo Smith, the great trumpet player," said Steve, who spent years assembling one of the largest record collections on the West Coast. "It is not yet recognized but it was, in fact, the first vocal blues record in the history of jazz that was made with a white man and a black man singing on the same level. There had been previous collaborations, but always with the black guy in a subservient, secondary role. Like Jack Teagarden singin' down to Fats Waller, callin' him 'boy.' Or the record by the Mississippi Sheiks, where they walk into a drug store and the man says, 'What are you boys doin' in here?' And one of 'em says, 'Oh, we just lookin' for some chewin' gum.' That sort of thing. In the 1920s, they actually printed 'Race Record' right on the label. But in 'Boogaboo Blues,' you have the band doing a vocal introduction to set up Jabbo, who sings solo, then an instrumental section, then the whole band comes in and introduces my dad, and he sings a chorus of it. I believe Charlie's tune was the first where race was not an issue."

Gaining momentum, and a larger stage, Charlie became well known as the front man for LaVere's Chicago Loopers, a sensational studio band that virtually founded a short-lived jazz label called Jump Records in the mid-Forties and featured Fatool, Matty Matlock on clarinet and various others from session to session, including Billy May on trumpet and Jack Teagarden on trombone. Charlie had the talent to play both trumpet and trombone in some first-class bands, and he was Bing Crosby's piano accompanist for a spell. As it happened, he and my dad both came to L.A. in 1937. They started working radio shows together in 1939 and were riding high by 1944, when Gor stepped down as NBC's musical director to work full-time on the network's weekly Auto-Lite show, with singers Dick Haymes and Helen Forrest (later replaced by Martha Tilton). They hit it off big-time, Gordon and Charlie. They both loved to drink, laugh and play real good.

"My dad drank heartily and then whoosh, right under the table," said Steve with a smile. "Oh, yeah. Terrible. But he was a lovable drunk. Unlike Johnny Mercer, as perhaps you know. Mercer could get so belligerent, it would make you sick. There was a time when he just verbally lambasted Matlock to pieces. Matty, the sweetest guy in the world. Mercer must have called him every bad name he could think of, and Matty was just about in tears. People were so afraid of Johnny, nobody ever did a thing about it. But not too long after that, my dad was driving Johnny and Ginger [his wife] home. Johnny was drunk, talkin' loud, and he started in on something, and my dad turned right around and said, 'Aw, John, you're full of shit.' And Ginger said, 'You tell him, Charlie!' I don't think too many people could get away with that, but Johnny shut up and didn't say another word."

You couldn't have hand-picked a better piano player for the Jenkins band. And as it turned out, Charlie could sing a little, too. Not like Mel Torme or Tony Bennett could sing, but in a heartfelt way that suggested deep knowledge and understanding—sort of like Mercer or Matt Dennis, or Sammy Cahn's engaging versions of his own stuff. Gor never had a problem using obscure singers to make records. He churned out nationwide hits with Don Burke ("P.S. I Love You"), Joe Graydon ("Again"), and Sandy Evans ("My Foolish Heart"), among others. If it sounded good, that ended all arguments—and in 1947, Charlie wound up with the Jenkins orchestra on "Maybe You'll Be There," a Sammy Gallup-Rube Bloom song that got to No. 3 on *Billboard,* stayed on the charts for thirty weeks and became my dad's first million-seller.

"I was a big fan of Charlie's singing long before we made that record," Gor said years later. "He knew all of Willard Robison's [blues] songs. 'Pigeon-Toed Joad' was my favorite, although when I think about his singing, I remember the look on his face when he sang, *'My son's in Jeff City, doin' ten to fifteen'* [from 'Sharecroppin' Blues']. A great line, sung by a great singer."

"Maybe You'll Be There" was a Milt Gabler production for Decca Records, and as Gabler recalled, "Gordon pulled a real good trick on that one—he started the song in the middle, using it as an introduction. And he did it with a mixed chorus. I think more than any other record, that one launched a whole new career for backup singers, because outside of the old Glee Club that Fred Waring used, this was the first time mixed voices were used in conjunction with strings in the orchestra to back up [lead] singers. Instead of an instrumental fill, Gordon put lyrics to it and used the words instead of strings. It was fabulous. Pretty soon, everybody was doing it at all the other labels. Gordon probably did more to start the singers' union than any man in the world."

The beauty of that song escaped the public at first; it became a hit nearly two years after the night it was recorded. And it's entirely possible that Gor's innovation escaped Charlie. "He was a little sick on that date," said Steve. "Had to drink a half-pint of gin to get through the session. Which I'm sure wasn't a big hardship for him."

My dad loved to tell the story about the time he flew Charlie to New York, where he was headlining at the Capitol Theater, to sing "Maybe You'll Be There." Charlie wasn't in the mood to wear his glasses for the gig, so he tried some contact lenses. "We were up on a platform about thirty feet above the audience," Gor said, "and Charlie had to make quite a long walk on his entrance, without much room. Well, he lost the contacts during the song. They fell right to the ground. I'll never forget the sight of him literally feeling his way off the stage, knowing he'd better stay close to the band or he'd have a hell of a fall. I can still see the violinists desperately trying to avoid his flailing arms."

On another occasion, "Charlie arrived at our Malibu place one hot afternoon, wearing a suit, vest, tie, the works. He was also carrying a load of gin, internally. He decided to dive off the board into the pool. Nothing wrong with that, except he still had on all his clothes, and also his glasses. When he surfaced, his glasses didn't. They were safe and sound at the bottom. We all stopped laughing long enough to get him out."

Gor brought LaVere and a bunch of familiar cronies onto the Auto-Lite show, arriving in June 1944 and working 188 shows through July 1, 1948. In what proved to be a golden combination, described as "The Gilbert and Sullivan of America" by one publication, Gordon wrote the music while Tom Adair, a splendidly bright and engaging fellow who co-wrote several tunes that were recorded by Sinatra (including "Let's Get Away From It All" and "The Night We Called It a Day"), handled the words. Crowds of fans and servicemen surged into the studio on Thursday nights to see a Broadway-style production with a full orchestra and chorus, some sixty-five people when you threw in the sound men and engineers. I always thought it was murder trying to write up a ballgame in twenty minutes, 'round midnight, at ballparks around the country. My father and Tom Adair had to come up with complete mini-operas each week for a show that would be broadcast live, and somehow, Gor also found the time to become a staff conductor for Decca.

"Gordon was so fast and prolific, he embarrassed people," Dant told me. "That is, if they weren't bitter or jealous about it. He was the fastest writer ever for arrangements. He could spin something out while he was eating breakfast, and meanwhile he's developing a style that's totally distinctive. I used to watch him. He'd arrange in ink, because he wasn't going to be erasing too much. I could put it down pretty quick, but I'd have to sit down at the piano and figure it out. He didn't need the piano. That's genius-type talent. And the real beauty of it was, he never made a big thing about it. He and Adair just cranked out those shows like it was nothing."

The Auto-Lite centerpiece was Haymes, a handsome, robust baritone who loved the Hollywood association, hanging out with the stars and answering the door of his ranch-style home in jaunty tennis outfits. He had replaced Sinatra in the Tommy Dorsey band in 1942, and for pure style and singing prowess, they didn't come much better than Haymes.

"He really was a wonderful musician and just an impressive guy," Gor said. "Good athlete, beautiful swimmer, good tennis player. We taught Dick how to read [music] right on the show. There was no choice; he had to learn new music, thoroughly. But he was a giant at breathing. He probably had better breath control than anybody I ever worked with, with the exception of Tommy Dorsey, who was kind of a freak. The boys in Tommy's band always said that he could inhale while he was exhaling. I refused to believe that, but it sure sounded like it at times. You never saw him take a breath, and I never knew how the hell he did it. But Dick would take a big one and go indefinitely, bars on end. Just scared you to death. My lungs would break just watching him. We made a bunch of good records and he always left me alone—as I did with him."

Haymes was a fine, prominent singer for years, but he never

reached the long-term potential he showed with the Dorsey and Jenkins bands. "I don't know the whole story with Dick," my father said. "I know he made a lot of money, and spent much more, and got in a terrible jam with the government over income taxes. He had a little alcohol problem, too. He had delusions of being a big star, not just a singer; he wanted to hobnob with Cary Grant and Fred Astaire, and he got in way over his head. Then he went broke and started drinking like crazy. In this business, when you're down, they don't call you too often. Once it gets out that you're in trouble, it's very hard to overcome."

MacLean: "I lived with Dick for a year and a half. I think the only time he was ever happy was doing that Auto-Lite show. For all the great singing he did, mentally . . . I'll tell you how dumb he was. He had an excellent manager, well regarded in town, and the guy got Dick a movie audition out at Fox. They wanted the young All-American boy to sing with Betty Grable, and he's the guy they picked. So he made four or five movies with Grable headlining, naturally. But that's not enough for Dick. He tells his manager, 'I'm never gonna sing another song with Grable. I've done some big pictures now, but she keeps getting the top billing.' The agent said relax, man, you'll get your chance, but no. I swear to God, he quit, and that was the end of Dick Haymes.

"The thing that got him in trouble was that Dick had never become a citizen. He was born in Argentina, of all places. He started owing money up to here, the government closed in on him as the years went on, and once he got to drinkin', he owed everybody in town. He owed me, and I'm sure he owed Gordon. Years later, I saw him out in the Valley at a club one night, and he hid from me. Finally I went back to the dressing room and found him there. 'I knew you were here,' he said. 'I thought you were gonna ask for the money I owe you.' Jesus, that guy . . . such a singer, and he loused up everything."

One of the great weeks for the Haymes crew, naturally, was the end of the war in 1945. My mother, then Beverly Mahr, had just come to the Coast from New York to work Hollywood radio. They knew of each other, vaguely, from the New York days, and Gor—who had just finished writing "Manhattan Tower"—happened to be looking for a singer. "Well, of course, the celebration went on for days," she told me. 'Everybody's drinkin' and yellin' and carryin' on. I guess we were both at a party somewhere, and he just came over and plopped down next to me. We talked for a while, and agreed that I'd come down to NBC for an audition the next day. So I did. And when you sing a solo and you're lookin' right at the guy … I mean, stand back! [laughter] You find out stuff on both ends."

The electricity in that room would have lit chandeliers in Peru. Gordon and Beverly *had* to meet—the nature of their work made it inevitable—and when they did, it was all over: glorious nights onstage together, a dizzying romance, then a madcap October 11, 1946, in Juarez, Mexico, where *both* of them were granted divorces and they turned right around for a quickie wedding (exactly a year later, they made it a bit more official with a ceremony in Yuma, Arizona). It sounded like a hopeless stunt, bound to fail. Nearly thirty-eight years later, on the day of my father's death, they were still deeply in love.

The more my dad found out about Beverly in those early days, the more he was hooked. She had known Charlie LaVere back home, having heard him play around town while she was attending Oklahoma University. Her father, Claude Freeland, had struck it rich in the oil business and was living the charmed life in Bristow, outside Tulsa. She had been a backup singer for Kay Thompson in New York, about the classiest job any young talent could get. She was hilarious—or at least Gor thought so. She spoke with upper-crust elegance, drifting occasionally to her down-home Oklahoma accent when the need arose. She seemed to enjoy exactly the same music he did, she played the piano beautifully, and she could sing the blues—authentically, after years of infatuation with the most talented and tawdry acts of the Deep South.

She probably did a bunch of interviews over the years, but I only found one, with Mike Dutton, the NBC producer who had eased into retirement with his own radio show. She was like my dad, sharing tremendous memories with the right company but making only fleeting comments to me. I interviewed her myself, or tried to, in the late 1980s—after my father's death and the onset of her Alzheimer's. Some gems came forth, between great surges of haze; it was a maddening experience. The Dutton interview, done sometime around the mid-Seventies, became my lifeblood. Letting her old accent resurface, she sounded like an ol' country gal on a roll.

"I got a good start on the blues," she told him. "Being born in Oklahoma [in February 1912], the Holy Roller churches were available to me. I used to go and sit outside when these hotshot girls— and I mean, the real flashers—would come in from Kansas City. They could dance and sing the blues better than anybody. That was the first time I'd ever heard the blues. My mother and father, to say the least, did not play that kind of music.

"See, our maid and cook, Pauline, came from Kansas City, and she got me wise to everything. She stayed in a little house just outside the door to my bedroom, and I used to slide over there to see what was goin' on. She knew about Bennie Moten and Bessie Smith, everybody, and she'd play me her records. We only had one place to buy records in Bristow, and that was Stone's Hardware. I didn't go there. Pauline had everything I needed to know about."

Dutton: "I think I heard one time that ol' Sonny Boy [Williamson] died from a stab wound to the head."

"Well," she said, "a lot of blues singers ended up in ... well, not a tidy situation."

"Who all did you like back then?"

"Oh, Chippie Hill, and of course Sonny Boy and Bessie, and a blues singer I heard down in New Orleans once, Cousin Joe. The lyrics were what I loved about the blues. After a while, the tune doesn't really vary that much. But it sure as hell ain't the Master-Charge Blues [laughter] or 'Well, I woke up this morning.' It's more like, 'My baby thinks I'm a black snake, 'bout twenty-nine inches long,' or 'Then my baby come in, had a fifty-dollar hat on a nickel head.' I'd say almost everybody who's ever been in jail sang the blues, or felt like it."

Like my dad, who knew who the really great piano players were, Beverly wasn't out to become the next Bessie Smith or Billie Holiday. She just understood that sound, took it around with her, and could reproduce the hell out of it on proper occasions. Although she never studied voice, she could always read music (Gor called her one of the best sight-readers in the business), and she was an accomplished piano, organ and ukulele player by the time she graduated from O.U. She made her pilgrimage to New York in 1934 as a pop/jazz singer, along with her sister, Julia, and a friend named Helen English. They'd been singing as a trio on a Tulsa station for several months, causing a nice wave of attention, and this wasn't one of those stories where a starving artist hangs around the Village for fifteen years. "We got an audition in New York the first day we got there," Beverly said, "and got hired on the spot."

A series of lesser radio shows became the big-time, very quickly, for the Oklahoma trio. Beverly always had the edge, because she could read and play the piano and had a knack for solo singing, but they stuck together in a number of groups, sometimes joining larger choruses, on the major networks. "New York was a perfect, wonderful place," Julia told me a few years before her death in 1998. "We'd window-shop and ride the subways well after midnight when the shows were over. We lived pretty well during the Depression. We were making more money than the president of the bank in

Tulsa, which was how I always judged it."

On the prestigious Philip Morris show, they were guided by Johnny Green, a prodigious talent (writer, conductor, performer, arranger) who put the radar directly on Beverly. "Johnny kind of had his eye on me," she said. "He asked me if I could go on a tour and sing solo for him. And I was like, 'I've heard this tune before, dad [laughter].' I loved him professionally and he was terribly smart, but I might have had lunch with him, that's it."

By the time she left New York, Beverly was a featured performer on several network shows and even had her own daily spot, "Beverly Calling," on NBC. But she had only one late-in-life memory of those days, something she cherished to the grave: earning a place in the chorus with Julia and Helen on CBS's Chesterfield Hour in 1936, featuring conductor Andre Kostelanetz and the fabulous, irrepressible Kay Thompson.

In the long history of entertainment, there hasn't been anyone like Thompson. When she died, in July 1998, she left a singular legacy to stand for all time. I think of her this way: There's a stylish, dapper gentleman in New York, dabbling in high society, determined to meet someone *unusual.* Enough with the knockout airheads and white-blonde bimbos; he wants stimulation, high intelligence, a dancer's poise, a jazz singer's rhythm and an erotic dash of intrigue. Of course, that person is a fantasy, so he settles for something reasonably close, and hey, what a festive wedding in June.

Then he discovers Kay Thompson, and he's ruined for life.

"If you don't know who Kay Thompson is," wrote Rex Reed many years ago in *Harper's Bazaar,* "you just flunked pizzazz."

She was simply exceptional at everything that struck her fancy: as singer, dancer, actress, pianist, composer, choreographer, author. At a limber 5-5 and 110 pounds, she seemed infinitely larger, just from the sheer impact of her presence. If she's not terribly famous, it's because she floated so effortlessly around the landscape, often behind the scenes. Old-timers around Hollywood remember her best as Judy Garland's singing coach and vocal arranger at MGM, the person who softened Judy's tone and livened up her body movements. "She's the one who put the sob in Judy's voice," wrote Reed. "The hand on the hip. The distinct bow, one arm perpendicular, the other behind her back—that all came from Kay." And while teaching subtlety to Garland, she brought out the belter in Lena Horne, who once said, "Professionally, Kay developed me as a singer completely. She is the best vocal coach in the world."

Kay was the kind of person you'd find in the suite of "Manhattan Tower"—at least in my dad's imagination. She did scintillating impressions, broke into impromptu comedy routines, knew all the best jazz players (her first husband was Jack Jenney, the fabled trombone player from the Isham Jones band). She could break into a wild, flawless jitterbug if things got a little drab, or make up a skit for three people right on the spot. Always impossible to pin down, she'd appear mannish to the first person you'd ask, supremely feminine to the next. In "Funny Face," the 1957 MGM film starring Fred Astaire and Audrey Hepburn, she took on a rare starring role, careening through Paris as fashion editor Maggie Prescott, and practically stole the movie. Her entirely original New York revue, "Jubilee Time" (1948–1954), with the four singing Williams brothers, was described by Walter Winchell as the best nightclub act in history. And in the mid-Fifties she began her *Eloise* book series, about a precocious six-year-old girl who lived in New York's Plaza Hotel. The four books were for children, ostensibly; once the adult crowd got hip, they sold over a million copies.

"The facts of her life are sketchy," read Hilton Als's obituary in *New York* magazine, "since she was entirely self-created." But Reed, recalling one of her grand entrances in detail, summed her up well: *"Boodle-dee-bopbop-bum-swe-bop."*

My mother hopped on the ground floor of Kay's career, and they were close friends for more than fifty years. Thompson became a recluse later in life, hiding mysteriously within the confines of her New York apartment (owned by her goddaughter, Liza Minnelli), but she always stayed in touch with Beverly and the rest of her Rhythm Singers from the Chesterfield days. Three of those women —Loulie Jean Norman, Gitchy Vass and Bea Wain—became my mom's lifelong friends.

"There was a fifty-piece band, Kostelanetz conducting, with Kay up front and the rest of us behind," said Wain. "Kay's phrasing and conception were wonderful, and she was an absolute genius; we all looked up to her. My goodness, we had fun on that show, especially the midnight version, which we'd do for the West Coast. One night Kay hit the big metal stand while she was conducting, and she had a great big diamond ring on. Clang! One by one, we fell out. Just laughing like crazy, and we never finished the song. What the hell, we figured nobody was even listening out there. But those were amazing times for all of us. We got to be so tight, we sounded like a bunch of sisters. It was very fresh and very young, and spontaneous. There wasn't anything that sounded like us."

I never heard this for sure, but I'll bet it was Thompson who took the raw Oklahoma out of my mother, smoothed it over and produced a sophisticated young performer. She told me later, over the phone, that Beverly was among her favorites: "Beverly was a leader, but she didn't know it. She told everybody what to do in a polite, quiet way, and she was awfully good. Just a marvelous girl, and very funny. You knew you had something when you heard Beverly. I thought someday she'd do some singing on her own."

As for the Rhythm Singers, said Thompson, "We were the first people to have a big singing group like that on New York radio. I knew Beverly and a couple of 'em could read, but I never wrote anything down, by design. It was all by ear. We were doing jazzy stuff, crazy accents, comic stuff, and that was the joy of it. I had nothing against sheet music and parts, but it bothered me to see a big bunch of heads looking down into the music. I refused to let anybody have it. Learn it, sing it, hold your head up—that was my sense of performing. I think we were a hundred years ahead of our time, although the people at CBS had no idea. They were so square, they thought we were just weird."

I made an odd discovery along the way, something neither of my parents ever mentioned to me or in interviews. Gor was arranging for a lot of people, along with Isham Jones, in 1936. One of those people was Kostelanetz, on the Chesterfield program. In a tattered newspaper article I found in an old family scrapbook, it was noted that Beverly performed on shows arranged (orchestrally) by Gordon. But they never actually met. Because they both did so much work, for so many different people, their lives crossed in a rush and moved furiously on.

Then again, both of their marriages made some sense at the time. Gordon and Nancy were in their glory, and my mother found a reasonably kindred soul in Carl Mahr, an unassuming gent who sang and played the piano. I'm about to dismiss Carl from the story, largely because my mother rarely said a word about him to anyone. Her friends couldn't offer much help, either.

"There just wasn't anything memorable about Carl," said Wain. "He was kind of a cold cat, didn't seem very romantic. He didn't have the type of musicianship that we were accustomed to. Plus, Carl's former wife, Jessie Mahr, was one of us, in the chorus. Pretty weird, you know? That always confused me, although she and Beverly seemed to get along fine."

Although my mother was well into Alzheimer's when I started researching her life, she had always been impossibly vague on how long she'd been married to Carl. "About a year," she once told me. Incredibly, when I finally saw the official papers, it turned out to be *eleven* years. "That whole period is like a black curtain for me," she said. "All I remember is that we drove to California together, and then I met Gordon. From then on, Hallelujah."

One of the staples of the Haymes show was "Six Hits and a Miss"—six guys and a girl singing rhythm, jazz and swing—and that's how Beverly landed on the same stage with Gordon. That group (which periodically had four male singers, or five) backed up Haymes, Forrest and the Jenkins band, occasionally doing numbers of their own, and my mom turned many heads as a soloist. Her voice was cheery and distinct, and there was such a confidence about her, it seemed that she was just passing through on her way to a crucial dinner party with Sinatra and Clark Gable.

Johnny Green, while admitting he had a little thing for Beverly, said it wouldn't have existed without her talent. "She was an arranger's dream as a singer, in her improvisation," he told me. "Like an Ella Fitzgerald or Sarah Vaughan; they sound like they *belong* with the song. I said, Beverly, I'm going to stop on that downbeat, and I want you to fill it. Then we'll come in on the end of your fill. And she did—it was written about in [newspaper] columns. She did it from left field. I loved her then, and I love her now."

The great arranger Billy May remembered Beverly, no problem: "Good singer and a good-lookin' chick, that's what I remember." And Peggy Lee, who occasionally called the house to speak to Beverly after my father's passing, regarded her as an equal. "She was just great," Lee said. "I always loved her singing. There was the hint of a jazz singer in Beverly, but she could sing anything."

There was one magical night on the Haymes show, my mother recalled, when she didn't get her usual ride home with the backup singers. Gordon, ready to make his move, took the assignment instead.

"I remember every little movement, everything about this," she told me. "We pulled into the driveway, he came around to open my door, then he took about four steps back and just held his arms out.

And I went right to him. And never left him. I mean, lightning had struck."

"That's what's called 'torrid,'" I said.

"Pretty torrid, yeah."

"It was like sparks in the air," said Loulie Jean Norman, who watched the romance fully blossom on the Haymes show. "It really was electrical. Both of 'em had found the love of their lives."

The cold reality was that Gor had two little boys at home, Gordon Jr. and Page, and a little girl, Susan, ages ten, six and seven. Moving on from Nancy wasn't going to be a problem; that appeared to have been written in holy scripture. But leaving the kids had to tear at his heart.

"Gordon came to me one day and said we had to talk," said Bruce Hudson, "and he ran the whole thing down. I said, boy, this is some step, walking away from those kids. But there were too many good things about it. I never thought it was that scandalous. What the hell, he got a blues singer and married her. You have to understand, there was nothing he could ever say to Beverly that she didn't understand. If they heard a note, they heard it the same way. If they heard Louis, they heard the same thing. He couldn't bullshit her, because she knew as much as he did—and I mean classical, jazz, whatever. Oh, it was a great one."

I found Marguerite Stevens to be a terrific source on the matter. A sharp and stylish woman out of Hollywood High, she lived for those nights with the radio, where she could hear her husband, Bob, sing with the best bands in town. She was getting the West Coast show, post-Key Club, and with her acute knowledge of music, she could hear those subtle effects of alcohol along the way. "You know, you kinda missed one there," she'd tell some horn player, gently. "Whaddya mean?" he'd protest. Then they'd hear it back, and Marguerite was invariably right.

"Bob and I went to Gordon and Nancy's house a few times for

dinner," she said. "Nan was very nice, but she could never find the time to listen to anything of his. I know she had a house full of hell with the kids, but she could never make it to a show, never turn it on and hear it. And Nan was slugging it down pretty good, I think. I remember one time she asked me in for a drink, in the middle of the day, and it wasn't until later that I realized she meant a *real* drink, not a glass of water. It's just that Gordon didn't get the attention. I don't think he felt much like going home. She didn't feel the things that he felt, or hear them, and gracious, Beverly felt and heard it *all*.

"Not only that," said Marguerite, "they laughed about so many things together. That's just about as close as a couple can get, when you get everything the same way. He thought she was the funniest person in the world. When the romance started, she was living on Ben Avenue [in the Valley] and he lived on Longridge, and they would meet at a midnight market on Riverside Drive. Beverly said, 'We used to hold hands under the lettuce.'"

They were laughing all the way to Mexico, in October 1946, when they decided to make things official. Some of the details are a bit sketchy, but the bottom line is that when they pulled out of Juarez, they were divorced from Carl and Nancy and married to each other. "We just figured the best thing was to get it done right away," my mom said. "Talk about quick; we had to get back to Hollywood that night and work the next morning. I'll never forget the guy who married us down in Juarez. At the moment of truth he says, 'And you, Beverly Fizzland . . .' And Gordon just broke up. It was the tackiest carryin' on, just the worst thing you could think of. But when we flew home we were laughing so hard, I didn't think either one of us would recover. You think of all these beautiful weddings, real fancy stuff, and here we are in Mexico with Beverly Fizzland."

Back home, said Frances Adair, Tom's wife, "Nobody really raised a fuss. It just seemed like a perfectly normal thing to do. They were very discreet, but there was no question among their friends that they'd get married. They were so much in love ... I didn't hear a single unkind word about them."

For me, though, there was the unfinished business of Nancy. I knew she was living alone out in North Hollywood, and I set up an interview with her in 1990. My father always kept up with his kids, but he seemed to have avoided his ex-wife at all costs. Consequently, I couldn't remember meeting her—not even once. But there I was, at her door with a tape recorder.

It turned out she'd been living alone for forty years. She did remarry, not long after the Jenkins breakup, but it was ill conceived and quickly annulled, to her everlasting relief. "And ever since then," she said, "just nothing, really."

I found the conversation strangely uplifting at times, because Nan had the same sweet laugh I'd heard my whole life with Susan. And she was quite cheerful the entire time. But I wanted to hear her side of things, and she did not hold back.

"We had a real nice marriage, I guess, although now as I look back, it was horrible," she said. "Gordon was always a womanizer, from way back in the New York days. Oh, God, about every six months, he had a new girlfriend—most always people he was working with. Singers, mostly. In fact, I think they were all singers. I can't tell you how many, because there were *so* many."

"That's wild," I said.

"Wild, is right," she said. "Nobody knew it, and we didn't separate over it. We just kept it quiet between the two of us. And I never accused him of anything. I look back now and wish I had, but I was this calm little person from a quiet home, where my parents never argued or raised their voices. I guess that was just instilled in me."

"You sure don't seem bitter about anything," I said.

"Not at all," she said. "I'm mad at myself, more than at him, for being so namby-pamby all those years. I should have taken the bull by the horns and just let him have it."

Gordon had only recently met Beverly when "Manhattan Tower" was recorded, in 1945, and my mom was the lead singer on the album. I'd always assumed it was about their soaring love affair, but Nan corrected me. "No, that wasn't about Beverly. It was Julie Van Ostrand, a married woman, a friend of ours whose husband was in the business. God, he was really hooked on her. Well, OK, there's someone who wasn't a singer [laughter]. I'd gone back to New York with him, so I was in on the 'Tower' thing. There *was* a constant party going on and there really was a waiter named Noah, just like the album. But when Gordon hooked up with this other woman, I just said to myself, I'm gettin' out of here. I went back to L.A.

"Bruce, you're gonna hate your father if I keep talkin' this way."

I mumbled something about its being perfectly fine, which it was. I was flustered and embarrassed, but not terribly surprised, not after a half-dozen people had told me how my father operated. "It's very wearing, to put up with something like that," she said. "Just terrible, emotionally. It affected my life. Still, I think I still have an inferiority complex because of it. Maybe that's why I've been by myself all this time."

Nan said she'd known Beverly a little bit, "and I always liked her, I really did. By that time, I was just beat to a pulp. I'd been asking him constantly if he wanted a divorce, and when it finally happened, it was like the weight of the world dropped off my shoulders. I was so relieved. The kids didn't know. We never bickered or argued, so they didn't know a thing about it. At the time, he hadn't been around the house much, anyway."

In the years that followed, she said, "He supported me and the kids, put 'em all through college, sure, he did fine. But he could never look me straight in the face. Couldn't carry on a conversation, couldn't look at me. He really had the guilt hangin' over him there. And that's too bad. Because there would have been times when I wanted to talk to him. He was obviously more attentive to the kids, but it wasn't until much later that they really got close to him."

I never detected a trace of anger from any of his three children, although surely they had cause. I was the one who got to live with Gor, in a beautiful two-story house on the beach. And my mother, viewed in a certain light, had stolen him away. But they never seemed to take it that way; they made regular visits to the house, always in an upbeat atmosphere, and they truly loved my mom. Since they all had roughly a ten-year edge on me, it was almost impossible for us to be close. (Just as an example, Page was a real hotshot at USC, and once or twice a year, while I lived in a ten-year-old's world, he'd throw a wild party at the beach house, complete with palm-frond huts, Fifties rock music and frantic making out.) But we had a common thread, as none of us had inherited the pure musical genes.

Gordon Jr. got by far the closest to the music business, spending many decades as the hip and highly respected booking manager for the L.A. Hollywood Bowl and Music Center. ("I guess I'd be a musician," he once said, "if I hadn't run out of will power, talent and patience. But those are the people I gravitate to.") Susan got one of the better secretarial jobs in town, at Universal Studios, and kept it for decades. Page went into accounting, which seemed kind of strange to me until he started raking in million-dollar salaries and hooking up with the Hollywood elite (for years, he was one of Barbra Streisand's top financial advisers). And he's invaluable to the family as the manager of my dad's royalties from A.S.C.A.P. and other sources. That's a tough gig, royalties. Through the years, untold musicians have been ripped off so badly by shady agents and managers, they wound up dead broke. My dad often promised that while we couldn't make a living off his earnings (split equally among the four kids), we'd have a little something coming in—and that has been the case, without fail. This is a man who makes a consistent six-figure salary, more than I ever made in my best year, and he couldn't be more dead.

As the years went on, and my dad's work options became a bit more scarce, he spent less time with those wild characters from the old days. There was a lot of heartbreak, too. Charlie LaVere died a little early for my dad's liking, at seventy-two, and Gor compared his reaction to John O'Hara's when notified of George Gershwin's passing: "I don't have to believe it if I don't want to." Dick Eckels took a terrible fall, later in life, leaving him permanently stooped-over and reclusive; they say he'd let Nick Fatool in the house every now and then, but virtually no one else. Charlie Griffard, whose distinct sound graced many trumpet solos, was found dead in his home, having apparently shot himself in the head (his close friends called bullshit on that one and targeted his widely despised wife). And singer Marv Bailey, who did countless sessions with my mother when "Six Hits and a Miss" was in vogue, got to the point where he couldn't come in exactly on the downbeat. "He never could read, and it started driving him nuts," said his old partner MacLean. "One day he called up and said, 'I can't make it today,' and we thought, fine, whatever. But that was it for Marv. He never sang another note."

It's funny how you remember silly details when a really tragic development comes down. We were enjoying a chicken dinner on July 23, 1961, when my dad picked up the phone and learned that Bob Stevens, whose tenor singing remains the sweetest I've ever heard in pop music (he sang the hit record "Unless," in the summer of 1951), had died of a heart attack at forty-nine. The news was inconceivably horrible; we were extremely close to Marguerite and their two kids, Rich and Rob, who remain among my best friends to this day. Rob, a budding singer himself, was the oldest; my dad figured he'd keep it together. But he wasn't sure about Rich, then a somewhat troubled fourteen. "I'll never forget," said Marguerite, "Gordon came to the house [in the Valley], held me tight and said, 'I've got to get Richard. This is no place for him right now.' I was so out of it, I hadn't even thought of all that. But we grabbed his clothes and off he went." (As Richard told me recently, "It was the right place to go—the beach house, where everything was always fine. There was no reason for me not to be there.")

Marguerite spent many months in mourning, wondering if she'd ever get back to our place, where she used to chat, soak up the sun rays and hear good music with consummate style. "I finally started going out there," she told me, "but I had no interest in socializing, or even talking. I needed to know they were there, but I just went out on the dunes or something. Then I'd get in the car and go back. And Gordon and Beverly understood that. I cannot tell you how wonderful that was. It was like therapy, and they just let me do it. That's so smart."

Tom Adair had been another constant visitor to the house. He and my dad had collaborated so often, they were like brothers when they sat down to work. They had written the music for the 1949 Broadway show "Along Fifth Avenue," which starred Jackie Gleason and had a seven-month run, and Tom went on to become a prolific songwriter for Walt Disney and dozens of hit television shows. One of his passions was going on vacations with his wife, Fran, and my parents, and after they all came back from Egypt in the mid-1970s, he sat down to recollect.

"Beverly has a charming peculiarity about her," he wrote. "She believes sincerely, and with unshakable faith, that in a previous life she had been an Egyptian princess. She was forever reading books of Egyptian history and acquiring odd pieces of jewelry. And she had never—repeat, never—visited Egypt. As we landed at the harbor of Alexandria, Beverly was finally setting foot on what she seriously believed to be her native land in generations past. We boarded a bus, and Beverly was right up front with a window seat. Outside, white-robed salesmen were hawking their wares. Suddenly, an old Egyptian man, curiously carrying no items for sale, stepped up to the open window. With an ancient and stately curtsy, he looked Beverly straight in the eye. 'Welcome home,' he said, and then melted into the crowd."

As I told Tom later, "That sort of justifies a lifetime's worth of weird." But the finest moment was yet to come. Later in that trip, they were visiting the pyramids, and Tom was still marveling over the bus episode. As they gazed upon the wondrous spectacle, Tom spoke up:

"Say, Beverly, when was the last time you were here?"

"Oh, about two thousand years ago."

"You wouldn't know the place," said Tom.

By the early Eighties, Tom and my father were both gravely ill. Gor was on the slow, irreversible downslide from ALS, and Tom was sinking deep into Alzheimer's hell. They remained close, corresponding when they could. My dad once sent him a joke: "The three coldest things in the world: The Pope's balls and a viola solo." But Tom was going completely off the edge. When my father died in 1984, Tom never digested the news. "He just went to pieces," said Fran. "He'd lost his closest friend in the world. We left California for Hawaii right then, and for Tom, that was the main reason.

"Alcohol started it, really," she told me in a gut-wrenching telephone interview from their Honolulu home in 1987. "Then came memory loss, a heart attack and, I'm sorry to say, over-medication. They kept him on an anti-depressant way too long, until he lost all his memory. His mind is completely gone now. It's like a living death."

Trying to keep her composure, she went on: "Tom doesn't even know his own son. Looks at him and sees nothing. He knows two things: my name, and Gordon. He doesn't remember his children or anything about his career, but in his mind, he talks to Gordon constantly. 'I saw Gordon today,' he'll tell me. 'We've got a project going. One of those big Sunday afternoon shows we were so good at doing.' God, I get the chills thinking about it. It's so real to him. It's the one thing in his life that he hangs onto."

Fran said she was so relieved by the notion of *any* conversation, she'd try to keep it going. "So how does Gordon look?" she asked him once.

"Gordon looks fine," said Tom. "He wants me to come live with him. He's not sick any more."

Tom died not long thereafter. Fran was nice enough to mail me a few things, including a telegram Gordon had sent after visiting the stark town of Newton, Kansas, where Tom grew up. It was a ridiculously barren outpost, not much more than two railroad tracks coming together. The telegram read, simply, "Say . . ."

* * *

On a late-December afternoon in 1989, my mother got a phone call from Kay Thompson. I knew a lot about Kay and asked if I could listen in for a while, but I had no idea what a privilege it was. Fully reclusive in her New York apartment, she hadn't granted a formal interview since 1972. Friendly phone calls, like this one, were her only contact to the outside world.

Well, it was the highlight of my mom's whole year. She'd been relentlessly despondent, beaten down by the dullness of a life without Gordon, and she just couldn't muster much enthusiasm about anything. But this was full glory. This was Kay. It might as well have been 1936 over the CBS air waves, swingin' and boppin' in a New York studio. Typically madcap, they talked about a grapefruit my grandmother had given Kay about a million years ago. They sang a silly, endearing song called "Tuesday Smiles." And they wished each other a merry Christmas.

"We were some very special people," Kay told her.

"Damn right we were."

"And we knew it, too," said Kay. "We liked everything we did."

"Natur-el-mont," said Beverly, intentionally torturing the French.

"You know, there hasn't been a grapefruit like that since."

"No, I don't believe there has."

"OK, Bev. Sing a song, and keep movin.'"

With that, my mother got up, poured herself a glass of wine and put on a mink coat that I hadn't seen in years. I went upstairs to find her gliding about the room, slowly, to a silent refrain. There was no time to waste.

"We rehearse at dusk," she said.

Chapter 8

The Cat Was Driving

E WERE GRACED ON THREE SIDES by desolation, the sublime emptiness of old Malibu. Things were plenty wild in the Malibu Colony, with its tales of extravagance, drunkenness and bitter divorces among the Hollywood elite, but that was ten miles to the south, an incalculable step toward civilization. My parents moved to Trancas Beach to get away from all that. In our part of the world, the lights were out and the doors were open.

To the east of us were the open hills, sparsely populated, green and lush until the periodic scorching by brushfire, then naturally restored to their old magnificence. Out front was soft, pure sand, the rough vegetation of the dunes and the great Pacific Ocean. To the north lay several empty lots, then a common sight along Broad Beach Road. And to the south, The Mystery House, as we called it. Hardly an original name, but well earned. Within those walls, the stars were never quite what they seemed.

In the wake of his divorce, my father had taken a small house on old Malibu Road, just off the Colony, to gain a measure of sanity. But he and my mother had bigger plans. As she once wrote, in private memoirs, "We were fond of driving north, finding new beaches and places to swim, cruising around in an old Plymouth with the top held down by a rotten-looking wire. One Sunday afternoon, we were shown a wonderful two-story house which had just gone on the market. I think it was the dunes that really sold us. We bought it for $31,500."

That was June of 1947, and while there wasn't much to see on Trancas Beach, there were a few solid landmarks. The stately three-story house on the far point was owned by cinematographer Lucien Ballard and his wife, actress Merle Oberon. Another home was stunningly nautical, basically an old ship that had been converted to beach-living quarters. Over time the Hollywood influence became loud and distasteful, tormenting the aesthetics with modernistic contours, pathetic seafaring themes and inappropriate stabs at sophistication (like the gaudy Moroccan-style mansion of the late Carroll O'Connor). But in the late Forties and early Fifties, Broad Beach met a rigid New England standard. The homes were hardy and worn, crafted along clean and sensible lines, with proper decks for entertainment and observation. A barefoot visitor could track sand into them without fear of recrimination, and they stood up to the wind and salt air.

Our place, we liked to think, had 'em all beat. Built around 1928 as a sort of Cape Cod west, it was a handsome tribute to charm and intimacy, all crannies and nooks and windows, by the dozens. The rooms were small, in retrospect, but in step with the period. The outside was all gray shingle, the perfect complement to any shade of sky, and there was an old-fashioned woodbox adjacent to the fireplace, loadable from the outside (I can recall desperate missions on rainy nights, struggling to pry open the big, heavy door and hurl the dampened logs inside, hoping spiders wouldn't crawl onto my arms). The inland side, one of the few legitimate "back yards" ever fashioned on Broad Beach, was a festival of bougainvillea, pine and Monterey Cypress trees, flower beds, rose gardens, and weather-resistant St. Augustine grass. But the crowning touch was the sunporch, a long and narrow extension jutting out toward the beach—"a bright and lovely room done in wicker with slip covers in sunny colors," my mother wrote. "Plants thrived in that room, and so did I." You couldn't get away with such architecture in today's world; the evil planning commissions would cite about nineteen code violations. But we got about a half-century of enjoyment out of that sunporch, where my mother spent countless afternoons playing the piano, napping in the softened sunlight and enjoying her record collection. (Did a few misplaced LPs melt in the sun? You bet they did. Part of the charm, we fibbed.)

It was kind of lonely out our way. A daily commute to Los Angeles was a practical nightmare, and it was a forty-minute haul to anyplace with a movie theater or department store. We were privileged kids, make no mistake about that, but for six solid years, we all had long morning bus rides into Santa Monica for junior high and high school. Writers and artists thrived in north Malibu, along with fishermen and plumbers and telephone linemen. The Hollywood people came grudgingly, as Malibu's beachfront property grew scarce, and Trancas eventually became cool. But even now, with a Starbucks across the street and the unthinkable notion of a Malibu High just two miles away, celebrities rarely *live* on Trancas. They take the houses as toys, something to show off on an August weekend or the Fourth of July. There haven't been many exiles like my father, who made a full-time commitment to a place where the Ventura County border lies just six miles to the north.

As my mom got a little older, and her diplomatic conversations gained a dash of salt, she loved to tell friends about those wild, early days. "Gordon and I would go out onto the beach without any clothes on, any place we wanted to, and we'd go right at it," she'd say. "What was there to worry about? There was nobody else around." And when someone did show up, it wasn't necessarily kosher. One day in the early Fifties, the flamboyant Zsa Zsa Gabor decided to make use of our beach—not *kind* of on the property, right in front of the house. Assuming that the place was deserted, she paraded through our back yard, entourage in tow, and made grand theater of her entrance. Well, my mom was home, watching incredulously through her picture window, and she charged right out there.

"Just what do you think you're doing?" she demanded of Zsa Zsa.

"Why, using the beach, of course."

"Not right here, you aren't."

"But darling . . . I am Zsa Zsa."

"I don't care if you're Jesus Christ, get the hell off our property," said Beverly, and off they went.

There wasn't much of a police presence in those days, just a local security guard named Homer Greer, motoring around in a marked car. You hated to imagine ol' Homer really springing into action, because he didn't seem to have the temperament, but hell, nothing much happened back then, and he knew just about everyone on a first-name basis. One night my dad was driving home, a bit sauced, with a six-week-old kitten in the passenger seat (a gift for me, I'd imagine; we always had cats around). It seems his car couldn't quite pick a lane, and Homer pulled him over. As the story goes:

"Homer, how the hell are ya?"

"Hey, I thought that might be you, Gordon. You were drivin' kinda funny back there . . . I was wonderin' if you might have had a couple."

"Aw, not at all, Homer. The cat was driving."

"Well, all right, then. You two have a safe ride home."

As an answer to all that quiet—Gor wrote and practiced from dawn to noon and then his work day ended—he built himself a little paradise. First came a swimming pool, which sounds excessive on the beachfront but proved to be a summertime gathering place, a marvelous tool for parenting, and a sauna-like retreat from the raging surf and high winds of winter. Then he built a full-tilt workshop, with all the latest in carpentry gadgets and power tools.

"I've become a carpenter all of a sudden," he once wrote to an East Coast friend, and he built dozens of handsome cabinets, chairs and tables to prove it. His triumphs in photography, as I look back, were stunning. He hand-developed his artful black-and-white stills, mostly of family and friends, set on the finest paper. And he had one of the first 16-millimeter cameras for layman's use, cranking out dozens of fully edited home movies. Back home from our greatest vacation—a full month in Hawaii, 1958, with Bob Stevens and his family—Gor produced a masterful film complete with titles (set against the shimmering pool background), slow motion, comedy speed-ups and fadeouts.

His musical workplace was the studio, another gray-shingled building, entirely separate from the main house. He built it so he could write, arrange and orchestrate "without having to hear the baby," and as I grew up, his all-business mood created a shield of intimidation. You didn't knock on that door unless you were delivering a direct message, usually from my mom, or word that his upstairs bedroom had come under attack. I got the full nocturnal measure of that studio in my teenage years, for once he finished work—sort of like the NBC radio days, when the show was over—Gor became a completely different person. My friends and I could play our favorite albums, at considerable volume. We could sample the piano, drums, organ, vibraphone or any of the guitars strewn about the room. And if we wanted to get technical about it, we could pretend we were in a professional-caliber recording studio—which it absolutely was. Gor spent a fortune on state-of-the-art audio equipment over the years, including the first 8-track mixing board ever produced (by 3M, in 1967) and the same European-crafted microphones used on his Sinatra dates. He did it for his own over-dubbing amusement, crafting big-band sounds using just two or three musicians or turning my mother's voice into an eight-girl chorus. He built a separate control room for sound insulation, installed thirty electrical outlets ("The electrician told me I have enough power to run a four-story office building"), shifted to a 24-track board, and hand-crafted a headphone system through which the listener could hear individual tracks.

I guess I could have gone that way, to the east, from the main house to the studio. I could have fancied the musician's life in the footsteps of my parents' careers. I always felt that I understood good music, and Gor once said he could tell that I had "it," whatever that is, by the way I whistled. But that was an eavesdrop; my jazz-riff whistling is a solitary affair, like singing in the shower, and pretty much the extent of my expertise. Over several years of piano lessons, I was terrified of performing and never got over it. Multiplying the discomfort, my father was stern and unforgiving as I lurched along. There were no kindly, patient lessons from the master; he preferred that I learn it from someone else, and he never seemed terribly impressed with anything I played. And while I did develop a passion for writing, the notion of songwriting amounted to a conversation in Arabic; I *really* didn't get it. The fact was, it all came naturally to him. He once spoke of his career as "a comfortable way to make money through the years without working." For me, the prospects always seemed daunting. The family standards were so high, I knew I'd never be in that league.

So instead, I went west. Straight into the ocean. I embraced sports, and conventional writing, and tried to end each afternoon immersed in the sea, one of life's most soul-satisfying, confidence-building, stress-relieving endeavors. Thanks to surfing and sportswriting, I'm still a little kid, in essence, as I enter my mid-50s. I never sensed any disappointment from either of my parents (although I'm sure it was there), and as I watched countless Malibu kids sink into oblivion, wasted by cocaine, weed, Jack Daniel's, a spoiled-rotten childhood or just plain indifference, I figured I was ahead of the game.

Unlike most everyone else who settled on Broad Beach, my parents truly understood what was going on out there in the waves. "Gordon and I swam in the ocean six months out of the year," my mom recalled in her memoirs. "We used to take floats out beyond the surf, swim a while, wait for a big wave and come flying in to shore. Most of the time we were alone out there, except for the seals that swam with us."

My father never said much about it, but he loved to go out and watch when my friends and I hit the water. It seemed to thrill him that we were having such a good time. Once, during my collegiate days at Berkeley, I tried to explain the surfing experience in a letter to Gor and mentioned the "timeless feeling" I experienced out there. It was 1966, not long after he had recorded the "September of My Years" album with Sinatra. This is what he wrote back:

"I think it must be like the feeling I've always had for music. It's a sort of welling up in the insides, a slow-moving explosion when I hear something, or even more, when I conduct or play. I am always trying for that better chord, that perfect wave, that gorgeous melody, resting peacefully in warm water. I know that the excitement I felt at fifteen was still present at the Sinatra recording; I felt that I could move my hands and create a great wave, one that would carry everyone in to shore. I slip off the board occasionally, but it never bothered me. I just got back on and started being Gordon Jenkins again.

"I used to conduct and write a lot of radio shows, real dramatic deals, where I had to follow the actors, be at several places at the same time they got there, and the more difficult it became, the more excitement I felt. I would get up on the podium (surfboard) and say to myself, 'I am Gordon Jenkins, and I cannot make a mistake.' When the show was over, it would take me hours to get back down where the other people were. Then I couldn't wait to get back in the ocean again.

"It sure beats being just plain folks, doesn't it?"

In a relationship marked by comfortable distance and warm thoughts unspoken, that was the best connection my father and I ever had.

There was something about that studio that kept me moving in a vaguely straight line. Thanks to my parents' exquisite taste, I constantly heard the best, whatever the mood: Ray Charles, Count Basie, Stravinsky, Renata Tebaldi, Mahalia Jackson, Lambert, Hendricks & Ross. Those were golden days for the long-lost experience of comedy albums—actually sitting down and listening to a stand-up routine—and I wore out the vinyl with Nichols & May, Stan Freberg, Woody Allen and especially Jonathan Winters, the king for all time. The Stevens brothers and I memorized every routine from a half-dozen albums, and to this day, we greet each other with Winters lines ("You're gettin' greedy about that, Brigham") that wouldn't mean a thing to anyone else. At times, there was high comedy in music, too. The incomparable Billy May cut an album called "Sorta Dixie" in 1955, with Eddie Miller and Matty Matlock and a ton of great Dixieland players, and while it was musically superior, it had the distinctive May touches that illuminated so many of Freberg's comedy bits over the years. Rich Stevens and I must have played "Sorta Dixie" a thousand times over the next few years, making Billy May an eternal hero of my life, and when I went to interview him, I felt like a photography student at the doorstep of Ansel Adams.

"One night, after 'Sorta Dixie' came out, I got a phone call," May told me. "It was your dad, dead drunk in London, telling me how much he liked the record. I was very flattered, because I'd been a fan of his from the Isham Jones days. But he went on and on, and I mean, *long* distance. The thing just knocked him out."

Our great invisible hero was Mr. Harry Warren, one of the best and most prolific songwriters of all time ("Chattanooga Choo Choo," "Lullaby of Broadway," "You Must Have Been a Beautiful Baby," and, of course, "Hooray for Spinach"). Harry owned the two huge parcels to the north of us—Harry's Lot, we called it, because it was tumbleweed empty and the last open space on all of lower Broad Beach. Seems the crusty old chap just didn't want to build *or* sell, and we reveled in his strategy, playing spring-to-autumn hardball games there until I was fourteen years old.

On the other side was raw intrigue: the Mystery House. For months on end it was dark and forbidding, no cars in the driveway, nothing around but some scattered debris and, we were certain, many ghosts. Like the kids in "To Kill a Mockingbird," scurrying around the perimeter of Boo Radley's place, we imagined great horrors inside the Mystery House. Was there really someone in there? Were there rats the size of boulders? One time a couple of us crept over there, did our usual tug at the door and found it open—but the prospects were so horrifying, we raced away.

The real mystery, as it turned out, was in the characters who made their way out from Hollywood. I can't remember when the house was built or who originally owned it, but Katherine Hepburn was extremely close to our southerly neighbors—Dr. Ruth Rahman and playwright Chester Erskine—and she routinely rented on Broad Beach, invariably joined by Spencer Tracy in the movie world's most discreet romance.

From all that I've gathered, our little spot reminded Hepburn greatly of Fenwick, a seaside refuge in Connecticut where her family owned property. She was known to paint beach scenes there, occasionally leaping into the icy waters to refresh body and mind, and Trancas became a pretty fair substitute during her spells in California. "She was quite fond of Beverly," Marguerite Stevens told me. "Every so often I'd see them out on the beach talking. She loved your house, because it reminded her so much of Cape Cod, and she would mention occasionally that she'd love to buy it if it ever came up for sale. I just remember seeing her walk out to the sand with a great big black hat on, and a white terrycloth robe, and she'd get to the top of the dune, throw off the hat and robe, and she'd have on this sensible, black, one-piece bathing suit and march right into the ocean, just cold as hell. Wasn't she amazing?"

Hepburn had fallen in love with Tracy during the making of "Woman of the Year," in 1942, and as most everyone knows, they carried on an illicit affair until his death in 1967. Some of their best times were on Broad Beach, occasionally right next door, where trusted folks like Erskine and my parents would never blow their cover. The astounding part is that I never saw Spencer Tracy—not even in 1963, when he developed a number of ailments and Hepburn moved him to Trancas for the summer. "If you passed the simple wooden house, you were likely to see Tracy's black Thunderbird in the carport," wrote Charles Higham, a Hepburn biographer, but Higham described the Malibu times as "unwatched. No one other than Kate will ever know what happened between them in those days they spent together away from even their closest friends."

In the mid-Sixties, about the time I started high school, the Mystery House became a beach retreat for Lauren Bacall and Jason Robards during their nine-year marriage. I said hello to each of them occasionally (Robards in "A Thousand Clowns" is the one piece of celluloid I'd keep in a bank vault), but my strongest memory is of Bacall's daughter, Leslie, from her marriage to Humphrey Bogart. It was just one sighting. She was about fourteen, a vision of loveliness. I was sixteen, and frozen solid. Wanted to say something, but in the presence of inconceivable beauty, I couldn't muster a word. Before I could recover, the place was taken over by Philip Carey, the hulking actor from the old Granny Goose commercials. Decidedly boring in comparison, Carey didn't last long—and then along came Dennis Wilson.

Dennis was a pretty regular guy—surely a refreshing development for those who put up with his eccentric brother, Brian—and he always had time to chat for a while. I had always hoped that Dennis, the cool drummer, would be the Beach Boys exception, a guy who actually surfed. He talked a good game, but every time the waves started pumping out front, he had something else to do. And he was up to some wild shit, be clear on that. I'll never forget the night I read a *Rolling Stone* article, in the wake of Wilson's death, and learned that he had been close friends with Charles Manson. This was before Manson's cult unloaded on Sharon Tate, and according to the article, the two spent many late nights socializing at "Wilson's beach house." Well, that would be right next door. Manson. Looming. Sneering. Gathering himself to really wreak some havoc. I'm pretty sure I never saw him, either, thank God. That was the last notable episode at the Mystery House, and surely its darkest.

As for Harry's Lot, the carefree hardball days couldn't last forever. The man finally sold his land, and in stirring contrast to the Mystery House, it became a haven for snobbery. First came Jerry Orbach (the fashion designer, not the actor), who married a former Miss Sweden and built a world-class tennis court encased by three towering cement walls. I didn't care much for Miss Sweden, who dismissed life's peasants with a haughty smirk, but I was obsessed with the court. Built by L.A. tennis legend Gene Mako, it was a forest-green masterpiece, complete with a riveting echo for balls particularly well struck. Occasionally a match would break out and I'd lurk on our upstairs deck, yearning to play the winner. But mostly, in typical Broad Beach fashion, the court just sat there, empty and immaculate. Finally, I did what any self-respecting neighbor would do. I trespassed.

It was a bit of a tightrope act, but by scaling my own brick wall and easing myself up onto the thin concrete barrier of the tennis court—a narrow but passable walkway—I could jump onto Orbach's cyclone fence and climb down onto his property. Once there, I simply opened his front door and ushered my guest into the tennis Taj

Mahal. We held nothing back, bringing drinks and sandwiches, setting up camp on the tables, yelling loudly on winning shots to hear that echo. This went on for several years, until the day I brought one of my girlfriends, the luminous Rhonda Mahan, onto the scene. We were hammering away when I noticed some movement inside the house. It was Miss Sweden and a distinctly younger man, the two of them in bathrobes. This had to be one of the great dual embarrassments of all time. My scam was brutally exposed, but on the other hand, I knew the dirt. The poor woman made a gesture that hinted, "By all means, play on," and we did, about eight strokes' worth. Then we packed up and left. It was years later, under new and even more negligent ownership, before I tried that stunt again.

Orbach's successor was Ronald Reagan, a man roundly despised in our household, but it wouldn't have mattered if we'd walked around wearing Republican party hats. He was just another Malibu phantom, virtually never seen on the beach or the tennis court. Of far greater interest was the arrival of Carroll Rosenbloom, a very wealthy man who had just bought the Los Angeles Rams. His wife, Georgia, was something of a laughingstock around town, a former Las Vegas showgirl who struck a cosmopolitan image but failed miserably in the execution. Carroll was a bold, life-of-the-party type who quickly endeared himself to strangers, but he was a big-league gambler with some shady connections, and his days did not end well. In 1980, I read newspaper accounts of his mysterious death by drowning in a lake-calm stretch of the Atlantic Ocean off Florida. A number of sources pointed straight to Georgia, figuring that she could do away with anyone, including her husband, without blinking an eye. Others speculated that Carroll's gambling debts got way out of hand. But here's one thing for sure: The man did *not* drown. I have a vivid memory of sprinting out the sunporch door and into some beautiful, pounding surf—and seeing Carroll already out there, laughing and diving under the waves with superb timing. So forget that Florida story. One alleged eyewitness said he noticed some skin divers in the area where Rosenbloom was swimming, and you can bank on that. The man was killed without mercy.

Georgia, of course, never broke stride. She took over the Rams, without knowing a single thing about football, and walked the sidelines trying to fake it. She fired her stepson, Steve, who had the executive know-how to run the team. She moved the Rams to St. Louis, an inexcusable act tantamount to shifting the New York Giants to Peoria. She kept the beach house for herself, instead of turning it over to Carroll's sons, then completely ignored it—to the point where the upstairs caught fire one day and remained in a sickeningly charred, crumbling state for months thereafter. Finally she tore it down and built an obscenely gargantuan thing without rhyme, function or compatibility (of course, it was occupied by no one). My favorite moment in the latter-day Georgia years: spotting a leftover Christmas tree through an open window—in June.

For the most part, celebrity sightings on Broad Beach were all class: James Garner tossing the football with kids who happen to pass his way; the enigmatic Steve McQueen and his very conspicuous partner, Ali McGraw, who embraced Malibu and a number of local causes; noted chef Vincent Price sashaying from one beach home to another with a tray full of food. But for anyone intent on joining the real world, it was a most unrealistic setting. My salvation was Santa Monica High, where a lot of the kids came from underprivileged backgrounds, where a lily-white suburban athlete learned the meaning of street-wise competition, where a music-starved kid could find a decent record store. My friend Jack Pritchett and I were devoted fans of Motown, rhythm & blues, and the all-soul radio station KGFJ, and somehow we learned of a little hair salon, run by black women, on the southwest corner of town. We weren't about to get our haircuts in there, but those women had a fantastic rack of 45s for sale, all the latest from underground soul artists around the country. An outright gold mine. We didn't have the most comfortable feeling walking into that place, not in 1965, but the women seemed humored by the nervous suburbanites in their tidy little sweaters. We couldn't believe our good fortune.

For my father, life was essentially the passing of time between trips to New York. With his Decca connections, his string of hit records, the lure of the nightclubs and Al & Dick's, he was a significant player in the big city, with a stylish apartment awaiting his arrival. He'd routinely pack up the family and head back there—twice for a full year or more. That was my best counterpoint to the soft Malibu life, even at a very early age, and it fully recharged my mother's career after an event (my birth) that had forced her into semi-retirement. She loved to tell stories of rocking me to sleep with her blues singing, late at night above the roar of uptown traffic. She talked about going to hear Louis Armstrong, Ellis Larkins or Bill (as she called him) Basie on the nights she could find a babysitter. But her favorite story, told only among friends, was of a New York night that went a bit foul.

It seems that my parents were throwing a party for a number of musicians, right around 1950, and I was safely stashed in a back room, sleeping away. Suddenly my mom heard me crying, and she came back to discover a fully loaded diaper.

"Don't worry about it," my father assured her. "Just mingle."

Well, that wouldn't do at all. She had gone through two miscarriages to produce this baby, her one and only. A good mother goes in there and deals with it. But it was bad news, logistically. There was no way to dispose of the grisly remnants without walking right through the crowd to the bathroom.

"And let me tell you right now," recalled Marguerite Stevens, who was in attendance, "that was not Beverly's style."

This was the great convergence of personas—the country girl from Oklahoma and the upscale New Yorker—and to get past this problem, she had to be both. It was her worst and finest moment. She grabbed that diaper and threw it right out the bedroom window, some ten stories up.

"Beverly, you *didn't*," said a horrified Marguerite.

"Girl, I sure did."

"And then," as Marguerite tells the story, "she mingled."

Only a few close friends ever heard that story, for my mother was generally defined by her elegance. She was the picture of charm and sophistication at our Malibu parties, always saying and doing the right thing at exactly the proper time. Which was great, because Gor's manners had taken leave about the time Red Grange scored his first touchdown for Illinois.

If he conducted a Sinatra recording session with a ham sandwich in his free hand, listen, he was hungry. If he broke wind during a really key stage of someone's conversation, well, he just couldn't hold back. If he walked out of someone's party around 8:45 p.m., leaving my mother to say some desperate farewells, it's because he simply couldn't tolerate the boredom. We'd be watching prime-time television—Ed Sullivan, the Perry Como show, something along those lines—and if a half-baked singer took the microphone, he'd simply get up and go to bed, without a word of explanation. I could sum up his entire social stance in a single word—"Bye"—and he absolutely connected with the Thoreau inscription that hung on his studio wall: "If a man does not keep pace with his companions, perhaps it is because he hears a different drummer. Let him step to the music which he hears, however measured or far away." If for some reason a visitor wasn't familiar with the passage, he'd swear it was written specifically about Gordon.

His old friend from the Webster Groves days, Wally Simmons, told me he'd been that way from the very beginning. "He was very strange in a lot of ways," Simmons said. "A lot of people didn't like him too much because they couldn't understand him. He was just lacking in real personality, I guess, not a real gushing, happy-go-lucky guy. He really didn't let you into his life unless he liked you, and if you were on the outside . . . not good. I remember one time way back in the early Thirties, there was a drummer in town, and Gordon must have said something he didn't like. This guy walked out in the alley of the musicians' club and hit him right in the mouth. Hell, Gordon never fought anybody; he didn't know what to do. But a bunch of his friends were out there, and let me tell you, that drummer didn't make out so good."

"Emotionally, he was very young," said Bud Dant, Gor's partner in composing from the L.A. radio days. "He hated the climbers, the self-promoters, and he wouldn't even begin to be nice to 'em. I never complimented him, as much as I wanted to, because he hated that jazz. Everything about him was just raw, as I think about it. He didn't study anything, he just knew. He was pure talent. No time for any frivolous bullshit."

"I'm more apt to say what I think than the next guy," Gor once said, "and that always makes you look like kind of a nut. I'm labeled an eccentric for that alone. I just about blew a radio station apart one day in the mid-Sixties. I had some bigwig from Victor with me, and somebody asked me what I thought of the Beatles. By the time I got through with that, they almost had me in jail."

Family friend George Lee was particularly amazed by the fact that alcohol wouldn't necessarily relax Gor's demeanor. "You'd never know he had a drink, even if he'd been pounding it all night. He always had that sober look about him. He could be jovial, yeah, but if something set him off, he'd get right up from the table and leave, that's it, you wouldn't see him again. Even if the conversation became dull for him, he'd go into the men's room and take off from there."

At the dinner table, home or away, he crafted his own strange planet. No vegetables, ever, not even for laughs; it was meat and mashed potatoes 365 days a year for decades on end. As Marguerite

Stevens told me, "I remember people saying, 'Are you really going to invite Gordon Jenkins to dinner?' Because he wouldn't eat anything. No salad, nothing that was green, God, he was a pain in the neck. After a while he'd just get up, motion to Beverly and they'd leave right then. People would be left saying, 'Did we do something wrong?' But that's just how he was. You got used to it after a while."

Not surprisingly, years of rude behavior earned him the reputation as a real pill. One of the cutting-edge British rock magazines did a small piece on him in the year 2000—for what reason, I can't be sure—and made reference to the "rare smile" on his face in a photograph. All I can say is, a lot of people missed out. On the inside of Gordon Jenkins's world, tough as it was to penetrate, things were just plain rockin'.

Kay Thompson was breaking in her acclaimed nightclub act with the Williams brothers in Las Vegas on a night when Gor happened to be there. "It was the second or third night at Ciro's and it was a huge smash, just incredible," she told me. "Even *we* were surprised. Tables were impossible to get, people shoving and fighting to get a seat, and the owner called me over and said, 'Let me tell you who's here.' I said, 'I don't want to know. Just keep the tables flying.'

"The audiences were so perfect, you couldn't believe it if you'd invented them," she went on. "Well, this one spotlight was moving through the crowd when all of a sudden there was this *head*, moving in time to us. You could see it above all else, just this wonderful head and face going, 'Yeah!'. I started smiling, because I knew that guy. It was Gordon, just sitting there keeping time.

[Kay begins singing, a tremendously upbeat, jazzy thing.] "He came back and saw us twenty-seven times," she said. "I tell you, that head said more about the act, and about him, than anything I could possibly tell you. He was so *alive*. Gordy was one of those great musicians who got heavily involved in these huge assignments, and I know he loved going out and seeing something that excited him. Like, '*Gee,* I'm glad I came.'"

He had a laugh so oddly separate from his everyday personality, you'd hesitate to believe it was really him. It was a great hooting sound (literally: "hoo-hoo-hoo!"), leaving behind the sour-faced fellow and revealing a giddy admirer of true talent. "Gordon was the world's greatest audience if he loved you," said Jane Rollins, who sang with the Bob Crosby band and married the famed promoter Jack Rollins. "To have him in the club, forget it. If you were a comedian, he had the world's funniest laugh, so penetrating and high-pitched. It was so distinctive, you'd think, my God, Gordon is in this theater somewhere." But it wasn't just humor that flipped the switch. True musical genius made him laugh. He'd crack up over a saxophone solo, a guitar fill, a singer's difficult note hit perfectly, not so much with the hooting laugh but a more subdued, relaxed version, as if to answer, "Oh, God, yes. You're killin' me here."

"An incurable romantic," arranger Nick Perito called him. "A perfectionist, a dreamer, a dramatist, a taskmaster, and yet a guy who could be reduced to tears of joy by any singer or musician who really knew how to turn a phrase."

He wrote letters of gushing praise, like an impressionable teenager, to entertainers who moved him. He surprised people with gifts or passages in a song. And if something wasn't going right, he just obliterated it from his life. Well before the days of remote control, he invented a switch that allowed him to silence the sound of our television sets during commercials. When he realized that his chain-smoking might be killing him, he stopped with shocking haste. I remember it well, a Sunday in the autumn of 1955. We were at a Rams-49ers football game, watching the likes of Hugh McElhenny and Crazylegs Hirsch race downfield, when he said, "I'm quitting today. You'll never see me smoke another cigarette." And he didn't.

He went from a daily two dozen to zero for the rest of his life.

Songwriter Floyd Huddleston and his wife, Nancy, became close friends with my parents, and Floyd couldn't get over the difference between the real and perceived Jenkins. "One time he recorded a song of mine, 'Baby,' with Ella Fitzgerald and didn't tell me about it. Finally I called him up one night and he said he wanted to play me something. Played it right over the phone. Absolutely broke me up. I don't know of anybody else in the business who would have done that. That's nobody but Gordon.

"Johnny Mercer told me a story one time, said he was in New York, making all kinds of money, and Gordon didn't have much at the time," Huddleston went on. "That's when he got that offer to go out to California to make movies, head up the whole Paramount music department, and he said, 'Johnny, I can't do this. I don't have enough money to make the move.' Johnny said he lent him about $1,200, a hell of a lot back then, to make the trip. A few months went by, and usually when he lent a musician some money, that's the last he ever saw of it. Then one night there was a knock on the door, and a guy was delivering a case of Scotch. Real good stuff, J & B or something. And each bottle had a $100 bill wrapped around it. Now, that's just creative and kind, and it describes Gordon Jenkins. Johnny told me, 'I never worried about letting Gordon have anything he ever needed.' He said he was just so much warmer of a musician than anybody he'd met before, that he thought deeper, had an insight to things that no one else had.

"One night we were in Le Petit Moulin, a terrific little French restaurant in Santa Monica, when Henry Mancini walked in with Michel Legrand, the guy who wrote 'Umbrellas of Cherbourg' and a lot of terrific stuff," Huddleston said. "Legrand says, 'Gordon, it's because of you that I compose. Everything I've ever done, I owe to you.' He goes on and on about Gordon being his hero and everything else. And Gordon could barely speak. I mean, it really caught him off guard. See, Gordon wasn't much for taking away. He gave."

Bea Wain recalled hosting a big reunion for the Kay Thompson Rhythm Singers in New York, after Wain had risen to stardom with the Larry Clinton band, "and we had no idea where Kay might be. She had become a total recluse, somewhere in the city. Everybody was having just a fantastic time, and we kept saying, 'If only Kay were here with us.' Well, somehow, Gordon managed to get a hold of her. He ducked into the back room to make a phone call, then came into the living room and said, 'There's somebody that wants to talk to you.' And you don't know how we adored her, how we worshipped her. Everybody got on the line; the call must have lasted an hour. Afterward, we were all saying, 'Such a coincidence.' We believed that for a long time. Gordon did a lovely thing without taking credit for it."

Marguerite Stevens: "He loved being in love, just falling-down, flat-out in love, and he loved other people who were in love. That's one of the things he loved about Bob and me. We were special to him because we were so in love, and we'd cry with him over pieces of music, and we'd hear things in his compositions that other people couldn't pick up. There was a night one summer when Bob had replaced Dick Haymes [as the Auto-Lite show's lead vocal]. Gordon called the house to make sure Bob could hit this one certain note, a really high one, but Bob was out playing golf. 'Oh, sure,' I told Gordy. But when Bob came home and I told him, it was like, 'You're kidding.' He was a little bit in awe of Gordon, and he wasn't at all sure about that note. Well, I was in the booth the night of the broadcast, behind the glass, and when Bob hit that high note and sustained, Gordon turned around and looked at me, and tears were rolling down his face. Mine, too."

Huddleston recalled the time he brought an obscure record down to the beach house. "It was raw material then, just a guitar and vocal by a little Mississippi girl named Bobbie Gentry. Later they added strings, called it 'Ode to Billie Joe' and it was a tremendous hit, but at the time it was just Bobbie singing and playing the guitar herself. Well, we put it on the machine, and Gordon was cryin' before too long. Said, 'That's the best thing I've heard in fifteen years.' See, the simplicity of it, the honesty, just killed him. Like Junior Samples, the guy on 'Hee-Haw.' Gordon just loved that guy. He was ignorant, but he was honest ignorant and funny ignorant. Gordon liked him so much, one time I went back to Nashville and Gordon said to get me an autographed photo. You want to talk country? I found out the Ramada Hotel room where Junior Samples was staying, and when I knocked on the door, somebody opened it, and Junior was on the toilet. Says, 'Come on back here.' Signed that thing while he was sittin' on the can."

I had the pleasure of interviewing a long, tall Texan named Jack Steinhauser, whose relationship with my father was nothing short of amazing. Jack was a traveling businessman in the early 1960s, and when he got home from an exhausting cross-country trip one night, he poured himself a cocktail and played an album, "The Magic World of Gordon Jenkins," he'd received on Father's Day. "I kept playing 'This Is All I Ask,' over and over," he said. "The lyrics just got to me somehow. My friends and I had always known the thread of sadness in his arrangements, how he so lyrically expressed how people feel when they're down and out, and we were avid collectors of his work. Perhaps due to my condition at the time—alone, looking at that second drink, feeling lonely—I decided to call Gordon Jenkins right then and there."

Thanks to an especially friendly operator, he got through to my father. They talked for a while, until Gor mentioned that it might be getting a little expensive, and tell you what, Jack, send a tape and we'll continue the conversation that way. "It took me about thirty days to get up the nerve to make it, but I finally did," he said, pausing for a moment. "I can get a little teary about this if given the chance … we wound up exchanging tapes for twenty years. Just talking, about everything. Golf, music, dumb politicians, sadness. We went from reel-to-reel tapes to 8-tracks to cassettes, the best move of all."

Jack's speaking voice was Grand Canyon deep and horseback country. He sounded like the actor Ben Johnson, some trustworthy rancher with a wry sense of humor, the kind of guy who rides across six counties to deliver a two-word message. The simplicity of that voice, and the mission behind it, moved my father tremendously. This was a man who once bypassed a $50,000 payoff because he wouldn't record Beatles music, but he devoted many hours of his life to Jack Steinhauser.

"One time I had a stopover in L.A. and Gordon invited me out for golf and dinner," Jack said. "It was wonderful. The thing I remember most, we stopped for ice cream and Gordon didn't have a cent. He told me, quite seriously, 'I've spent my life devoted to the principle of spending every dime I can get my hands on.'"

It was 1987, three years after Gor's death, when I spoke with Texas Jack. "Those tapes were so much fun," he told me, "and I miss it. Badly."

Gor always struck me as having a singular perspective on things, far removed from other parents, and it often proved to be as soothing as the onshore breeze on a Malibu afternoon. When Jack Pritchett and I embarked on a three-month Europe trip in 1971, Gor knew we'd occasionally seek out ways to get high. Those were the times, and places like Amsterdam and Copenhagen offered a tantalizing lure. I was up in Berkeley, clearing the way for my graduation from Cal, when he wrote me this passage:

"As far as pot is concerned, it's your business. I smoked more of it than you probably ever will [in the Forties], although we were all slowed down a little when one of us got a year in Atlanta for giving a stick to a girl, who gave it to a soldier. The extremely momentary pleasure of the weed sort of faded at the prospect of a year in the pokey. The fact that the sentence was unfair and unreasonable is beside the point; he still did the year. Beverly and I both feel that it should be legalized. That still doesn't keep me from pointing out to you the possible consequences in that square world we are in. People are very afraid of anything that is not just like them, and long hair has become the universal symbol of people that bomb schoolrooms, commit mass murders, and push dope. Now, you and Jack know that you aren't that way, and your parents know it, but that cop in Istanbul who wants his name in the paper doesn't know it, or care."

I found that astonishing. During my college years, none of us felt that our parents had the slightest idea what it meant to be lounging on an apartment deck in the sun, toking, and listening to Crosby, Stills & Nash's "Guinnevere." But my father knew the feeling exactly. Just plug in some Dixieland, and the two worlds meet.

Along those lines, just recently I heard from sportswriter Lyle Spencer, who first triggered the notion of writing this book. "My dad was old school," he wrote in an e-mail, "a sentimentalist who unfortunately became a drunk, frustrated over his own thwarted ambitions. He put it all on me at a young age, and it was a heavy burden to bear. I was always so envious of your dad, the coolest ever. I'll never forget the day he busted us in his studio with weed, listening to Motown, and he kind of smiled and shut the door. It blows me away to this day."

There are letters and memories and the fine recollections of friends, but I never heard my father sit down and sort it all out: his theories on fame, lifestyle, the things that matter and the junk to be discarded. That just wasn't his style. Through a series of radio interviews, a somewhat clear picture emerges. In composite:

"When I had my first hit record, everybody was makin' a big fuss over me and I was quite happy. The rest of 'em didn't mean much to me. The first time I saw my name in lights on Broadway at the Capitol Theater [for "Manhattan Tower"], I thought, gee, headliner, that's great. But I never looked at it again and never took a picture. I just never cared about pursuing it. I could have made a bundle going out on the road to do concerts and make my name as Gordon Jenkins, the performer, but none of that did anything for me.

"I've won a bunch of trophies and stuff over the years, and I have no idea where they are. I had gold records around, and I lent them to people to get their pictures taken with them and never got them back. I don't even know where my Grammy [1965] is, and I don't really care. For some reason, I just don't react to those things. Generally, especially as I've gotten older, I know in my own mind whether I've done a good job or not. I'm more selective, and I know what's going to stand. There was more talk about a possible Grammy after the 'Trilogy' album with Sinatra, and some interviewer said to me, 'Wow, isn't that exciting?' I said, 'No.' Because it isn't. It's mostly about politics, and a bunch of people who don't necessarily know what they're talking about.

"I had a lot of fun. You'd be hard-pressed to find any fella during my lifetime who had that much fun. Not counting the divorce; that wasn't fun a bit. But as far as the business has been concerned, it's all been fun. I always went off in a number of different directions, but the most fun, I think, was writing the words and then doing the orchestration and conducting the band when we made the record. That's fun. If nobody buys it, I can't help that. Hell with 'em. I'm in the bar by then."

His longtime business manager, Harold Plant, recalled many occasions when Gor chose his lifestyle and principles above all else. "The Beatles thing required no thought whatsoever on his part, because he had no respect for their music," Plant said. "But I remember someone talking to me about Gordon being musical director on a new television series starring Dean Martin. Would have made him a fortune. He said, 'No, I don't think too much of him as a singer.' The show lasted a number of years and was very successful, but with Gordon, it never even reached the point of how much money or prestige. He simply wouldn't do it.

"I think Gordon was one of the most democratic people I ever knew," said Plant. "If he liked someone, anyone at all, he'd offer his services as their cocktail pianist. And he did that, many times. He knew just about every song ever written, and he could play it in any key, and he'd do that by the hour. He didn't care if you were rich or poor, black or white, what your religion was, he either liked you or he didn't, and the relationship went accordingly. I remember him telling me that Louis Armstrong was the greatest man he'd ever met. Not so much on talent, but that he had the greatest outlook on life. And that, to me, was Gordon. He had the best outlook of anyone I ever knew. Now, I never met Louis. . . ."

As artfully as he could craft or reproduce a piece of music, Gordon Jenkins couldn't sing it. And I mean, not even a little bit. "I'm the worst singer in the world," he once said. "Worse than anybody. That's one record I hold without any competition, the worst singer in the music business. It will never be questioned. You can't even find a rock singer as bad as I am. Seriously, I'll challenge anybody in the world. In the old days, music publishers wouldn't even let me demonstrate my own songs. They were afraid they'd miss something, like a good song would sail right by 'em if I was singing it."

The beauty of our home studio was that he could record anything, even for his own amusement, with multi-track professionalism. Trying to keep a straight face, he'd sing all four parts of a perfectly awful barbershop quartet. He'd have my mother sing lead, then weigh in with horribly off-key fills. Most of the takes collapsed in laughter, the familiar "Hoo-hoo-hoo," suggesting ventriloquists or startled owls. For the music historians who portrayed him as the most dour, serious man this side of Leningrad, the scenes would have been quite revealing.

In the manner of a master comic, his humor never surfaced in conventional ways. It was zany, often corny, always a little different. When I was about twelve years old, we were riding a crowded elevator in a fashionable New York hotel, both of us in suits and ties. As the floors shot by to uncomfortable silence, he announced, "I hear Bruce Jenkins is in town." For the next few moments, a dozen strangers tried to determine exactly what that meant. Bruce Hudson, known to be savagely tight with a buck, once won a $2.50 bet on the golf course; Gor paid off with 250 pennies in a Sara Lee pie tin, encased in concrete. One night a golfing buddy called to wish him a happy birthday, breaking into song as soon as Gor picked up the phone. "I know who it is," he answered, "but I don't recognize the tune." And he could be funny without even trying. He never could accept the fact that he was gaining weight, especially in the gut, after being one of the world's skinniest healthy men for most of his life. He seemed to think that he'd wake up one morning as a strapping 140-pounder, good as new. Yet the diet grew worse, and the waistline followed suit. One night Jack Pritchett and I were in the kitchen, whipping up brownies or some such thing, when Gor came through the front door. Willing to try anything to drop some pounds, he was wearing one of those ponderous "weight belts" that were so fashionable for a while. And he was eating an ice cream sandwich.

"I remember two great stories about Gor," Jack told me. "I guess Sinatra had a thing about change, never liked to bother with coins, and if he'd go out drinking, after a few hours at the bar there would be all these quarters and dimes lying around. They might have been a hassle for Sinatra, but not Gor. He told me that whenever he got the chance, he'd scoop 'em all up when Frank wasn't looking."

The other story harkened back to a high-society party that Gor happened to be attending in the early Fifties. "The way Gor told it—and I love it that he'd bust himself," said Jack, "he was hanging out in the corner of the living room, trying to look suave and debonair as he smoked a cigarette. In doing so, he casually burned a hole into an oil painting."

A lot of nice things came our way after he died, including letters he'd written. One of them, to my half-brother Gordon Jr., addressed the subject of puns. "This all reminds me of Don Ho and his large family," he wrote. "Let's see, there was Westward, Land, What, Heigh, and the one who always did Santa Claus at Christmas, Hoho. Then there was the uncle, Gung."

He sent out a Christmas card one year to all of his golfing buddies—mostly pilots and airline employees and all of them quite willing to make fun of themselves—from the Las Posas Country Club near Camarillo. It came with the following message:

> *So up to the putting green all of them flew,*
> *With a cart full of beer, and George Figley too.*
> *And then in a twinkling I saw on the range*
> *Some swings that were weird, and wondrous strange.*
> *As I strolled away, trying to stifle a fart*
> *Down the fairway Saint Nicholas came in his cart.*
> *His stance, it was open, and then it was shut*
> *And he looked like Lou Erickson missing a putt.*
> *He was chubby and plump, a jolly old rake*
> *And I laughed when I saw him put two in the lake.*
> *And then, his frustration and anger all spent*
> *Mumbling short oaths, down the fairway he went.*
> *And I heard him exclaim, as he drove out of town*
> *'Merry Christmas to all, and keep your head down.'*

It was Sinatra, of all people, who proved the perfect foil for Gor's vaudevillian humor. The two of them exchanged light-hearted correspondence over the years, often triggered by something they'd seen in the newspaper. As an example of the whole silly business, my father discovered an article in *Hi-Fi* magazine about a European composer named Carl Orff.

"Reminds me of a song," Gor wrote to Sinatra. "'Let's Carl the Whole Thing Orff.'"

Chapter 9

The Sinatra Interview

B Y THE FALL OF 1990, I had waited more than three years for a Sinatra interview. It gets to be sort of comical at that point. Friends start wondering if you made the whole thing up ("No, really, he wants to do it"), and you figure it won't happen in a million years. But on a weekday morning that November, a call came in from Dorothy, the secretary I'd been pestering every three or four months. Frank wants to see you. Today. Be there by five.

I would have dropped anything to be there. Pleasantly, there was nothing to drop. I was living in the Malibu house at the time, idling along on a separate book project, and it would be an easy drive to Sinatra's home on Foothill Drive, just east of the Beverly Hills Hotel.

I could feel the strength of my father's music as I pulled into the driveway. It was a vital component to the scene. Over the years, my newspaper interviews ranged from the satisfying (Magic Johnson, Tiger Woods, Martina Navratilova) to the bizarre (transsexual tennis player Renee Richards) to the arduous (Billy Martin, Bobby Knight), but nothing compared to this. Aside from the occasional Larry King spot, I wasn't aware of Sinatra doing any one-on-one interviews. This was strictly a tribute to Gor, and without having a say in the matter, I walked through that door with one of his signature arrangements ("When the Wind Was Green") rushing through my head.

The foyer was absurdly jammed: yes-men, servants, hangers-on, and the imposing Jilly Rizzo, Sinatra's close friend and connection (one of many) to the mob.

"Jilly, it's Gordy Jenkins's son," Sinatra said. "You believe this? Is he a dead ringer, or what?"

"Son of a bitch. No kidding, Frank."

"He wants to talk about the old man. We're gonna drop into the back room for a while."

And in an instant, everyone was gone. I don't know if Sinatra snapped his fingers, or just vacated the place with a glance, but the people just vanished. Soon it was just the two of us, on facing sofas in a private room, with an attractive woman asking if I'd like a drink (Screwdriver, in Gor's honor). Sinatra appeared to have bourbon, with a splash. "We've got an hour," he said.

In his pale yellow sweater and white shirt with the collar out, Sinatra struck a comforting image from the Sixties—perhaps a celebrity golf tournament, or an old album cover. He was seventy-four years old and cogent, still ahead of the game, though it wouldn't be long before his memory and perception began to fade. This was a particularly good day, and as his mind drifted back in time, there were moments when his face took on that formidable "From Here to Eternity" look. I brought two tape recorders (no way would I screw this up), activated them simultaneously and took a swig of the man's best vodka.

More than anything, I wanted to know about Gor's command of the orchestra and his stern handling of Sinatra. The subject brought a smile to his face. "It almost took me back to my childhood, those record dates," he said. "My daddy was a pretty straight-ahead kind of man, you'd never talk back to him, and that's one of the things that grabbed me about Gordy. The fact that when he walked into the room, everything stopped. There was attention. And I never saw it with anybody else. I worked with a whole bunch of guys, beautiful people, but they were almost too soft for their own good. Gordy's presence demanded attention. I don't know if you ever saw that in him...."

"That's my whole life," I said.

"But when Gordy stepped in front of the band, something happened. You dig? I don't want to take anything away from the other guys I worked with, but Christ ... I never saw a man step up in front of an orchestra and get that much attention without saying a *word*. You'd go into the date, and the guys are unpacking and yakking and everybody's laughing and having fun. But when you heard this [taps the table loudly, four times], there was silence. Absolute silence. It's like when we were five years old and the teacher came in and said, 'Quiet!' and everybody sat up. I've seen that in people over the years, big business meeting, and when the key guy walks into the room, everybody just realizes it instinctively. Anybody who can do that has got some kind of authority. And I loved Gordy for it, because I needed that from time to time. You can't just run around wildly all the time, or you'll wind up in the can."

He broke out laughing right then, and it was a great laugh, easing the tension and taking me about thirty years back in time. I remembered that laugh from recording sessions and out-take segments I'd heard from other dates. Most likely, my dad would start laughing, too. There weren't many people who could affect his concentration when he held the baton, but Sinatra could do it every time.

"I have to say beyond question that Gordy was the most solid and best-equipped musician, orchestrator and conductor that I ever worked with," he went on. "I don't mean the other guys weren't, but there was something different about the way he worked. It was *serious*. When we sat down, it *went* – right away. We settled down and arrived at stuff without fooling around, and—I don't know quite how to say this—there was something growing, all the time.

Something new and better than before. He was of great assistance to me as a vocalist, because he knew a hell of a lot about it, stuff people don't even understand. He knew a tremendous amount about vocalizing. We'd walk aside for a few minutes and he'd make a suggestion, like, 'You're leaning too hard on these four bars,' and so on. He was wonderful at dissecting what the problem was."

"For someone to lay that on you," I said, "he'd better know what he's talking about."

"Oh, absolutely," Sinatra said. "I would trust him from here for Chrissake to San Francisco and back. It wasn't just the knowledge that he had, or all of his years in the business, it was *how* he came to me that was so uplifting. Because what the hell, I can't read a fucking note. I just know what I hear, and Gordy understood that. He had ears like a fox. I mean, like an animal in the woods. If there was a clinker—which happens all the time in our business, from the vocalist all the way down to the fourth trombone player—he would hear it and correct it. So whenever he wanted to explain something to me, it was pure. Absolutely pure. In fact, everything about Gordon Jenkins . . . he was almost *all* pure. I don't give a god damn what you want to talk about, he was clear, right straight ahead. He was a taskmaster and I loved him for it.

"And then, of course, there was the other side of Gordy," he said. "At the end of the date, or a gig in Vegas, whatever, we'd go to a bar. We'd lift a few, laugh and have fun. Forget about all the stuff we'd done before that. It was a totally different world, Gordy was suddenly one of the guys, and there was no difference between any of us."

"I didn't realize you guys were that close off the set," I said. "He left the impression that you didn't do much socializing together."

"No, we got together an awful lot," he said. "There were times when I went on my own and said, Gordy, I have to talk to you. I need some help, I need a friend. And he'd just look at me and I knew he understood completely—what I was saying, and what I was *about* to say. That's what knocked me out. That he knew where I was coming from, where I was going, where I wanted to go. And could I *get* there. That's the whole idea. You see, our association was much more than conductor and vocalist. We were two friends, close friends, and he knew as much about my problems and my life as I did myself. I don't think anybody else knew half of it, because I never trusted people to talk to 'em that way. I trusted Gordy, and he never let me down. I mean, I never heard an echo from something I might have said to him. Never! Jesus, I loved him. I just miss him terribly."

As I listened to the tape later, I stopped cold at this point. Gor always used to joke about his out-of-the-studio relationship with Sinatra—as if there wasn't one. "If Frank made a right turn after the date, I'd go left," he'd say. "Otherwise, next thing you know you're in a bar and some drunk comes up to Frank—'My wife's in love with you, ya bastard!'—and takes a swing at him. That sort of thing. Not for me." But it wasn't like that at all. They were the world's saddest men because they talked about their sadness and a thousand heartbreaks over the years. They made terribly sad music together because they understood it, and each other, better than anyone else. My father not only kept this to himself, he wouldn't even admit to *seeing* Frank after a date. Everything Sinatra told me along those lines was a wild, wonderful mystery, slamming me hard from deep left field.

"Jesus, I can't find any more adjectives," he went on, and there was a long pause. "He was a genius, absolutely, and I don't mean just in music, but in life. He could tell something was wrong just by looking at me, or the way I was acting, or the way I was speaking to somebody."

"You mean heartbreak kind of problems?" I said. "Lost love and such?"

"Yeah. Family breakup and stuff like that. It hurt me so terribly much, and he knew it, he sensed it, because he'd been there. I think he sensed sadness in people quicker than anybody I ever knew before or after."

I ventured, "If anybody wants to get in touch with their own sadness, my God, put on 'September of My Years' and you're there. You're in it."

"Isn't it marvelous? So wonderful. Jesus Christ [voice becomes lower and quieter] . . . I drink to him. And we'll see him, too. I have a funny feeling that we're all gonna be someplace together. I believe it, and I will continue to believe it. I was born a Catholic, although I didn't live it too well. . . ."

"Few do."

"Yeah, but I didn't practice it that well. I'll go in and kneel down once in a while, maybe go into the booth with the man, and tell him some hokey things I did. But now I've come to an age where I can work it out pretty much in my own head, you know? What the hell."

He thought for a moment. "I always got a kick out of it, guys who didn't really know Gordon would come up to me and say, 'He's pretty deep, man. Awful quiet.' But he was a guy who swung pretty good in his early days. When we started working together, every once in a while he'd come into the date, get up on the stand and he'd have a fuckin' bottle of booze right there next to him. 'That's for when we're finished,' he'd say, and it was marvelous. He'd have a bottle of Jack Daniel's. I don't even know if he was drinking Jack Daniel's, but he'd have it up there. Hell, every so often we'd have a little taste beforehand."

"That sounds like my father all the way."

"Oh, yeah. Maybe I'd have a bottle of champagne, and we'd have some of that jazz. Have a little nip."

Gor was known for his bold forays into the Las Vegas gambling world—sometimes winning big, occasionally blowing as much as five grand at a time—and I'd always assumed he went it alone. Now I wondered if Sinatra had been right there with him.

"Sure, and I always knew where to find him," he said. "The goddamn roulette wheel."

"He'd spend hours at home working on systems," I said. "Half the night goes by without a word—he's figuring out ways to beat the wheel."

"Yeah, and in the casino I'd come up behind him and say [ominously], 'How we doin'?' He wouldn't even look around. He knew that voice like he knew his own. 'Not good,' he'd say. 'This fuckin' bum is the worst dealer I've seen in my life.' And I'd say, 'Maybe I can get him to fix the game [laughter].' Because I knew all the guys who were dealing inside the joint. But Gordy was too pure for that."

There was so much more ground to cover. I sensed an imaginary hourglass running low. So I threw out some rapid-fire subjects, starting with "Manhattan Tower."

"I fell down on the floor. Take a note to God, I fell right to the ground. Because there had never been anything written or spoken or performed about a city like that. It really knocked me out."

On my mother's singing:

"Oh, yeah," he said, in a low, almost guttural sound. "Oooh, yeah. What a sound. What a sound! Wasn't that marvelous? I must come and see her [at the beach]. We're gonna build a house out there now. Hell of a singer. You play her for an instant, you know who it is. Like Crosby—that's Crosby. Or Kate Smith, hokey as she was. But Beverly had that wonderful thing that came out of a group. You'd have four hundred singers around town and one voice would come out like that."

The "September of My Years" date:

"I'm leaving myself out as a vocalist, but it's one of the most moving popular works of all time. *The* most moving. And I play it often. I paint at home, in the studio, and I play the same goddamn tapes every day. I love the sound and the effort that went into it, the lyrics and the orchestration. It's part of my life."

On Gor's decidedly Jewish-sounding string arrangements:

"It's almost as if he *was* Jewish. He had more Jewish fans than I ever heard in my life. Particularly in New York, kids born of Jewish parents and brought up as Jews, they'd say, 'Jeez, this guy—is that his real name, Gordon Jenkins? You sure he's not Jewish? His music gets down *into* us.' I said, 'Maybe someday you'll get to meet him, and you'll understand. That is, if you can get him to talk.' Sometimes I'd give him this big buildup to people, and they'd finally meet and he'd say like one word. But forget it when the music starts playing. I'd watch the string guys in the orchestra, and Gordy's just killing 'em with this stuff."

On the quirks of his recording style:

"There were times when Gordy had me sit behind the orchestra. First guy who ever did that, by the way. He wanted a balance, and in the back, there was never a mixup or a bad time mixing the vocal and the orchestra. Nobody ever thought about that before. I sat against the wall with my microphone, so the orchestra could play as freely as they wanted and he had better control of them. And I think we discovered something quite marvelous. I had guys tell me later on that it worked for them, too."

On his favorite arrangers:

"I was fortunate in the very beginning to have Axel Stordahl, who had a very small education about orchestration. He did some very pretty things, but they were lightweights, like feathers. But it was the beginning, so it caught on. Axel was a bad third trumpet player who had no lip at all. I used to tease him about it. But what a sweet man. Very quiet, and while Gordon under pressure would probably bite you a little bit, Axel didn't know how to do that. He was just a guy conducting with a pipe in his mouth. And every time he had a chance, he'd go back to Norway. He was born there and he'd go back for two or three weeks, for Christ's sake.

"Nelson, of course, was wonderful. There was that little gimmick he had, chord changes that would show up every once in a while, a little dissonance here and there. Absolutely a champion. I was lucky to find three guys—Nelson, Gordy, and Don Costa. The other guys were very good, but not championship. Not enough here, not enough there, you know? Or maybe they just didn't have the time, and it was kind of a rush job. But not everybody can overcome a champion.

"I remember saying to Gordy, I've got a song ['Laura'] that I'm just nuts about. I think we oughta sit down in the studio, give me a downbeat, and let's make the best goddamn record of that song. 'Cause everybody was crazy about it then [1957], and it had been beaten to death. That's my favorite song of all time. The introduction Gordy wrote to that ... Oh, Jesus. By the time I got around to hearing everything he'd put down on paper, I was fucking nearly in tears when we were ready to make the record. I had a fuckin' lump in my throat this big. Oh, boy ... that's when you really needed Gordy, to do stuff like that."

"I've heard that story about recording 'Lonely Town,'" I said. "How you were so moved by the arrangement, you said he had saved your career."

"That's true. I was in trouble. I had problems in my personal life and my career, too. What I heard that day, I felt it was something that was gonna lift me up. That's the only way I can explain it. I'd never heard anything like Gordy's arrangement before. And nobody else had heard anything like it before. That's when I really realized what he was doing for me."

Sinatra had become deeply saddened by the end of the interview. It was 6:30 p.m., the late-afternoon sunlight had given way to darkness, and there were tears in his eyes. He looked at the floor for a moment, then raised his glass to me. "It's such a goddamn shame," he said. "I had so much more stuff I wanted to do with him, and *now* is the time I wanted to do it. We knew a great man, my boy, in every sense of the word. He was sensitive, he got angry, he was caustic, he was warm ... well, cheers. Here's to him. I can't say any more."

Chapter 10

Nat, Ella, and Like That

M ILT GABLER WAS ADDRESSING A GROUP of Decca executives in Los Angeles one afternoon when he became overwhelmed with appreciation. The studio mastermind started talking about my father, the company's No. 1 asset at the time, and what he meant to the music business.

"If Jesus had been a musician and come down to this earth, there were two guys," he said. "Gordon Jenkins and Nat Cole. Gordon would have been the white Jesus, Nat the black Jesus. They always thought properly, said exactly the right things, did impeccable work. Without fail. They were like Jesus. That's kinda how I felt about Gordy."

I was at lunch with Gabler in Connecticut when he told that story, and it just about knocked me over. "I went a little off the deep end," he admitted, "but I really meant it."

Partly due to circumstance, and partly because Cole died so disturbingly early (just fifty years old, of lung cancer, in 1965), I never saw much of him. My mother and Nat's wife, Maria, were very close friends, and I once participated in a piano recital that included his two daughters, Sweetie (later to become famous with her given name, Natalie) and Cookie. But to me, Nat was a photograph: the elegant posture, a cigarette in his hand and the promise that on a record date with my father, not a thing could go wrong.

The association began in 1939, when Nat walked across Sunset

Boulevard from a little nightclub and played piano with the Jenkins band on "Swing Soiree," the NBC radio show said to have been the first in Los Angeles to consistently play jazz. I'm sure Gor would have followed Nat's career with religious conviction if he'd never sung a word; when he did go that way, my father actively sought him out.

They did three albums together, all on Capitol: "Love Is the Thing," in 1957; "The Very Thought of You," in 1958; and "Where Did Everyone Go," for which all twelve songs were recorded in just two days in August 1962, three years before Nat died. And their work together was immortalized in the highly regarded film, "My Favorite Year," which opened with "Stardust" and perhaps the finest introduction ever arranged for that song.

"I always dug Nat, from the moment I first saw him," Gor said. "Such a gentleman and *such* a good musician. He had perfect pitch. The advantage of that was, I could bring him in anywhere I wanted to. I could write any kind of trick chord, or a harmonically structured introduction with a simultaneous key change, and it was all easy for him. I could never have done that for Dick Haymes, or anybody who didn't have that pitch, because they'd be guessing. In fact, with some singers, you have to get down to a child's level, a rock-and-roll level, so they won't have any trouble coming in. With Nat, you always knew he was gonna be there with the right note at the right time. It wasn't any earth-shaking thing, but it sure impressed the hell out of musicians. He was an instant sight reader, a wonderful jazz piano player, and always sober, soft-spoken and on time.

"Nat approached the sessions differently from Frank or Judy, where there was a lot of give and take. He never told me much what to do. He'd heard things of mine that he liked, so he figured I would know. Hell, he did everything good. As far as I know, he never made a mistake. He had a very high standard level of performance—probably higher than anybody—as far as the first team being there all the time. Frank might have been tired, or had a date, or he didn't want to do something again if I asked him. With Judy, I just locked the door of the studio and *made* her do it again. I never heard Nat make a recording I thought he should have done over."

Gor said Cole didn't want to do "Stardust" because it had been recorded about six million times. "We conned him into doing it," he said. "That's the closest I ever saw him to being even slightly temperamental. We did one take and he said, 'That's it. Next?' And he sang the hell out of it. I was crazy about Nat."

To hear a lot of people in the business tell it, the Jenkins-Cole master stroke was their version of "Paradise," which had gained some popularity over the rock 'n' roll airwaves through a junky rendition by April Stevens and Nino Tempo. That's how I knew the song. When I heard Nat sing it, I realized how far I'd been led astray. Then I went to see Dave Dexter Jr., and got a pretty fair idea of the record's impact.

Dexter had been writing about jazz since 1935, as a newspaperman, author (*The Jazz Story*, 1964) and editor/critic for *Downbeat, Metronome,* and *Billboard.* He had known and interviewed Billie Holiday, Louis Armstrong, Woody Herman and Duke Ellington, for whom he produced several records. Charlie Parker called him "High Dexterious," quite fondly. And after joining Capitol Records' original staff in 1942, along with my father, he stayed with the company for thirty-one years, moving up to full-time producer. His son, Mike, a standout high-school athlete in the San Fernando Valley and a bodysurfing partner of mine in Malibu, introduced us—and I felt a strong sense of urgency. A couple of years before I interviewed him, Dexter had six strokes in six days.

I found him in failing health but, at the mention of the old days, lucid and enthusiastic. He told me of a project he called "My Life on Record," his personal history of favorites over the years. "Considering that the tape begins with 'Blue Prelude' and ends with 'Paradise,'" he said, "I'd say your dad had a pretty strong influence on me."

Dexter said he began collecting records when he was four years old, growing up in Kansas City, "and this tape traces my entire life as connected with records. There must be two hundred bands and singers featured on it, mostly in excerpt form, and I put an awful lot of thought into it. I knew almost everybody and collected records all my life, and when I came up with what I consider the most perfect record ever made, it was 'Paradise,' Nat Cole with the Gordon Jenkins orchestra [on the 1958 Capitol album "The Very Thought of You" and the 1961 Capitol release, "The Nat King Cole Story"].

"In the first place, it's the only pop record I ever heard that probably the first fifty times I heard it, I'd start crying," he said. "The way those strings go up, the way they jump an octave at the end . . . I'd probably start cryin' now, 'cause I haven't played it in several months. And mind you, I'm a jazz guy. That's my real bag. But it's so beautifully orchestrated, and Nat was at his very best. That record . . . I just don't see how a man can think that way, and write down those notes . . . marvelous. You think I'm exaggerating. I tell ya, I cried. Time after time. It gets down to those last sixteen bars, those strings . . . and I don't feel I'm an emotional guy."

My parents kept the Cole connection going with Maria, who made many visits to the beach house over the years. She was very mannered and elegant, with a speaking voice like Lena Horne's, and while she once admitted having terrible short-term memory, "I do remember the night that Nat asked me to marry him," she said. "'Manhattan Tower' was playing on the radio, and honey, that was no accident."

As Maria recalled, "Nat would always tell me that Gordon was the only person who could do those things with strings, to really embellish what he was doing on ballads. He once told me Gordon was the only person he worked with where he was totally at ease, where the session just flowed and there were no problems. The arrangements were just *there,* perfect, and you can hear it in the records. I always felt Gordon had in his music what Nat had in his voice, and they really were wedded; I never saw two more intense people about their work. Anyway, one night in 1947, Nat got through playing a club at around four in the morning, and he was driving me home. 'Manhattan Tower' was playing, and the setting was just right. What a way to propose: middle of the night, summertime, just beautiful. It was so romantic."

My father once said that one of his biggest regrets was that he never cut an album with Barbra Streisand (he was thrilled by her work; time truly stopped for him when she appeared on television). But he worked with just about everyone else. A few highlights along the way:

One Day in Mecca: On March 8, 1950, the year that saw Jenkins reach the height of his record-chart popularity, he had an extraordinary day. He recorded two songs with Billie Holiday, "God Bless the Child" (a cover of her epic original) and "This Is Heaven to Me," at the Decca studios in Los Angeles. Then he turned around and recorded "My Mother's Rosary" with the legendary Al Jolson on the same set.

None of the records made any kind of splash, but it was a double-barreled glimpse at some penthouse talent. "I had a lot of fun working with Billie Holiday," he said in an interview with Chuck Cecil. "I'd seen her so many times on 52nd Street, many years before, and we'd done one radio show together for NBC, so it was a thrilling experience for me. I guess she had her wild days, but they weren't around me. She showed up on time, knew the songs, did exactly what she was supposed to do, and went home."

The sessions couldn't have been too memorable, because Gor didn't recall doing "God Bless the Child," one of Billie's greatest songs. "The funny thing is, my dad didn't, either," said Steve LaVere of his father, Charlie. "We were going through a bunch of stuff and he said, 'Can you believe this, I did a session with Billie Holiday. I don't remember that.' I said, 'Oh, of course you do,' and he looked at me like I was nuts."

The records don't hold up too well today, largely due to the painfully white-sounding chorus in the background, a style that was wildly popular on most of my dad's records at the time but, with Holiday, didn't fit the artist. Gor had an infinitely better session with her in New York, October 1949, with a chorus-free ensemble and the great Bobby Hackett in the brass section. Hackett and the second trumpet do a tasty little harmonic thing on "Somebody's On My Mind," and Gor crafted some sweet, simple arrangements on "You're My Thrill," "Crazy He Calls Me" and "Please Tell Me Now," with Ms. Holiday sounding very much on her game.

Conducting Jolson was a more familiar experience, as Gor had worked with him several times during his pre-war radio days at NBC. "Jolson had the reputation of eating orchestra leaders alive," he said. "He completely ruined one guy's life, just about put the guy in a sanitarium, but that's because he kept letting Al walk all over him. I was tipped off on how to handle him by Victor Young. He said, 'Jolson will come in late, make a big scene and start throwing his weight around. Then you'll have to stop him. Once you do that, everything will be all right.'

"I remember Jo Stafford was on the show and I was rehearsing her," Gor said, "and sure enough, Jolson doesn't show up. An hour late, he finally walks in, pushes Jo off the stand and says, 'I'm ready to go.' I said, 'I'm not.' He says, 'Whaddya mean?' I said, 'You go sit down. I'll call you when I'm ready.' And you have to remember, this was *his* show. I looked down and all the guys were packing up their instruments; they figured we were through. But Jolson looked at me, said 'OK,' and sat over in the corner like a child, with his hands folded in his lap, making sure everybody saw him.

"Finally I finished with Jo. I said, 'I'll take you now, Mr. Jolson.' He said, 'Are you sure it's gonna be all right?' Now he's playing another part, because he's an actor, which I found fascinating. And we never had another angry word—except for one night when I beat him for a buck-eighty at gin rummy. He accused me of cheating, threw the cards on the floor, went in and asked his valet for $500 to go to dinner and left me sitting there with the cards."

Strictly from a working standpoint, "Jolson was a big, big talent. There's nothing like this guy around any more. Musically, he was nothin'. I almost got sick when NBC wanted me to do the show, because I'd heard him sing without seeing him. I thought he was awful. But when you see him . . . oh, boy. He was a big star in pictures, but that was nothing like seeing him in a room. His talent was thrilling, it really was. He captivated all of us. All of the musicians that hated him, they didn't feel that way when it was over.

"I'm a talent worshipper. I've got to make allowances for people with that much talent. I don't see why they've got to be like the guy who sells you the bakery stuff. People with talent are entitled to aberrations that you don't expect from a cab driver. If they throw a temperamental fit, I'm not gonna be there. And if for some reason I am, I'll stop 'em."

Ella Fitzgerald: There are simple, rhythmic album titles, like "Nashville Skyline" or "One-Man Dog," and then there was Decca's style in the early Fifties: "Miss Ella Fitzgerald and Mr. Gordon Jenkins Invite You to Listen and Relax." While they were at it, they should have added, "Tell You What, We Got Olives, Too." The cover shows a young woman on a couch, wistfully petting her cat, with a phonograph on the floor alongside a bunch of grapes. Pretty much all you need for a really nutty evening.

The remarkable thing about this album is that it doesn't sound like either one of them. You won't find anything like "Ella Sings

Gershwin," but there's a distinct appeal to this serious, forthright approach, and in a strangely refreshing way, Ella's voice is breathtakingly beautiful. My dad's arrangements lack their usual trademarks and there's a bit more brass than his fans might expect, but for any objective observer in retrospect, the combination works well, particularly the cuts "Black Coffee" and "A Man Wrote a Song." This is assuming you can even find the album in the first place. You get the feeling that cat took off with the grapes.

At the time of the recording, in 1949, Columbia was the only label with so-called long playing albums, at twenty-three minutes a side. Decca was slow to adopt the format, and when Fitzgerald went into the April 28 recording session, she figured the four cuts she made with Jenkins would be released as 78s. They were, but they also formed part of one of Decca's first LPs, finally released in 1954. The rest of the selections were cut that September, and in the words of a *Chicago Tribune* critic, "Ella gives her best and simplest performances."

Jimmy Durante: Nora Ephron makes movies the way my dad made music—tenderly, with themes of rapture. What many feel is her definitive work, "Sleepless in Seattle," includes Nat Cole's "Stardust" and a couple of Jenkins sleepers, "As Time Goes By" and "Make Someone Happy" from his album with Jimmy Durante.

Around that time I read a newspaper quote from Ephron, saying that the whole basis of the soundtrack was the Cole album "Love Is the Thing," which she called "the great makeout album of my teenage years." In her adoration of the Gordon Jenkins arrangements, "I became sort of obsessed with him, saying his name over and over to music people I talked to."

I eventually caught up with Ephron at her New York office, and the whole pleasant story came to life. "I spent half my time as a Los Angeles adolescent lying on my bed, face down, listening to 'Love

Is the Thing',", she told me. "It was the most fabulous over-the-top romantic album imaginable. When I began thinking about songs for 'Sleepless,' I knew immediately that I had to begin with Jenkins, that the whole emotional idea of the movie—'somewhere out there is the right someone for me, and what if I never find him?'—was the exact thing I'd been thinking while lying face down on my bed.

"I especially thought about the Nat Cole version of 'When I Fall in Love,'" she said, "and one of my great regrets is that we didn't use it instead of the new version we recorded for the movie. But anyway, when Marc Shaiman agreed to do the music, I kept saying Gordon Jenkins, Gordon Jenkins, Gordon Jenkins. I also said to Marc that I'd loved the Jimmy Durante version of 'Young at Heart' he'd used in 'City Slickers.' A few hours after this conversation, Marc's partner returned from a trip to a record store downtown with a Jimmy Durante album ["Way of Life"] with orchestrations by Gordon Jenkins. All I could think was, there is a God."

Bing Crosby: Most people favor Crosby's 1944 version of "San Fernando Valley," one of my dad's most popular and widely recorded compositions. It's a catchy little number, sung by a master, and it sold like crazy. By all rights, it should have triggered a long and successful collaboration. Thanks to Crosby, a big-league grouch when he set his mind to it, the relationship went sour—for life.

"I always wondered about that," said Sam Weiss, the highly successful music publisher. "I said to Gordon, 'What the hell happened between you and Bing?' And he says, 'He was goddamn stupid, if you want to know.'"

It started with a phone call, Weiss said. "Bing had put a lot of money into a movie he was producing on his own. It seems the producers, the top guys, didn't like the music and he needed some changes. They recommended Gordon, Bing was all for it, so he called Gordy to set the thing up. Problem was, Gordy was real busy at the time. Said, 'I'd love to help you, Bing, but I've got a lot going on here. I've made promises. I've made deals.'

"Well, that was the end of Gordon Jenkins for Bing," Weiss said. "Bing's attitude was, 'The nerve of that guy, after we made that hit record,' and I knew Bing real well. He had the idea he could control everybody. But he had no business getting mad at Gordon, none at all. Gordon was very honest. You couldn't fool around with him."

"And the thing with Gordon was hardly an exception," said publisher George Lee. "Everybody thought Bing was very warm and sweet, but he was a very cold individual. The kind of man who'd turn you off in a second, and that would be the end of it for all time."

(There were ways of dealing with Crosby, but you needed moxie and perhaps a little kick-start. Roger Kelly was a storied amateur golfer in the late 1930s and 1940s, as well as a fabled drinker, and he played some of his best rounds drunk. Once he was playing a $100-a-hole round with Crosby, who had a habit of walking off the course if things weren't going just right, and sure enough, after Kelly won the first three holes, Crosby pretended to be sick. Later, a well-lit Kelly found Crosby at the bar, the two started arguing, and they wound up in the clubhouse. With a quick nod and a handful of cash to the clubhouse attendant, Kelly shoved Crosby into a double locker and padlocked the door.)

"The thing with Bing, you had to stick with him," Weiss went on. "No matter what happened, he was right and you were wrong. Give you an example: Lennie Hayton was Bing's best friend. They'd done shows together, played in the [Paul] Whiteman band, worked in the movies and everything else. But Lennie got this huge crush on Bubs Husing [whose ex-husband, pioneer sports broadcaster Ted Husing, was very close to Bing] and eventually married her. See, Bing was an orthodox Catholic who didn't believe in divorces or any such thing, and it just infuriated him. Once Bing got word of that, he threw Lennie out on his ear. Didn't talk to him for *twenty-five years*."

About five years after "San Fernando Valley," Weiss said, "Gordon came up with a very important song, 'Maybe You'll Be There,' on Decca, the one Charlie LaVere sang so nice. I was Bing's flunky at the time, and he picks out this song and does it on the Kraft show. 'Here's a great, great song,' he tells the audience, 'done by my very good friend, Charlie LaVere.' I said, 'Bing, Gordon Jenkins did that record. It all belonged to him, with that great arrangement.' He says [disdainfully], 'Who cares?' That's how mean he could be. It hurt Gordon, but it was still that same dig going on. Later I got a hold of Charlie and asked him, 'You didn't put Bing up to that, did you?' He said, 'Hell, no! I was so embarrassed, I couldn't see.'"

It went on like that for years, forever. Gor wasn't about to come begging to Crosby for work; he had plenty, with classier people. And Bing never let go of the grudge. "Gordon and I would see Bing in the street, or at NBC, where both of them worked," said Weiss, "and Bing would just keep on going. Wouldn't look at either one of us. He never talked to Gordon to the day he died."

Benny Goodman: This one had a happier ending. Goodman could be a little sour, too, and he once asked something of my father that caused an interminable pause in their working relationship. And then, nearly a half-century later, everything was fine again.

"That story dates all the way back to 'Goodbye' in the early Thirties," Gor said. "I was really the first arranger Benny ever had—before he got Fletcher Henderson or any of the other guys. I helped him pick some guys for his first dance-band radio outfit, and you know how 'Goodbye' turned out. Well, he wanted to cut in on my share of the royalties from 'Goodbye,' and I didn't want him to. He was quite unhappy about it. I never did the favor of cutting in people on any of my stuff, and I never cut in on anybody else. It was quite prevalent, but I didn't do it. So we had a little falling-out. He's an easy person to have a falling-out with."

As Bruce Hudson recalled, "Gordon and Benny were good pals—as good as you could be with Benny. They were kind of similar, in some ways. Benny could be very tough on his musicians, just drop 'em in an instant, and Gordon was capable of that, too. Gordon fired very easily. You can't play too busy, you can't send your uncle, you can't have a friend. Because when the baton comes down, you have to play, and play it right. The first time. The thing is, Gordon had a really soft side that Benny didn't."

"Benny has such high standards," Gor said in a 1978 interview, "he expected everybody to be perfect. He was a little like Sinatra that way. Just the slightest mistake or lapse in musicianship in the band, and he'd start givin' them The Ray, that terrible look he'd lay on people. If you couldn't stand up to it, you had a big problem. Oh, he was something. He changed people's lives. Literally drove them to mental problems, he was so tough to work for. I always thought he expected more than people could give, and Frank was like that, too. Everything's great if you're doing your job. It's when you goof that the trouble comes up.

"I sure had a lot of fun writing for Benny while it lasted. I figured I'd never hear from him again, and all of a sudden [in the mid-Seventies] he called up and wanted some arrangements for an album. Then I wrote a clarinet concerto for him [in 1977], which he performed with the Richmond Symphony—legitimate stuff, no jazz—and we were both quite happy with it. So I talk to him once in a while. But you talk about traditional; this guy wanted to record an album with one mike—monaural—like he did in 1935. People had to argue like crazy to talk him out of it. I think he really believed that nothing could quite match that original sound. Hell, I don't know, maybe he was right."

The McGuire Sisters: It is widely assumed that the McGuires were discovered by Arthur Godfrey, the entertainer and talent scout, shortly before their first big hit, "Goodnight, Sweetheart, Goodnight." Not true. As Phyllis McGuire told me in a 1999 interview, and Milt Gabler confirmed, they were discovered by Gordon Jenkins in 1951.

They had come out of Middletown, Ohio, "three of the most gorgeous, 5-foot-10 black Irish girls you ever saw in your life," as Gabler put it, and they had been church-choir singers back home. "I think we only knew three pop songs, if that," said Phyllis. "We were never supposed to be in show business. We had gone to New York on a lark." They got an audition on NBC radio and did an eight-week stint on the Kate Smith show, but quickly found they were running out of luck.

"We thought, well, time to go back to Ohio," said Phyllis. "We figured we had failed and we were totally downtrodden. But there were two people, NBC producer Barry Wood and a director named Kevin Johnson, who thought we had some talent. They asked if we'd like to go with them to meet this wonderful gentleman. We figured we were heading home unsuccessful, so why not? Well, they took us to this apartment, where a man was sitting at an upright piano. It was your father, and of course, we knew the name. We said, 'Well, Mr. Jenkins, we'll sing the only pop songs we know.' Which was 'Pretty-Eyed Baby,' 'Miss You Since You Went Away, Dear,' and an *a cappella* version of 'Mona Lisa.' He flipped over our sound, and the way we looked, and he took us right down to Milt Gabler at Decca, where we did the same three songs."

Gabler: "So in walks Gordon with these three dreams, and as he went to the piano, I said, 'Gordon, they don't even have to sing. If you say they're good, they don't even have to audition.' Which was a put-on, of course, but how could they be bad if Gordon liked 'em and they looked like that? The problem is that we had the

Andrews Sisters on Decca, and we thought the McGuires should go some other way, so we put 'em on my Coral label. Since Gordon was a Decca artist, he couldn't record 'em, but we snuck him in there, anyway. He orchestrated and arranged our first four sides for Coral, without getting credit. Pretty soon the shit hit the fan at Decca, like, 'Why the hell don't we have these girls?'"

"A few weeks later, Arthur Godfrey called," said Phyllis. "We went on his talent show and won, and things just took off from there. For some reason we're always associated with that show, but it was Gordon who discovered us and had the vision to put us on Coral. I'm very proud to say that."

Peggy Lee: My father's 1952 single with Lee, "Lover," was a revolutionary hit and remains a standard in the pop-record industry. I knew I had to find her, and it wasn't too difficult. She called my mother to say hello one day in 1988, and I jumped right in.

She was in terrible shape, and apparently looked worse, and I was appalled as she ran down her many ailments: two serious lung infections, double-bypass heart surgery, a fractured pelvis, diabetes, heavy medication, sporadic confinement to a wheelchair. "I think I've had everything but AIDS," she told Beverly. "If I weren't so healthy, I'd be dead."

"My lord, it's good to hear from you."

"I've thought about you a thousand times," said Peggy. "Somehow, I'm still out there on the road."

"You have to," said Beverly. "If you stop, it goes away. You just keep movin'."

Peggy was movin' pretty good in the early 1950s, when she and Gor hooked up for a number of singles. She'd been a nationwide favorite since making her name as the singer with Goodman's band in the early Forties, and she was about to change record companies. "I was with Capitol, which had made a giant record of 'Lover' with

Les Paul," she said. "They didn't want to do it again, and I was passionate about it. It was something inside my mind and I couldn't let it go. I actually switched over to Decca because of that. Fortunately my contract was up, and Gordon was very ready to record it."

Lee had a singular plan for that song, something she had uncovered in the dark recesses of a movie theater. "It was some B picture about the French foreign legion," she said. "There was a very handsome man who had joined up because he'd been rejected by his lady friend, and there were these fabulous images of horses running off into the distance. It sounded like Latin rhythms to me, the horses' hooves and different gaits. I remember sitting there and making it sound like galloping on my lap. And it seemed that if the key was raised, it gave the impression of the horses going faster."

This "Lover" would be a far cry from Les Paul's version, and "it was absolutely her idea," Gor said in a 1977 interview that I ran past Lee. "She just laid it out for me—not literally the musical notes, but the tempo and the Latin drummers, the whole pseudo-sexy feel of the thing, changing keys a couple of times, the whole thing was dictated by her. Everybody's running around saying what a brilliant arranger I was, but the whole conception of the thing was hers."

"Well, that's ridiculous," Lee told me. "I just had an idea for the rhythm section, nothing to do with the whole orchestration, and he brought my concept to life. I had no idea that he could embellish it so beautifully. I think he made one of the classic arrangements of all time. I got letters from different arrangers telling me they were grateful for a new way to do music. That was the thing about Gordon in general, with 'Manhattan Tower' and so many things he did. He just seemed to surpass what other writers did."

Strange bird, that Peggy. That's why my dad loved her, for her genius and creativity and eccentricity. Dave Dexter Jr., a producer from her Capitol years, recalled a session in which she was singing a ballad and suddenly stopped cold. "It's not right in here," she declared. "I'm not seeing those purple clouds that I like to see. Those big purple clouds floating across the room."

"I forget who was running the date," said Dexter, "but he didn't bat an eye, because he knew Peggy. He said, 'Maybe if we change the lights around,' this and that, whatever, and it seemed to help her. That's Peggy. She sees purple clouds and stuff."

The omnipresent Milt Gabler produced the "Lover" session for Decca and recalled, "She was a very sensitive person, a poetic person, same as your father was. She used to make me put flats and screens all around her, so she would be isolated from the band. She just didn't want to feel that there was anybody else in the room besides her. And it worked. She could record poetry with a harp, and if you gave her a blues or something with a beat, she was dynamite. She had it all."

Lee's sense of isolation was remarkable on "Lover," because it's one of the most raucous, complex pieces you'll find. The Latin percussion is nothing short of frantic; instruments surge in and out, right along with a powerful male chorus. If you wanted privacy in that setting, you were truly in your own little world. And as they said, that was Peggy.

"Was it a fun thing to do?" a British interviewer once asked my father.

"No. It was a pain in the ass [laughter]," he said. "Oh, my God, what a disaster. I must have had forty guys, then we had four Latin cats, and they were out in center field someplace—way the hell out. We're goin' at a big, fast tempo, and it's just murder trying to keep the thing together, and then Peggy stops and announces that she can't sing in tune because my drummer isn't playing on the cymbal. She *must* hear him play on the cymbal, or she can't sing. It was a buzz cymbal, a great big thing with a little piece of metal to give it extra vibration. She just wanted the guy to keep pounding that thing all the way through.

"I said, 'Peggy, if he plays on the cymbal, this is gonna be the worst shambles you ever saw in your life.' And for the moment it went right down the drain; she went home and gave up the date. What are you gonna do? That's not my fault. I just went down to the saloon. But when we called a new session about three days later, some other drummer showed up, and we went ahead and made the record. Peggy just sees and hears things differently than other people. Good singer. *Real* good. 'San Souci,' which she wrote, is on the flip side, and that's the one I liked. It was recorded extremely well for those days. I didn't like 'Lover' that much, because it had already been a hit. You don't bring those things off twice."

The record-buying public didn't agree, nor did historians establishing the landmarks of pop culture. For Peggy Lee, it was the culmination of a year's work. She was in tears when she heard the playback, and she was still crying when she left the studio. "The emotion is what it's all about," she told me. "Your father was very quiet and strong and capable on the dates. On the breaks, he'd tell jokes and laugh uproariously. Then he'd go back very seriously into this music that could make you weep—and I don't mean 'Lover,' so much, but so many other things he did. I think he became increasingly lauded over the years, because it took people a while to understand everything he had going. Some people. Not musicians. They knew it all the time."

Chapter 11

On the Contrary

WE VENTURE NOW INTO THE OPPOSING CAMP, a strange and bitter world inhabited by New York radio personality Jonathan Schwartz and, to a lesser degree, the characters of a meticulously crafted book about Sinatra's musicianship, *Sinatra! The Song Is You.* They make us realize that in certain corners of the world, there is no room for sentiment or schmaltz. They prefer their music dry and breezy, without the burden of tears, and if Nelson Riddle can do all of the arrangements, it's champagne and caviar for everyone.

Thank goodness for them, I say. Any good story needs a conflict, and once you've heard someone like Schwartz, or author Will Friedwald, you have a fresh and damning view of my father's music. The irritating part, for me, is the warfare. There are no vague areas for certain camps of Sinatra fanatics. You sign up for one side or the other, OK? Riddle or Costa. Riddle or Jenkins. Stordahl or May. And whoever falls short of your lofty standard, make sure he takes some abuse along the way.

I've always thought that if revisionist history allowed someone other than Nelson Riddle to arrange "Witchcraft," "I've Got You Under My Skin" or "Summer Wind" for Sinatra, there should be a federal investigation. (I once got a copy of "I've Got You Under My Skin" with the instrumentals only, no Sinatra, and it holds up splendidly all by itself.) My life was never the same after I heard Riddle's

"Route 66," the jazzy theme to one of the best shows ever aired on television (starring George Maharias and Martin Milner in the early Sixties). It was just about the coolest, most sensible piece of music I ever heard, and I idolized Riddle from that day forward. When it came to Sinatra's confident, upbeat, high-society tunes, Riddle was a beacon of perfection every time.

Not that it's any great revelation, but Riddle could hit the sad notes, too, and no pop record collection would be complete without his "In the Wee Small Hours" collaboration with Sinatra. What I'm asking is, why not a little Gordon Jenkins, too? Why not have time in your life to really dwell on his sadness—and Sinatra's, and perhaps your own—in a dark and quiet room? There should be no fear of crying, no harm in appreciating a brand of despair so vividly captured in words and music. That's what happened when Sinatra and my father got together. That's the sole reason Frank ever sought him out.

I had been told that Jonathan Schwartz was the No. 1 all-time Jenkins detractor, and I couldn't wait to see him. I knew we'd be in complete agreement on certain things, like "Trilogy," parts of "Manhattan Tower" and some of the Judy Garland material. I've got a distinct personal limit on schmaltz, and sometimes my father crossed it with plenty of room to spare. But I also got the feeling I'd be the only person in the room with an open mind. Wow, was I correct.

There are three things you have to know about Schwartz, the first two being (a) at his best, he is exceedingly charming, and (b) he's had a hell of a life. The son of Arthur Schwartz, who wrote "Dancing in the Dark," "Alone Together" and many other top-drawer songs, Jonathan grew up with a writer's talent and a powerful, stirring voice for radio. He became a novelist, short-story writer, cabaret singer and fixture on WNEW, the New York radio station that pioneered FM radio in the late 1960s, and WYNC. He is also a fan of the Boston Red Sox, following that much-cursed outfit with a brand of desperation peculiar to Red Sox Nation.

The third thing is that he can be almost criminally dangerous, willingly throwing punches to make a point, and his combination of brilliance and smart-aleck opinions has made him a sort of Howard Cosellian figure, both hated and revered, among East Coast sophisticates. Schwartz was so vehement in his distaste for my father's role in "Trilogy," vilifying it relentlessly on WNEW, that Sinatra actually got him thrown off the air for a while. And this was Schwartz in "A Day of Light and Shadows," his book about the Red Sox and the maddening stretch drive of 1978: "I had wept and raged. I had participated in two fistfights, had terminated a close friendship and had gone out in search of a neighborhood fifteen-year-old who had written RED SOX STINK in orange crayon on the back window of my car. I had set out after him with vicious intent."

I found Schwartz at his midtown New York office, near Carnegie Hall at 56th and 7th, in May 1989. Over the phone, I assured him that I was coming in peace. I was greeted by a vital, energetic fifty-year-old with a suntan that didn't seem fully earned, that sort of orangish look that comes from sitting under a sunlamp (just a guess, but after growing up in Malibu, I'm familiar with the subject). Jonathan said that he appreciated a son of Jenkins coming to see him "congenially and happily, with full knowledge of my discontent," and I offered very little in the interview. I just turned on the tape recorder, threw out the occasional hint, and let him vent.

He opened his diatribe with an indictment of "Lover," my father's hit record with Peggy Lee. "I took great exception to that record," he said. "My father hated it, and my feeling was a reflection of that, but there's no forgiving the Jenkins treatment of that melody. It was, of course, a waltz, one of the most beautiful songs of all time. To hear it become so successful, under such conditions, was a puzzlement to me. I also felt that "Inchworm," such a lovely, plaintive little item, was ruined by your father's music behind Danny Kaye. Just the writing for the strings, so overblown in its arrangement . . . I wasn't terribly educated musically at that time [1952], but I felt something was afoul there.

"I went through probably a month of being attracted to 'Manhattan Tower,' because I'm a New Yorker, and it spoke of romance in my future life. I had no critical evaluation to render at that time. I now deeply regret that 'Manhattan Tower' was created, because it spawned other concept albums, including 'The Letter' by Judy Garland, and that's how 'Trilogy' came about. [Producer] Sonny Burke said, 'Let's get Gordon to do something like 'Manhattan Tower,' and because Sonny and Gordon had worked together since the Forties, I knew that was going to be a collaboration of awfulness. I mean, I was furiously trying to ward it off. Shooting off letters to Sinatra, to anyone who would listen, saying, don't *do* this. Don't let Jenkins do this! Get some people from the theater who could make a brilliant thing for you. My recommendation was the collaboration of Alan J. Lerner and Leonard Bernstein. I was horrified what might happen to that third record in the hands of Gordon Jenkins. And it turned out I was right. Jenkins was savaged all across the land in print."

"Well, that's not entirely true," I said. "Leonard Feather [for years one of the most highly respected jazz critics] raved about it in the *Los Angeles Times,* and he wasn't alone."

"Leonard Feather is an asshole," said Schwartz, and he edged closer to my tape recorder to make sure it registered. "*Leonard Feather is an asshole! Jonathan Schwartz says so!* Any jazz musician who doesn't need him will tell you that. Anyone worth his salt will tell you that Leonard Feather can be bought, that he's a disreputable figure, a terrible writer and a lousy jazz critic. People who need those Calendar reviews won't speak up, but I don't need those Calendar reviews. He wrote that sycophantic Sinatra stuff for the *Times,* which is thrown on Sinatra's doorstep, and now Leonard Feather has a chance to be invited down to the compound."

That's a shocking and quite likely preposterous set of accusations, but I had no knowledge of Feather's inner dealings and didn't care to investigate. The whole idea of this interview was to let Schwartz speak his mind. And I told him, hey, "The Future" sort of left me cold.

"To me, it epitomizes the overkill and the reverence for Sinatra that I find so distasteful," he said. "I love Sinatra, but I criticized your father's end of 'Trilogy' and Sinatra got me thrown off the air. I was relieved of my job at WNEW on a Tuesday, the 25th of May 1980, and I was suspended for six months. And then I was reinstated, as if nothing had happened. But for years, I had publicly expressed a concern about Jenkins in popular music. It had nothing to do with the man personally. I always heard he was a hell of a guy. It was the overkill of violins, the reckless presence of Tchaikovskian strategy, which was particularly galling to me in view of the excellence of Sinatra's singing. Gordon's name will go down in history as a part of American music in the twentieth century, but I felt in the Forties and Fifties he brought American popular music to its knees, just by those violins. Juxtaposed with Nelson [Riddle], it seemed all too obvious where the problem lay, because Nelson, if anything, was an understater. Particularly when he wrote for violins.

"The album 'Only the Lonely,' which is considered one of Sinatra's finest, was originally assigned to Jenkins, but he couldn't do it due to a prior commitment. Riddle took it over and wrote these haunting charts on some great and very bluesy songs—which I feel is Jenkins's great weakness, because he would apply Tchaikovsky to Harold Arlen, and you just have oil and water. That album also has Gordon's own song, 'Goodbye,' and Nelson just wrote a great, great arrangement for that."

I asked Schwartz what he thought of that song. "I've always

loved it," he said. "I think it's a wonderful song. [Begins to sing] *'But that was long ago . . . now you've forgotten, I know. . . . '* But Nelson's arrangement is so subtle and graceful and understated."

Schwartz admitted to enjoying one Jenkins-Sinatra collaboration, "the very first one, 'Where Are You?'. For the most part, Jenkins is more subdued than usual. It was a very serious album, the first torch album since 'Wee Small Hours,' and I was appalled at first. All of these violins! I just couldn't believe it; took me many years to get past it. But I never got past anything else."

Even "September of My Years"?

"Had Nelson arranged that album, it would have been a masterpiece. Again, Nelson is such a part of my displeasure with Gordon. The overstatement of violins runs *rampant* on that album. The Tchaikovsky of it is just maddening. As excellent as the singing is, there are many moments that with a quieter voice, the point could be made. That's my total objection to Gordon. To me, 'It Was a Very Good Year' is the least offensive. But the whole idea of the album lends itself to the sentimentality of Gordon, which I found so abusing. What can I say? It's just my opinion, you know?"

Schwartz said he never spoke to Sinatra about his complaints, "and I really couldn't. I'm not about to say to Frank, you know, 'You could have done a lot better.' How could he have done better? The record sold millions, and he credits Gordon with having saved his career with the 'Where Are You?' album. I don't know how he could possibly feel that way, but he felt he was beginning to lose his voice, not trusting his own instrument, and then along came Gordon.

"It's the Jenkins sentimentality and the harmonies that have driven me nuts through the years, and I've said so on the air. It seems to me what you should do, as an orchestrator, is to be quiet, and you'll be heard far more. 'We can *hear* you, Gordon, we can hear you,' is what I've said through the years. I mean, 'No One Cares' is a disaster. A sorry disaster, because that was Frank singing at the top of his game. I'd like to take back 'September of My Years' and 'No One Cares'—and really, 'All Alone' might be the most egregious of overly sentimental arrangements. Just awful."

I asked Schwartz about the Jenkins-Nat Cole partnership, particularly "Stardust," and got a wall of indifference. "All of their work has that problem for me," he said, "but I never had much interest in Nat. There was no need for me to listen to a Nat Cole-Gordon Jenkins album when I was stuck forever with the wine of choice, which was Sinatra's albums. I never heard a new thing out of Gordon's writing from the time he started with Frank. Whereas Nelson astonished me to the end."

I found it odd that he actually liked "Manhattan Tower" for a while, only to despise it in retrospect. "I'm sure it reflected a young man's excitement and love for the city, and it's probably worthy material," he said. "I remember there were a couple of appealing songs—like 'New York's My Home'; I found that kind of exciting, and still do. But its major disaster wasn't realized until years later, like cancer. See, one of its assets was that it was totally original. No one had ever heard anything like that. But by the time 1980 rolled around, we had heard all too much of it. It spawned Mel Torme's awful 'California Suite,' which is just a disgrace, and I'm close to Mel, but I can't tell him, because he loves 'California Suite.' Like I say, the holocaust of 'The Future' was spawned by 'Manhattan Tower.' So it had its major disruption thirty, forty years after the fact.

"And I know I speak for a lot of people in my criticism," he was quick to point out. "Jazz musicians, pianists, it's universal. Particularly jazz players, who are the most economical of musicians. Like, if you just listen to Gordon trying to swing [bitter face], it's just impossible. And I really wonder, since you're Gordon's son, how many people would be inclined to tell you the truth."

I was stunned, disappointed and only slightly angry at the finish. I'm rather non-confrontational, and this is a man who cultivates his sharp-witted weapons of debate and seems to be at his best when riled. But it was interesting: As I was leaving his office, a bearded fellow by the name of Larry was coming in; he looked to be about forty years old.

"So, Larry, what do *you* think of Gordon Jenkins's music?" Schwartz asked him.

The man was taken aback, but the subject was not unfamiliar to him. "Great stuff," he said.

"Well, there you have it," said Schwartz, smiling, and I hopped on the elevator.

I felt strangely exhilarated for the rest of that afternoon in New York, having located the enemy and experienced his passionate viewpoints firsthand. "Great voice," I scribbled in a taxicab message to myself. "Disturbing tan." But as I heard the conversation played back later, I began to isolate some of his comments. If you're so dedicated to Sinatra that you don't have time for Nat Cole, isn't that pushing the obsession a little too far? Would a rock-and-roll aficionado swear off Elvis Presley's early (and best) work because he spawned so many imitators? And this business of the anti-Jenkins stance being "universal" among musicians—that was beyond appalling.

I have no doubt that countless jazz players heard my father's music and ran for cover. As Will Friedwald points out in *The Song Is You*, a number of pop musicians are in that camp, as well. But just for the record, I felt compelled to put together the all-star team of people who revered the Jenkins style, unconditionally, and couldn't have cared less if he even *had* a son: Benny Goodman, Judy Garland, Louis Armstrong, Frank Sinatra, Nat Cole, Peggy Lee, Kay Thompson, Count Basie, Dick Haymes, Martha Tilton, Mel Torme, Steve Lawrence, Eddie Miller, Nick Fatool, Matty Matlock, Milt Gabler, Pete Seeger, Isham Jones, Jack Jenney . . . those would be my early draft choices.

And in the opposing dugout: Jonathan Schwartz?

Still, I wanted to stay true to my book's premise, to weigh in occasionally as Gordon's son but mostly to tell an objective story through the recollections and opinions of others. I casually mentioned Schwartz in virtually every interview, just to see if people had a reaction. The most diplomatic observation, interestingly, was Sinatra's.

"Jonathan? He's kind of a lofty ... he's always been sort of in the clouds," Sinatra told me. "All over the world, millions of people are having a great time with Gordy's music. They're hugging each other and loving each other, just having fun with the thing. Listen, Jonathan's a very bright guy, and a friend to me, and he was one of my biggest boosters at a time when I was really down, years ago. But he's basically a New Yorker [snaps his fingers to a lively tempo], you know, he's got that jazz going all the time. Sentiment isn't really his thing."

I'll admit that I was moving steadfastly through the Jenkins camp, not dropping into any Miles Davis strongholds, but I rarely heard another positive word about Schwartz. A brief sampling:

Alan King: "Well, Schwartz's father was a giant in the industry, but that doesn't make Jonathan any kind of expert. Listen, there's nothing wrong with being schmaltzy. So was Puccini, for Christ's sake. That's my mother's cooking. If Gordon dripped with schmaltz, Puccini dripped with tomato sauce, and it was beautiful."

Nora Ephron, who told me that she spent half of her adolescence listening to a Jenkins-Nat Cole record: "I spent the other half listening to Sinatra's 'Songs for Swingin' Lovers,' orchestrations by Nelson Riddle," she said. "A kind of yin to Gordon Jenkins's yang, don't you think?"

Mega-manager Jack Rollins: "This Schwartz is a very odd character. He's got an ego from here to Main Street."

Rollins's wife, Jane, who sang on "Manhattan Tower": "Well,

isn't that his name, Jonathan 'E for Ego' Schwartz? He's the only person I've ever heard put down Gordon, and I'm always in my car. I'm never in a position where I can call him up and argue with him."

Nick Fatool: "Enough with the knocks. Nobody in the business ever had a bad word to say about Gordon. Nobody who was good."

Sammy Cahn: "Let me explain something about schmaltz. I'd rather have it than not have it. I don't consider it a flaw. I know too many people who are afraid of emotion, and that's what it is—emotion. Laying it out. The violin has the great, great capacity to move people, and Gordon knew that better than most. I personally am most moved by strings. I mean, you can't have too many. Too few, yes. Too many? Never. How ya gonna hate violins?"

Billy May: "So he's the king of the Jenkins haters? Oh, my God. I think with most of these guys, they get an opinion, and it gets cemented in, and they never open up their mind to it. I'm guilty of the same thing with rock and roll, of course, but if you're playing records on the air, what's constructive about that kind of attitude? If you're gonna make a point of tearing into somebody who's really good—the hell with that."

Friedwald's *The Song Is You* is a vital, important work, discussing Sinatra's musical career—and only that, forget the social life—in great detail. An entire 44-page chapter is devoted to my father's work with Sinatra. And while Friedwald tosses out several compliments and elicits others, he can't help himself in a crusade to put Jenkins down—and he makes a few mistakes along the way. He describes Gor's piano style as "rudimentary" and "hunt and peck," when in fact he was an accomplished pianist who could play virtually anything (the one-finger approach was not an amateur's impediment but a gimmick that turned out to be successful). He hangs the wrong title on the Broadway play my father orchestrated in 1936, calling it "On With the Show," and describes "Manhattan Tower" as "an immediate best-seller," when it actually took two years to catch on. According to Friedwald, "most sidemen remember Jenkins as being at least a little bit uptight," when in reality his regular guys savored his generosity and hard-drinking style off the set. And when Friedwald writes that "the nicest compliment that most musicians care to pay Jenkins" was that he was "a real gentleman," he misses the mark so badly, you wonder if he talked to *anyone* who worked with my father.

It seems Friedwald was most interested in finding musicians who didn't care for Gor's work, as we see in this passage: "Bill Miller [Sinatra's pianist for many years] named Jenkins his least favorite arranger: 'I didn't like his writing at all; his stuff was so dull and boring. The piano parts were so simple that they were terrible.' He was a little more old-fashioned than Riddle and May, Dick Nash explained: 'He didn't have the knowledge of the newer harmonies that would work and fit, like the flat ninths and raised ninths, and flat fives, and so forth. He didn't utilize a lot of the new technology, so therefore it was kind of old hat and boring.' Milt Bernhardt [whose trombone solo is a highlight on "I've Got You Under My Skin"] elaborated: 'I'm not a big fan of Gordon Jenkins, and everybody who ever wrote an arrangement felt the same way. Nelson wouldn't bum-rap him, and neither would Billy May, but if they were pressed, they would say, 'Well, Gordon doesn't really know an awful lot about harmonies and orchestration'—and he didn't. When he took somebody else's song, the harmony was right out of the lead sheet. He couldn't expand on it. He couldn't alter changes to make them prettier.'"

It goes on like that. Friedwald's withering indictments of "The Future" and "The Letter" are shared by many critics, and I have no problem with an honest rip. But perhaps he goes too far in describing the Jenkins arranging style as "kitsch," or when he finds elements of the "hokey and pretentious" in "September of My Years," or—this one really pushed a button—describes my mother as a "blues singer," in quotes. Like, wink-wink, nudge-nudge, she's gotta be kidding.

Not long after Friedwald's book came out, I heard a scathing rebuttal from disc jockey Sandy Singer, a Sinatra aficionado who has worked in radio for some fifty years. "Bill Miller said Gordon couldn't play music worth a damn?" Singer said. "Maybe if Gordon thought Miller could play piano worth a damn, he would have used him on one of his sessions." As for Friedwald, said Singer, "I refer to him as F. Consider it short for anything that may come to mind. I have found him to be one of the all-time great users of people and the worst kind of hypocrite. After reading his blistering attack on Gordon, I made it a point to ask him why. He told me what a big Gordon Jenkins fan he was, that he owned some thirty albums of Gordy's. He explained the chapter this way: 'Those were the words of the musicians I interviewed, not mine. Some of the things were so bad, I left them out of the book.'

"Not knowing Friedwald or his work, I had to take him at his word. Then I happened upon a book he wrote using his own words, *Jazz Singing*. There were eight references to Gordon, and he made some kind of backhanded assault on Gordon in every one of them. When I wrote him about this one, he failed to reply. And yet, when he was paid to write the liner notes for the Gordon Jenkins Collection CD release, he had nothing but glowing things to say. Just wave the money in front of his eyes and he'll write whatever you want. What a whore."

From a technical standpoint, it was easy to say that Gordon Jenkins was a screwy arranger. "You have to remember that Gordon wasn't a formally educated musician. He taught himself everything," said his longtime trumpet player, Bruce Hudson. "To his dying day, he would subdivide a bar wrong. Fred Neff, his copyist for years, told me, 'You ought to see this stuff when I get it.' It was playable, but not formal. For example, if a bar is four beats, you write the notes so it divides in the middle. You have four eighth notes of an eight-beat bar. Well, he'd write it where it would hang over into the next half. Not every bar, just the occasional strange one would creep in there. He read music beautifully, opera scores, anything; why he didn't write it that way, I don't know. Maybe he was writing so damn fast, he didn't pay any attention. Hell, if he hadn't been cremated, he'd be whirling in his grave right now, saying he was right. But here's the flip side of that: One time with a four-trumpet section, he wrote the fourth part first, a harmony part. To do that, you've got to know in your head what the first three are doing. He wrote the whole goddamn fourth part as a challenge, just to show us.

"But the thing you need to know more than anything, he wrote with more heart than any other three arrangers put together," said Hudson. "I spent many years playing with Meredith Wilson and a bunch more with Carmen Dragon, and with those guys, you just worked to make a living. They were formal musicians who wrote from their education. There was no heart in 'em to write good, and that's the truth. They didn't have it. With Gordon—and I'd say the same thing about Jeff Alexander [from the old 'Amos & Andy Show'], you really felt like something was goin' on."

"Of all the people I worked with, I always thought he put more soul into his music than anyone," said clarinetist-saxophonist Matt Utal, for years a mainstay of the Les Brown and NBC studio bands. "To me, he was just a genius. There was nothing trite about anything he ever did. Looking back over my years of playing, there were few things I'd say were really highlights. I think playing on 'Seven Dreams' and in Vegas with Gordon would be among them."

I had a fascinating visit with the multi-talented Johnny Mandel, at his home just a few miles up the highway from ours in Malibu. Walking into his office, I was immediately struck by a photograph from 1953. There's the Count Basie band, Marshall Royal and the fellas, and the first white man Basie ever had: Mandel, on trombone. He went on to play with the Joe Venuti and Jimmy Dorsey bands, wrote arrangements for Woody Herman and Artie Shaw, studied symphonic forms at Juilliard, arranged for the TV program "Your Show of Shows," won an Oscar in 1965 for "The Shadow of Your Smile" (music only) from "The Sandpiper" and became a fixture at the Grammy awards show, getting twelve nominations and five wins.

Mandel wore a warm smile through much of the conversation, effusive in his praise but also taking a very objective look at things. "I pretty much agree with what people said about his arranging in the Friedwald book, although I wouldn't say my comments are an indictment," he said. "He was an old-fashioned arranger, and deceptively simple. He was a creator of moods, is what he was, and he got a sound out of strings like nobody else. That's why Sinatra loved him so much. But it was very simple stuff. He kept his harmonies very simple. I don't think the harmony actually went past Tchaikovsky. I mean, he seldom, if ever, got into any kind of Debussy or Ravel things at all. He was just a late romantic, the way he wrote, and nobody ever got an orchestra to sound like his. You hear it and it's Gordon, period.

"To be quite honest, I was more a fan of his songwriting than his arranging. I mean, 'Goodbye' and 'This Is All I Ask,' how do you write better songs than that? I'm two generations ahead of Gordon and basically a be-bopper at heart, but no, I don't think he did know a lot about harmonies or orchestration. Harmonically, he didn't go past 1930, really. There wasn't a single thing in those arrangements that was being done after 1930. What he did, he wrote very tight triads all the time, three-part harmony, and he used the right kind of string players; to make that stuff sound right, you really have to be good. Four-part harmony started coming in around 1931, 1932, and I don't think Gordon ever embraced it. That's one of the reasons certain musicians didn't like it too much; it wasn't all that much fun to play. But it sounded right. It was the perfect thing for what he wanted and what Sinatra wanted. He kept everything very simple and never got in the way of a singer—mostly, I think, because he wrote good songs and he understands how you can screw one up. Listen, the romantic feeling he got on 'September of My Years'—Nelson, Billy May, myself, nobody could have done that like Gordon. We could do it good, but not like Gordon."

Within about two weeks of the Mandel interview, I was over at Billy May's place in San Juan Capistrano. May was eighty-three at the time of the interview, not moving too well but a hundred percent sharp and perceptive. He couldn't wait to talk about the Friedwald book, because he felt that he'd been badly misrepresented.

"A lot of the stuff he has about me is bullshit," said May. "The kind of thing where someone told a story, and it gained a little fiction, and by the time Friedwald got through with it, it was completely blown out of proportion. I don't think he knows enough about music to know the difference."

I told him of my surprise to read the comments by Miller and Bernhardt. "I feel so bad for Bill Miller; he's a good musician who went through a terrible tragedy," said May. "He was living in Burbank when a flood came, killed his wife and washed everything he had out into the street. You can understand it if the guy sounds a little bitter sometimes. I don't get what he's saying to Friedwald; maybe he based his opinion on the fact that by the time your father was doing that stuff for Frank, he wasn't writing very interesting piano parts. Plus, your dad mostly used Charlie LaVere, who was a great guy and a hell of a piano player.

"What Milt said about harmonies and orchestration, that's wrong," he said. "But Milt, you know, he's looking out mostly for Milt. Trying to make himself a big man. Yeah, he did the trombone solo on 'I've Got You Under My Skin,' whatever. He runs the Big Band

Society and makes sure that he's a big shot. He's kind of a poor man's Milton Berle."

I told May about Mandel's thoughts about harmonies, and he said, "I never thought of it that way. For one thing, there isn't a *thing* wrong with being influenced by Tchaikovsky or Rachmaninoff, in any way. When I started out, I was writing whatever sounded good to me. When I heard that Fletcher Henderson four-way saxophone thing, where he figured out a little gimmick with diminished chords on the passing tones, that was kind of an education. Then it reached a point where guys were writing five-part harmonies, and I wrote a lot of that for the [Glenn] Miller band. But the whole idea that five-part is better than four, or four is better than three, that's a bunch of shit. Christ almighty, Gordon *could* have done anything. He just put down what he wanted to hear."

(In a tattered family scrapbook, I found a 1938 article from *Tempo*, the industry magazine, in which Gor discussed his theories on arranging. "I believe that an arranger will get farther in his profession if he leans toward a good, solid ensemble rather than tricky effects achieved with small sections of the orchestra," he said. "I am opposed to excessive use of harmonization involving the uses of 6ths, 9ths and extra voices. An arranger should be able to write interesting scores without falling back on these devices, which are now getting too commonplace.")

As for Friedwald's portrayal of Gor as a sour, distant individual, "Well, now you're talking about someone who doesn't know Gordon at all—and didn't try to find out," said May. "I'll tell ya, man, Gordy was as much fun as anybody. He liked to drink and laugh and play great music, like all of us, and he was just generous as hell. I always got a huge kick out of him. But he would have despised a hack like Friedwald. Maybe that explains it."

As the theories about my dad's work raged on, I established a golden connection with my friend Scott Price, who has authored some of *Sports Illustrated*'s most incisive pieces over the last few years. Scott's a true original, in his writing and lifestyle. He tools around in a 1960 Plymouth Fury, sings Nirvana at the top of his lungs and does frantic rock-drummer impressions when he's had a few beers. Yet he has a firm and studious grasp on American popular music. He had me for life after I visited his home in Miami one afternoon. He had five CDs playing at random, and the five were Sinatra, Chet Baker, Hank Williams (not the lamentable character from Monday Night Football, Hank Jr., but his accomplished father), Johnny Hartman and Dexter Gordon. After seven or eight cuts, I longed for a sleeping bag. There was no point in moving, even an inch, for several days.

Once or twice a year, we'd find ourselves working in New York together. By accident one night, we stumbled into a perfectly ordinary-looking little bar around 2nd Avenue and 52nd, advertising itself in 1950s-style red neon, and the jukebox was glorious—luring us in for good. Without fail we'd open with "Witchcraft," absolutely the one song I'd take to a desert island. Nelson Riddle's intro to that thing, and the first few bars from Sinatra, are the definition of cool for all time. Next up would be Tony Bennett's "I Wanna Be Around," something so tight and perfect (it can't be more than two minutes long), you just want to kill yourself, because nothing on earth could be better. Then Bobby Darin's "Beyond the Sea," a finger-snapper that goes *so* well with that first cocktail in your hand, and "Summer Wind," another Riddle intro for which the world must stop. Those were the musts, in that order. Life could not proceed if it wasn't handled exactly that way.

From that point on, it was open season: Louis Prima, Elvis Costello, Van Morrison, any direction under the sun, and there were a couple of "September of My Years" cuts on there. Now, I would never play anything that I really admired from my father's arsenal, in any setting. I come from a family of intense listeners, and I get in real deep, and once I've gone below the sea level of noisy barroom conversation, I can feel the tears welling up. So no Gordon Jenkins from me. But Price never knew that, and he'd always pop in "When the Wind Was Green" or "It Was a Very Good Year." I'd stare at him through a haze of distraction, trying to keep the conversation going, slightly rattled yet secretly delighted he'd gone that way.

"Riddle *and* Jenkins!" he'd shout above the din. "I've got to have 'em both. What the hell, this isn't 'The Crazy World of Arthur Brown.' Remember that? 'I am the god of hellfire, and I bring you Fire.' That's it! That was the whole career for Arthur Brown. Sinatra gave you everything. I want Billy May and Don Costa, too, but I've got to have Riddle and Jenkins, OK? These idiot one-or-the-other guys make me ill."

Bill Madden, of the *New York Daily News*, was another sportswriter who loved to talk music, especially Sinatra, whenever we got together. Madden took me up to Elaine's, pointed out the Manhattan notables in the crowd and introduced me to Loren Korevec, a marvelous piano player who seemed to know every great song ever written. What old-time character he lent to the place, knocking down tunes from years ago, singing beautifully, sort of a Hoagy Carmichael over there in the corner. (Elaine fired him a few years back and ditched the piano altogether, a cold-hearted maneuver that defied all logic.) Korevec flipped when Madden pointed me out one night, and the next thing I knew, he was singing, *"As I approach the prime of my life. . . ."* Madden had set that up. Later in the evening, as we hung around the piano, Korevec would occasionally shout "Gordon Jenkins chord!" right in the middle of a song.

I knew there would be some passionate opinions on "The Voice," an e-mail exchange for Sinatra lovers, and there was one contributor with especially strong credentials: Vinny Falcone, one of Sinatra's primary conductors over the last fifteen years of his life. Falcone was the house pianist at Caesar's Palace in 1977 when he got a gig with Sinatra, then being conducted by Bill Miller. Sinatra decided to give the kid a trial by fire, and in a decision that some found surprising, he bypassed Miller and made Falcone his Las Vegas conductor in 1978. Falcone went on to work with Bennett, Jack Jones, Andy Williams and several other first-rate singers and became firmly established in the business.

"Jonathan Schwartz is a friend of mine," Falcone told me in February 1999, "and that's forever a point of contention between him and me. Jonathan is a very, very intelligent man, but when it comes to analyzing Gordon Jenkins, he's a damn fool.

"Frank used to talk to me constantly about your father. He looked upon him as a personal equal—that's how much he respected him. I knew his work to begin with, but once I heard Frank's end of it, I was especially interested. One night at Caesar's Palace, your dad came in to see the show, and he introduced himself to me backstage. He said, 'Can you take some constructive criticism?' I told him it would be an honor, and he said, 'I only give it to people I like.' So that put me at ease.

"He began to tell me some of the things he'd learned over the years, and he gave me a tip that probably is the greatest single piece of advice I ever received from anybody. And that was to never take my eyes off the singer. The orchestra needed to see my hands, not my face. He explained to me what to watch for, the dynamics, the entrances, all these ways to keep the orchestra close to a singer, and he explained it in such a way that I began to do it immediately. It served me so well over the years, I can't tell you what a boon it is. And it's something few other conductors do, or are even aware of.

"One of the things that's so amazing is that when you hear a Gordon Jenkins arrangement, you know it immediately. Not that other arrangers weren't in his league, but when you have something that's so quickly recognizable, it sets you apart from other people. And you can't imitate Gordon Jenkins. You either *were* him or you weren't. That's why you don't hear anything like him, then or now, and that's what separates the men from the boys. The idea of someone else arranging "It Was A Very Good Year"—are you kidding? To me, if anybody else tried that, using contemporary harmonies and who knows what else, it would sound like shit. Just like if you took 'This Is All I Ask' and did it any differently, it wouldn't be right."

Falcone found the criticism of "Trilogy," particularly from his friend Schwartz, "just unconscionable. I rile at that. For one thing, I admire all of Frank's arrangers. There's a greatness to all of them, and a variety that makes the body of work so exciting. But Jenkins had a talent that embraced an area where no one else could go, and I believe there's a real genius in 'The Future.' If anyone says otherwise, that is illustrative of their ignorance, someone who truly doesn't understand what's going on. All those nasty critiques—people are just so fucking stupid, it disgusts me. They have no idea. And it hurt your dad, too. He was very hurt by the criticism of that album. I say if you can't do better, keep your damn mouth shut."

So that's the long version of the whole bloody mess. Opinions zing back and forth; who's to say who's right? But there's a shorter take, highly preferable for those in a hurry. It came like a bolt of lightning one night during one of Kay Thompson's phone calls to my mother. I listened in, as usual, and at one point I asked Kay about the Schwartz crusade, sort of a "what's up with that?" kind of question.

"Honey," she said, "Jonathan wouldn't know."

Chapter 12

The Weavers

I MET PETE SEEGER'S FLIGHT on a warm summer evening in New York City, 1987. With a case in each hand—his banjo and guitar—he arrived in jeans, black tennis shoes and a striped shirt with the sleeves rolled up. He looked precisely as I'd imagined him: confident, gentle and alive, with a little gleam in his eye. He struck me as having the most erect posture I'd ever seen, a positively upright figure at the age of sixty-eight.

We had a mission that night: to grab two chairs at the Village Vanguard, a historic little nightclub in Greenwich Village, and talk about Gordon Jenkins. With a single bold stroke in 1950, my father got the Weavers on record and triggered the popular folk-music craze in America. I interviewed all of the living Weavers in my travels (Lee Hays had passed on) and learned of a warm, deeply respectful association that changed the music business forever.

The Weavers would have made it eventually, but Gor was the person who defied convention, right-wing alarmists and skeptical executives at Decca Records, where he had reached the peak of his powers and was routinely billed as America's leading hit-maker. He could call his own shots—and he needed all of that authority to stand behind the Weavers and get them into the studio.

It's hard to tell who was more shocked, the Weavers or Decca, at the residue of those recording sessions. Within weeks, the two-sided record of "Goodnight Irene" and "Tzena, Tzena, Tzena" was a runaway hit, at that time among the most successful in history. After years of anonymity, playing in fields and stark halls and around campfires, the Weavers could hardly turn on the radio without hearing their own voices. Around the country, people were picking up guitars and singing along—badly, in most cases. Among the more talented set, folk groups like Peter, Paul & Mary, The Kingston Trio and the Limelighters had their inspiration. The Weavers started it all. "And the thing I most fondly remember about that whole period," Seeger told me, "was knowing Gordon."

Seeger, as described years later in *Rolling Stone,* was "a banjo player living in a cold-water flat on MacDougal Street in Greenwich Village with a wife, two young children and no money. He had dropped out of Harvard and hit the road with the banjo on his back, learning hard-times songs from people in the lumber camps and coal mines of Depression America. In New York he joined a band (the Almanac Singers) with Woody Guthrie, and they wrote folk songs together, championing the downtrodden common man in his struggle against capitalist bloodsuckers."

Guthrie was a man of great strength and conviction, author of many songs (including "This Land Is Your Land") and a full-blown legend; folk enthusiasts could only imagine the possibilities if he'd formed a long-term performing partnership with Seeger. It didn't work out, Seeger said, because "Woody was just too undisciplined as a performer. The chords he'd play were always different. He'd hold a note out, more or less [laughter]. And besides, he could only take New York for so long. He was a man of the American South, and occasionally he'd just leave to go hitch-hiking. 'Got to re-charge m'batteries,' he'd say."

Seeger formed a more lasting bond with Lee Hays, a large, heavy-set man with a penetrating intellect and a deep, rumbling voice that seemed delivered straight through the roots of Arkansas soil. In New York they connected with a younger pair, Fred Hellerman and

Ronnie Gilbert, who had begun singing together as counselors at a children's camp in New Jersey. As Hellerman described it during our interview at his home in Connecticut, "We'd get together in Pete's basement, the little brownstone on MacDougal. Of an evening, we'd have Pete and Woody, Josh White, Leadbelly, Burl Ives, just sitting around swapping songs. We were the only people in the whole damn city that were interested in that kind of music. Hell, get those people together in the Sixties and you'd fill Yankee Stadium. But that's the great thing about New York. Even if it's just two people, I don't care how esoteric their interests, they're gonna find each other. I mean, if you're interested in ninth-century Chinese pottery from the province of Umblang, with only the left-handed handles on it, those people are gonna find each other. That's how the folk-music scene was then. People huddling together for warmth."

The four-strong Weavers were formed in 1948. "Pete came from a very aristocratic New England family," said Hellerman, "a good and sophisticated musician, although he's horrified at the thought. He wouldn't dare let anyone know that. I was a kid from Brooklyn, a chronic truant in high school. I was down at the Paramount Theater, where all the good truants were in those days, standing in line, getting in to hear Benny Goodman, Glenn Miller and Tommy Dorsey." Gilbert grew up singing pop songs, in the Gilbert & Sullivan vein, and her formidable voice, sweet but positively booming, carried through the hallways and onto the streets. They all came to the Broad Beach house in Malibu over the years, but my lasting image is of Hays, a massive presence, filling up the large chair in our living room. That was customarily my father's seat during social gatherings, but once the 250-pound Hays planted himself, that was that. I know my father was delighted to see Lee Hays anywhere, under any circumstances. He was smart and different, country to the bone, and just funny as hell.

"Lee had come from a Methodist household, and he rebelled

against it, felt it was hypocritical," Seeger said. "His father talked about the God of love, and yet he would discriminate against blacks, tolerate lynchings. Lee split with his family and hooked up with a group that was helping black and white sharecroppers organize unions. Eventually they were run out by the Klan; burnt the whole place down, I think. Lee knew the seamy side of American life, as most radicals did."

Hays liked to drink a little, to say the least, and he had a willing companion in my father. Another dear family friend, Bruce Hudson, remembered Hays as "a big old guy who hated airplanes, and when we did 'Goodnight Irene,' he was drinking a fifth of Old Grand Dad a day. I went up to him one time and said, 'Lee, I understand you don't like to fly.' 'Well, I'll fly,' he said, 'but I never put my full weight down.'"

Hays died in 1982, not long after a superb documentary, "Wasn't That a Time?", chronicled the Weavers' success and a lively, emotional reunion some thirty years after their breakthrough. Hays is a hearty presence throughout, "and that's what pleased me the most about the movie," said Hellerman, "that Lee is documented. Lee was always an old man, from the time we met. Always a hundred years older than everybody else. He practiced his whole life, and when he finally got there, he was *on*."

Seeger: "I've often thought that history gets made when people come to the same conclusion from different directions. You had Lee from Arkansas, me from New England, Fred and Ronnie of a Jewish background here in New York City, and if we'd all come from the same place, we wouldn't have been so interesting. We were full of surprises; we even surprised ourselves from time to time. Sometimes we'd argue for a week over one or two notes. It was a very democratic group, without a real leader. We had variety and unpredictability. Back then, we had no idea in advance what we were going to do."

"We really got together for the fun of it," Hellerman said. "We sang for unions, at picket lines and hootenannies, but we had no anticipation of getting jobs. Even Pete, the most accomplished of us, couldn't get jobs on his own." But the Village Vanguard, near the corner of 12th Street and 7th Avenue, was a looming oasis. Max Gordon founded the 123-seat club in 1934 as a haven for Village bohemians, and a number of folk singers—Ives and White included—got their start there.

"I first saw the place in 1938," said Seeger, "when the actress Judy Holliday and three other people put on political skits and parodies. They were called The Reviewers; Judy was very unknown at that time. They were young [political] lefties and absolutely brilliant. I believe Harry Belafonte really started gaining attention at the Vanguard, and Leadbelly performed there often. Through many visits I got to know Max Gordon, and I got him to hire us for $200 a week—at that time, a pretty good amount—for two weeks. I think my wife, Toshi, worked out the deal. She even got us some cheap coats, white shirts and ties so we all looked more or less similar."

It was the Christmas season of 1949. The first few nights were dismal, with no more than a dozen customers hanging around, and the Weavers would go right into the audience to perform. "We always thought that if we sang loudly and strongly and hopefully enough, we might make a difference," Seeger said. "We mostly did material that had come from field hands and convicts. We sang songs from the Spanish Civil War—in Spanish. We sang 'Tzena, Tzena, Tzena' in Hebrew and we did songs by Leadbelly and Woody. Lee started developing his great talent as a storyteller, telling jokes in between the songs, and after a while, by gosh, we were a halfway seasoned group. Greenwich Village, then as now, was full of intellectual ferment. Humor was all around us, as well as talent, and we had to live up to it."

As *Rolling Stone* noted years later, "The Weavers' appeal was inexplicable to folk purists, who noted that most of their songs had been around forever, in obscure versions by blacks and rednecks who never had hits anywhere. What they failed to realize was that Seeger and his comrades had managed to filter the stench of poverty out of the proletarian music and make it wholesome and fun for the Eisenhower-era squares. Six months passed, and the Weavers were still at the Vanguard, now drawing sellout crowds, even the odd refugee from the swell supper clubs of Times Square.

"One such figure was Gordon Jenkins, a sallow jazz cat with a gigolo's mustache and a matinee idol's greased-back hairstyle. Jenkins loved the Weavers, returning night after night, sometimes sitting through two consecutive shows."

My father couldn't have cared less that the Weavers had a decidedly left-wing slant (and in fact had more than a passing association with the Communist party). For him, good music was the end of all arguments. I don't think he ever voted, such was his disdain for American politics. "I don't think he knew who the President was," said Hellerman, laughing. "But God, I can still see him there in the audience, just alive with energy. And that laugh—that marvelous, marvelous laugh. I think he came thirty-one nights in a row. It got to the point where if he wasn't there, we'd call his hotel to see if he was sick. Here's how enraptured he was: The Vanguard's public telephone was not enclosed; it was right out near the stage, down a hallway. One time Gordon was back in California and he called up, collect, just before showtime. Told Max Gordon to leave it off the hook so he could hear it from there."

"I just flipped over the Weavers," Gor said in a radio interview. " I thought it was thrilling; I was hypnotized by the group. Nobody had ever recorded songs like that—well, maybe Burl Ives, although nobody was buying it back then—but to me it was class. Absolute high-class for what it was."

According to Hellerman, it took Gordon "forever" to get up the courage to introduce himself. Seeger remembers him being "pleas-antly drunk" at the time. But that was folk music's seminal moment, its long-awaited ticket to the mainstream. Without the slightest care what Decca bigwigs Dave Kapp and Milt Gabler might think, Gor promised the Weavers a recording session—and despite their earthy, non-commercial roots, they loved the idea.

"Being a big-band guy, I really loved most of the work Gordon had done," Hellerman said. "Just knocked me out completely—Peggy Lee, Louis Armstrong and such. What I admired was his musical sense of humor. People take themselves too damn seriously, and there aren't many—Billy May, your father —who know how to make a musical joke. Not the cheap shot, where you stick in a musi-cal quotation from somewhere else [think "Happy Birthday" or "Yankee Doodle Dandy"]. But something that was good and orig-inal and just plain humorous.

"The one piece I really didn't like was 'Manhattan Tower.' Al-though I was always able to be completely honest with Gordon, he was so particularly proud of that piece, I never had the heart to tell him what I thought. It was just entirely too sentimental for me. That wasn't my New York by any stretch of the imagination. I mean, what should I say, he should have written something about the slums of Harlem? Hell, nature has never known a more sentimen-tal slob than your father."

Gilbert: "That record was how I knew and loved Gordon, from afar. He was such a wonderful romantic, and that was about the same kind of sentiment I had at the time. Sappy? Well, yeah, we're all sappy, and when we're at our sappiest is when our best work comes out. We're not censoring ourselves or saying it's not sophis-ticated enough."

Big orchestra, full chorus, major recording studio—the Weavers had never known such sophistication. But they had to get past the Decca people first. As Gilbert recalled, "I can still see Dave Kapp giving us the once-over in that office, smoking a cigar, scoffing at Pete's political reputation. He said, 'Listen, I know you guys' stuff. It just won't be heard on the jukeboxes. Do you want to be good, or do you want to be commercial?'"

Hellerman: "That's when Lee came up with his great line: 'Dave, we want to be *good* and commercial.' And here's all these stuffed-shirt guys trying to explain themselves, like, 'Well, it's not pop,' or 'Gee, it's not classical,' or 'It's not my department.' Kapp just walked right out; didn't even stay for the interview. Poor Gordon left the room, devastated, and that's where it stood for a while.

"In the interim we got a manager, Pete Cameron, who set us up with Mitch Miller and Columbia. We were sitting in Miller's office, contracts and everything right there in front of us, but we weren't feeling that great about it. One of us said, 'You know, the least we could do is call Gordon.' And we did. He was back in California; we probably woke him up. He says, 'Don't do anything. Call you back in a half-hour.' That's when he called Kapp and said he'd record the Weavers if he had to tape the thing and pay for it himself. I'm certain the only reason they consented was because it was Gordon. You know: 'Well, it's Gordon's folly, he's a big artist, we'd better keep him happy.'

"Afterwards, when everybody's drinking champagne over our hit records, they were all taking bows—Kapp, Gabler—and they didn't have a goddamn thing to do with it," said Hellerman. "Poor Dave was taking bows over that for years. Meanwhile, without Gordon, Decca has no record."

Noted publisher Howie Richmond, who worked with the Weavers' material, had been involved in the Mitch Miller negotiations. Secretly, he was happy they went with Jenkins. "Gordon had a feeling for the material," he said. "I felt Mitch would have given them a chance, but they never recorded with anyone as well as with Gordy. He breathed his soul into that material; I think he really was in love with their music. Hell, Gordy was my idol from the 'Manhattan Tower' days. Everything he did had genuine character and outstanding talent, and he had great humility as a person. To me, meeting Gordon was like meeting Babe Ruth."

Seeger: "I confess that I was pleasantly surprised by Gordon's very unassuming, gentle manner. He didn't sound high-pressure; he wasn't tossing around big names or anything. And I'd hear other people: 'Oh my God, you're recording with Gordon Jenkins? Do you know who *he* is?' And I'd say, 'No, who is he?' I didn't know anything about the pop music business, and I had a rather dim view of it. But we were in our own way very professional people. We could read music and we had some experience working with microphones.

"Gordon had a suite at the Carlyle," Seeger went on. "He wanted to record one of Guthrie's songs, 'So Long, It's Been Good to Know Ya,' which Woody had written down in Texas after the big dust storm of 1935. Dave Kapp said, 'Well, you've got to have new words. Those dust-bowl words don't make any sense, and who's interested in dust bowls, anyway?' So Woody came up to Gordon's suite, spread a big piece of wrapping paper on the floor and began scrawling out new verses."

The Weavers recorded that song, along with "When the Saints Come Marching In" and "Wimoweh," a melody that late arrivals might recognize from the 1960s hit "The Lion Sleeps Tonight." All of those songs became hits through the Jenkins collaboration. But the centerpiece, and the one that started it all, was "Tzena, Tzena, Tzena," a song of community celebration that the Weavers had always sung in Hebrew. For recording purposes they kept only the title, which meant "Come out, come out." Gor came up with a new set of lyrics, which in retrospect evokes the memory of a Frank Sinatra line many years later: "The way Gordon Jenkins writes strings, if he were Jewish, he'd be unbearable." A lot of his string players could have sworn that he was Jewish, and his imaginative "Tzena" lyrics wound up having an impact many years after his death:

> *Tzena, Tzena, Tzena*
> *Can't you hear the music playing*
> *In the city square?*
> *Tzena, Tzena, Tzena*
> *Come where all our friends will*
> *Find us with the dancers there.*
> *Tzena, Tzena, join the celebration*
> *There'll be people there from every nation*
> *Dawn will find us laughing in the sunlight,*
> *Dancing in the city square.*
> *Tzena, Tzena, come and dance the Horah*
> *Sing with me, we'll dance together*
> *Tzena, Tzena, when the band is playing*
> *My heart's saying, Tzena, Tzena, Tzena!*

Quite sadly, "Tzena" had no life after 1950. A lawsuit surfaced in Jerusalem over the adaptation of the original lyrics, whose author, Yehiel Yaggiz, had passed away in 1948. A long dispute unfolded over copyright laws and licensing rights, and it was ruled that the song could not be played with the modern-day lyrics my father had written. But Yaggiz' partner Issachar Miron, who wrote the music, never lost touch with Seeger. He loved the Jenkins version and told me, "Unexaggeratedly, I fought for their resurrection for fifty years."

Miron's phone call was delightful and quite unexpected. His English was rich in texture from the homeland, at times difficult to understand. Although he had lived in New York for many years, he had Americanized himself only in the ways he deemed necessary. I felt that his voice might rise to the Hebrew at any moment. "Your father's words were not only marvelously contemporary for that time, but quite daring and prophetic," he said. "He took the two words, meaning 'Come out'—which in this instance was something like a wolf's whistle at the girls in the neighborhood—and created an English proper noun out of it, namely a lovely girl named Tzena. In addition, he had the foresight to infuse a vision of international peace, with all peoples meeting and dancing together. This was a wartime song originally, a celebration of victory by the Jewish brigade of the British army. It was the soldier boys coming home, telling the girls to not be afraid in this terrible world, to come out and have fun. But in your father's lyrics he was inviting everybody, including the adversaries, to come dance in the city square. The idea being that in such a joyous act, we can learn to live together."

Miron paused for a moment. "Of what ancestry is your father?"

"Welsh."

"Well, the same heart that beats Jewish, beats Welsh," he said. "And if it beats loud, it is unbeatable."

As the Weavers' recording dates drew near, Jenkins had managed to convince everyone that his crazy scheme might work. A number of Greenwich Village denizens scoffed at the notion of the Weavers trying to co-exist with strings and woodwinds. It struck many of them as a complete sellout. The Weavers could not have agreed less. "Your father was so respectful of the material, we found we weren't required to do anything but sing the way we ordinarily sang," said Gilbert. "Although the folk purists put up a great big stink, when you listen, there's no messin' around with it."

Hellerman: "The truly remarkable thing about working with him was that he was so in awe of us. He never once even *asked* us to change a note of what we did. He wrote around us. And if anyone else had tried to change a note, he would have killed them. I remember that date so well. Guys were hanging from the chandeliers, it was so packed in there. When it was over, the musicians stood up and applauded. It was very touching. That sort of thing didn't happen too often, but everybody just *knew*. First two bars into 'Tzena,' you knew that thing was hell and gone. And it was. It became a hit in about twenty minutes."

The record came out just before the Vanguard closed for the summer (no air conditioning) in June 1950. "I had just gotten married," said Gilbert, "and my husband and I set off on a honeymoon camping trip across the country. One night we stopped by a café for coffee, and as we walked in the door, 'Tzena' was playing on the jukebox. Here we're way out in the country and an Israeli folk song is playing to us. As we continued on, all the way to the coast, it came out of every jukebox we hit. Unthinkable! The Weavers were wandering through this maze of mainstream music, not knowing where the heck we were going, what we were doing there, or if there was a way back."

Seeger: "1950 was a rare opportunity to hear myself coming out of a jukebox. It happened then, and in 1951, and never again. All I could do was laugh; it was so unexpected. I remember once hearing my voice, and all I could do was roll on the floor with my heels up in the air. I felt as though I was Eliza the flower girl, suddenly being dressed in a gown and taken to the queen's ball."

The flip side of that record, "Goodnight Irene," was an afterthought—"a song we'd sing at the Vanguard after twenty encores, when we couldn't get off the stage," said Hellerman. "'OK, let's sing Irene,' that sort of thing, with everyone singing along with us. Nice way to end the show, but we didn't think it would figure in the recording sessions."

"I guess Gordon had seen us so often, he couldn't get that song out of his mind," said Seeger. "I know Max [Gordon] didn't like it. Thought it was too sentimental. But Gordon wanted badly to record it."

"Irene" had been popularized by Huddie (Leadbelly) Ledbetter, a brilliant and highly troubled man, just before he was sent to the penitentiary in Texas for murder in 1918. "Adding verses as they came to him," wrote *Time* magazine, "Leadbelly made 'Irene' a prison favorite. Five years later he got out of jail on pardon, bounced into Louisiana's state prison farm for assault with intent to kill, and 'Irene' went right along with him." Seeger met and collaborated with Leadbelly years later in Manhattan, and he had worked to make the lyrics a bit more soothing for a general audience. The original closing verse—"Sung by de man, wid his head hung down, cryin'," Leadbelly once remarked by way of introduction—was a good example:

> *I love Irene, God knows I do*
> *Love her till the sea runs dry.*
> *An' ef Irene turns her back on me,*
> *I'm gonna take morphine and die.*

Seeger: "If nothing had happened with 'Irene,' we wouldn't have been surprised. But I was pleasantly startled at the unusual way Gordon started the song, with a solo, very romantic-sounding violin, and from that point we sang the song exactly as we always had. Well, 'Tzena' had zoomed up to No. 1. A couple of weeks later, 'Irene' zoomed up and passed it, and *stayed* there, for *weeks.*"

Three months, to be exact. The two-sided hit sold some 1.7 million copies, a staggering figure back then. While "Tzena" disappeared under the oppressive copyright dispute, "Irene" became a standard, sung by Sinatra, Jo Stafford, Gene Autry and Dennis Day, among others over the years. "Nothing ever compared to the original," said Chuck Cecil. "It really changed the way we thought about and listened to folk music. It had always been pretty rough, and the Weavers themselves were rough until your father gave 'em a little polish. He made it palatable to the tastes of the 1950s, and it's been palatable ever since."

About a year later, Jenkins and the Weavers recorded "Wimoweh," described by *Rolling Stone* as "by far the edgiest song in the Weavers' set. Prior to this, Jenkins had been very subdued in his instrumental approach, adding the odd swirl of strings to the Weavers' cheery singalongs. 'Wimoweh' was a great Vegas-y explosion of big-band raunch that almost equaled the barbaric splendor of the Zulu original. Trombones blared. Trumpets screamed. Strings swooped and soared through the miracle melody. And then Pete cut loose with all that hollering. It was a revolutionary departure."

While Seeger called that song "just about my favorite to sing for the next forty years," it was rather clumsily revived by the Tokens in "The Lion Sleeps Tonight," with some poor soul trying to copy Seeger's epic falsetto. "That was a typical case of bad words being put to a song," Seeger said. "'In the jungle, the mighty jungle,' and all that. Let's hope it will be mercifully forgotten. One of the principles of the folk process is, the good gets remembered, the bad gets forgotten. That's why I remember Gordon's sessions. He believed that music in some unexplainable way can do things to millions of individual lives, can do something for a nation, for the world. I doubt anybody could ever prove it, but I've always felt that, too. Otherwise you wouldn't find people so particular about *not* putting something on the air."

When I first contacted Seeger, in early 1987, I was delighted at the passion he invested in my project. He sent a note from his home in upstate New York: "It occurs to me that since Max Gordon and the Village Vanguard are still there, it might be fun to have a little reunion down there with you." I happened to be in New York to cover the U.S. Open tennis tournament that September, and Seeger flew into LaGuardia Airport from Bluefield, West Virginia, where he had been performing, just for the night. We jumped in a taxi and headed for a little Village café called the Triangle, where he ordered a "hamburg" and was approached by an admirer—one of many that night.

"Pete Seeger," the man announced.

"I think so," he replied.

Once inside the club, he sat peering into the distance virtually the entire time, looking somewhat Lincolnesque with his hand on his chin. But he smiled pleasantly. His voice was soothing and earnest. He privately accompanied the club's jazz combo with a lively "hambone," furiously slapping his thighs with open palms, superbly on time to a complex rhythm. And he unleashed a stirringly melodious whistle, the sound falling somewhere between a bird and a reed instrument. "When my voice goes, I whistle more," he said, and I made a little note to myself, saying I couldn't imagine a whistler running two notes together in more perfect blend.

"I used to be six-foot-one and a half," he said. "I'm shorter now. I believe the cartilages in one's backbone compress, and one grows shorter as the decades go on. I do get some physical exercise, though. I feed three fireplaces by chopping wood. There's something deep in our chromosomes, the undeniable urge to go 'whack!' I could use a chainsaw, but I'd prefer not to."

He never strummed a note that evening, but he seemed comforted having the banjo and guitar, a custom-made 12-string, at hand. The cases abounded with stickers, loudly proclaiming lifestyle and philosophy: Proud to Be Union. You Can't Hug Children With Nuclear Arms. If the People Lead, Eventually the Leaders Will Follow. Swords Into Plowshares.

"You know, there was quite a split among the folklorists when the Weavers went with Decca," he said, "over whether it was a good thing or a bad thing. I saw both sides of it, tried not to get involved. I was overwhelmed by the sensitivity of your father's treatment. And I think sometimes a nation gets lucky for a period of time when something honest gets through."

Safely inside the Vanguard, Seeger found himself resurrecting some long-dormant stories. "Carl Sandburg dropped down to hear us one evening," he said. "Some newspaper reporter discovered he was there, and bustled over: 'Mr. Sandburg, can you tell me what you've been working on lately?' Sandburg, with great seriousness, said, 'Well, I've just taken to the publisher my latest book, called 'The Story of an Habitué.' And of course, the reporter is scribbling it all down. 'Now I'm starting on the sequel,' he says. 'The Son of an Habitué.'"

The Vanguard had become strictly a jazz club around the mid-Fifties, home to Ellis Larkins, John Coltrane, Thelonious Monk, Sonny Rollins, Dexter Gordon, an endless list. Many names and eras had come and gone. But Max Gordon was still there in 1987, frail and white-haired, at the age of eighty-five. His hearing and eyesight were fading, he walked with a cane, and the seas seemed to part at the whims of his movement. He managed a rare smile at the sight of Pete Seeger, and all the memories that came with it. Fine days, they were. And not terribly long-lasting.

By 1952, the Weavers had been driven back into obscurity by the stifling hand of anti-Communist America. They were very conspicuous radicals in the era of blacklisting and Senator Joe McCarthy, and they paid a heavy price for it. "We had something of a distant relationship with the Communist party," Seeger told me. "We'd sing mostly at street rallies, union meetings. We didn't think much of the party meetings, because they were all full of long words. But we felt they were more or less on the right track. I'd say we had a light-hearted attitude toward the seriousness of the proletarian revolution. We were very intrigued by the challenge to try and be honest singers while not being revolutionary singers."

The Weavers, and Seeger in particular, became targets of pointed accusations by *Red Channels,* a publication that identified what it alleged were subversives. With "Irene" still tearing up the charts, the group was picketed outside the Strand Theater in New York. A television show was canceled; bookings dwindled. Decca was asked by distributors and stores to remove Weavers albums from the shelves. At Springfield, Illinois, they were greeted by a head-line across the local paper: "Weavers Named Reds."

Gilbert: "You know those old movies where the criminal stops by a newsstand, picks up the paper and sees himself in the headline? That was us. It was a scary time, just full of harassment, fear, secret get-togethers. And we couldn't get our records played. They stopped us cold."

One of the group's managers, Harold Leventhal, noted, "There were a number of people in theater and films who were targets of similar attacks, but the Weavers were the only target in the music industry. And nobody in the music business came to their defense."

"I don't know if that's necessarily true in Gordon's case," said Hellerman, "but at that point there was nothing he could do. He always maintained his integrity when it came to the Weavers. In fact one time, after we had been blacklisted and thrown out of the ballpark, he invited me to come and sing on a record date, a sort of pseudo-'Irene' kind of song. I got Lee in on it, too. The record actu-ally came out, but some cocksucker DJ—Bill Randall was his name —blew the whistle. But that was Gordon all the way; there was just a built-in decency to the guy.

"I remember when Decca stone-cold dropped us," said Heller-man. "Dave Kapp said he needed some kind of statement, so Lee wrote him a wonderful letter that concluded, 'In short, we deny the allegations and defy the alligators.'

"It's hard to describe that climate," Hellerman went on, "when you're walking down the street, you're approached by someone you know, and he ducks across to the other side. Can't afford to be seen talking to you. Even now, it's hard for me to realize that, but by

God, you can bet your ass it happened. It was insanity. Just by showing up at our concerts, people would put themselves at risk. Wives would lose custody in divorce cases because they attended a meeting!

"Pete was the most visible, the most successful of us, so he was the better target. But they nailed all of us. And we continued to have trouble for years. In the Sixties, at the height of the whole folk thing, ABC had a big show called 'Hootenanny.' Had every cocka-mamie singer you ever heard on there, but they wouldn't let Pete on. I remember people like Joan Baez and Judy Collins refusing to perform, out of protest. And the response was, 'Well, Pete doesn't seem to fit.' Like Willie Mays doesn't fit into a baseball show."

I asked Hellerman if Seeger had ever been a member of the Communist party. "You know, if you'd asked me that six months ago, my answer would have been incredulous to you: I don't know. Now I'd say yes. Only because there was a film, called 'Seeing Red,' and Pete talked about his brief time in the party. Before that, I couldn't have told you. It was something we just never talked about. It was irrelevant; wouldn't have mattered. Myself, I've always answered that question very freely: None of your goddamn business."

Hellerman recalled a particularly disturbing incident in Akron, Ohio, the day after a McCarthy informant had testified against the Weavers in Washington, D.C. "You could feel violence in the air," he said. "I've never felt such imminent danger. We did the show opening night and left, feeling like we were an hour ahead of the posse. The next day when we got off the plane in Columbus, they had a news conference right at the airport. Someone approached Lee and said, 'Mr. Hays, it is alleged that you delivered the oration at the funeral of Robert Reed, an alleged Communist organizer.' Lee . . . God, this was wonderful. He said, 'No, that isn't quite accurate. Bob Reed was not an alleged Communist organizer, he was a *well-known* Communist organizer. Secondly, I didn't deliver the main funeral oration. I delivered one of many.'"

Hellerman had to pause for a moment. He was losing it. "Lee was such ... [sobbing] Oh, Jesus ... There was such dignity to him. I think if I know anything in my life about dignity, it's from that moment. And I have a feeling they all felt very ashamed."

The Weavers broke up in 1952, less than two years after being the hottest recording act in the country. "We weren't really sorry," Seeger said. "We were no longer singing in Ciro's or the Waldorf Astoria. We were singing in Daffy's Bar & Grill on the outskirts of Cleveland. It was kind of a silly way to spend your life. So we quit for the time being. A sabbatical, we called it. And as Lee said, it turned into a Mondical and a Tuesdical."

Hellerman: "In our earlier days together, we really hated playing in nightclubs and vaudeville. We'd say, 'Oh, if we could only do concerts.' Later, after *Red Channels*, we found that the only way we could come back was by doing concerts. That's how Carnegie Hall came about in 1955. We found to our surprise that the act of coming to a Weavers concert was taken as 'making a statement.' It carried a sense of defiance."

Carnegie Hall marked the first time the Weavers had performed together in three years. It was a landmark event—the members of The Kingston Trio said that's the night they decided to form their group—and its momentum kept the Weavers together until 1957, when Seeger left the group. "I couldn't take care of my family and be a member of the Weavers family," he said. "It was just too much. Musically, after working with Gordon, it became less and less interesting."

It wasn't nearly the same without Seeger (he was replaced by singer-banjo player Eric Darling), but Hays, Gilbert and Hellerman kept the group together. Their last performance, in Chicago, came on December 30th, 1963. "We just got tired. We got to be terribly self-conscious about what we were doing," said Hellerman.

"Our most rewarding time was the first six months at the Village Vanguard. We didn't have time to be arty then. The juices were flowing."

"What always struck me," said Gilbert, "is that we never met anyone else like Gordon when we started to become popular. He was a gentleman. He gave us the wrong impression of the kind of person we'd find in mainstream music. It wasn't him."

Over the years, my father's take on the Weavers became increasingly jaded. He would remain devoted to them, as people and musicians, but he despised what happened in the wake of their success. "Jesus Christ," he muttered to himself one day. "I've ruined the music business."

In a 1978 interview with Chuck Cecil, he elaborated: "'Goodnight Irene' opened up a lot of doors I'd just as soon have kept closed. It was a good record, but it did more harm than you can possibly imagine. Everybody in the world started doing what they thought were folk songs, which developed into everybody on the street writing songs of their own, and it became just a flood of crummy songs and crummy groups. They figured, gee, if they can do it with a guitar and a banjo, so can we. And now you've got a junk music business. The Beatles did the same damage; when they started writing their own songs, every kid on the corner became a songwriter. And just because you're copying somebody else, that doesn't make you a songwriter. If everybody in the world decided to be a plumber, there would be a lot of rotten plumbers. There are only so many talented people in a generation. Spread it around, and all it gains you is rotten."

Hellerman: "It really did change everything. All of a sudden everywhere you went in the Village, some folk group was playing. I remember one time we were up in Minneapolis at the same time the Andrews Sisters were in town. One of them, I think it was Laverne, was a little bombed, and she goes [slurry], 'The Weavers. Great group. Know why the Weavers are a great group? I'll tell you why. Imagine yourself at a diner someplace, bunch of truck drivers sitting at the counter, and a Weavers record comes onto the jukebox. One guy turns to another and says, shit, I could sing better 'n' that.' And there's a truth to that, there really is. Suddenly, hit records were very accessible. I mean, you're not gonna listen to Benny Goodman, Gordon Jenkins or Tommy Dorsey and say that."

Hellerman was sixty years old at the time of our interview. "Let me show you something I really treasure," he said, revealing a letter written by my father in 1980. It went this way, in part:

"As you may have heard, our house burned to the ground in the 1978 Malibu fire. It was a hell of a shock, but we survived, thanks to the insurance company, and we have re-built on the same lot. We hereby invite any and all of you to drop by whenever you hit this part of the land. I often think of those marvelous nights at the Vanguard. A little concentration and I can feel my heart racing, and the tears. You formed a very special place on my musical cloud, one that I have desperately hung onto, and I love you for it. Peace, Gordon."

Hellerman wrote back a few months later, after the 1980 Weavers reunion that was such a resounding success. It was written on a classic old Royal typewriter, complete with corrections made in ink. Hellerman admitted that he owned but couldn't yet trust a computer, "with which I'm trying to come to some kind of mutual understanding." Of the reunion, which led to the "Wasn't That a Time?" documentary, Hellerman wrote, "Certainly we've had many occasions to mention your name, reflecting on you fondly and reminding ourselves of the huge debt that we owe you." He mentioned that Lee Hays was "literally coming apart—first one leg came off a few years ago, last year the second leg, then pacemakers, etc. One of several consequences was that we were limited to two nights by Lee's fragile shape, and I feel so bad about the thousands of people who had to be turned away.

"As for the concerts themselves, it was thrilling, Gordy, and moving and full and rich. I wish with all my heart that you could have been there to share it. From the moment we walked out and stood there helplessly, while the audience did *their* number on us; through listening to Ronnie truly sounding better than ever; through the singing of 'Goodnight Irene,' which I enjoyed more than I can ever remember—it was an emotional feast that was almost too much to bear. And when it was over, after feeling drowned in this tidal wave of love, Mrs. Hellerman's boy found that he had to get upstairs very quickly where he could finish going to pieces in the privacy of his dressing room ... And I better quit talking about it now, 'cause I can feel it starting to happen again."

Gilbert, also sixty at that time, was fantastically warm and energetic during the time we spent together. "You know, I married a guy named Marty Weg, and Gordon used to call him Weg-Face. He'd say, 'You get rid of Weg-Face, because you and I could make beautiful music.' And you always knew it was a joke; that wasn't anything you could take seriously. But there was such a sweetness about him, and you just knew that he and Beverly, they were ... [tears] ... they were *it*. I'm so sorry he's gone, honey. You go give Beverly a big hug for me." And she wrapped me in her arms.

After many years without contact, I renewed my relationship with Pete Seeger in the late Nineties, when he and Issachar Miron successfully got "Tzena, Tzena, Tzena" back into circulation as a peace song for choral groups. Seeger was typically vibrant, thoroughly energized by this new project. "It could be worldwide," he told me over the phone. "You might have the Croatians making up a verse and the Serbians making up a verse. Or sung in rounds: English first, then the Hebrew, now the Arabic, until they're all singing it together. A great big jumble of sounds. Then someone raises his hand and the whole damn audience is [dramatically, right into the beat] '*Tzena, Tzena, Tzena....*'"

I got the chills right then, racing up my arms and through the back of my neck, for my father had taken my place on the telephone. It was just about the sweetest thing he'd ever heard, and he was laughing out loud.

The Weavers (left to right): Pete Seeger, Lee Hays, Ronnie Gilbert and Fred Hellerman. Jenkins heard them at the Village Vanguard in 1949 and personally launched their recording career. (Photo courtesy of United Artists Corporation)

Beverly Jenkins, enjoying the beach life in the desolation of Malibu, 1955.

Beverly (second from bottom, right row) developed a lasting friendship with the great Kay Thompson (front and center) after singing behind her on CBS radio in the mid-1930s.

Beverly at the peak of her career, as a member of "Six Hits and a Miss" on CBS radio, 1946. Friends weren't surprised when she and Gordon broke off their respective marriages to be together.

"BUT I LOVED HER"

Words and music, Gordon Jenkins

SHE WAS BOS-TON, I WAS VEG-AS, SHE WAS CREPE SU-ZETTE, I WAS PIE. SHE WAS LEC-TURES, I WAS MO-VIES, BUT I LOVED HER SHE WAS MO-ZART, I WAS BA-SIE, SHE WAS AF-TER-NOON TEA, I WAS SA-LOON. SHE WAS JU-IOR LEAGUE, I WAS DODG-ERS, BUT I LOVED HER, MORN-ING, NIGHT AND NOON.

OP-PO-SITES AT-TRACT, THE WISE MEN CLAIM, STILL I WISH THAT WE HAD BEEN A LIT-TLE MORE THE SAME: IT MIGHT HAVE BEEN A SHORT-ER WAR, IF I HAD KISSED HER MORE SHE WAS PO-LO, I WAS

Alpheus Music Corp

Jenkins's original chart for "But I Loved Her" and *(opposite page top)* sheet-music covers for the hit records "San Fernando Valley" and "Homesick, That's All." Jenkins and Sinatra exchanged good-humored notes for years, including *(opposite page bottom)* this example from Sinatra's desk.

F R A N K   S I N A T R A

"It'll never work, Virgil . . . I'm herbal tea and yogurt,
and you're cola and Twinkies."

WHY CAN'T YOU WRITE LYRICS LIKE THIS!!

The absolute peak: Jenkins and Sinatra recording the Grammy-winning "September of My Years" album in Hollywood, 1965. (Photo by Ed Thrasher)

Jenkins and Sinatra immersed in the playback of a just-recorded track.

The family Christmas card, 1957. It doesn't get a whole lot tackier—
and that was the idea.

Broad Beach, 1950. This was our back yard. If you widened the shot by a half-mile in either direction, you probably wouldn't see another person.

Family photo, mid-1950s. Behind us: the so-called mystery house, where Katherine Hepburn and Spencer Tracy spent many a quiet hour.

The beach house. My father had the foresight to buy this place in 1947, when north Malibu was mostly a rumor.

Above: Recording the "Love Is the Thing" album with Nat Cole in 1957; inscription from Nat's wife, Maria.

Left: Jenkins was so thrilled to record with Armstrong, he cried tears of joy during the session. The hit record "Blueberry Hill" was a product of their collaboration.

Jenkins with Judy Garland during their 1957 engagement at the Dominion Theater in London *(left)* and a recording session in the 1940s. In a most professional way, they were crazy about each other.

The album covers for "Where Are You?" (1957) and "No One Cares" (1959). When Sinatra needed an arranger for his torch-song albums, he usually turned to Jenkins.

Sinatra and Jenkins on the same wavelength, recording "Send in the Clowns" in 1973.

From the "Trilogy" sessions in 1980. Sinatra sent Gordon this photo with the now-faded inscription, "This comes with my love, affection, and a million bars of admiration. Peace, Francis."

Above: Jenkins and Sinatra were more thrilled with their "Trilogy" collaboration than some of the critics. *Below:* Sinatra used two of his other favorite arrangers, (left to right) Billy May and Don Costa, to complete the album.

With Harry Nilsson and creative genius Derek Taylor in London, 1973, for the recording of "A Little Touch of Schmilsson in the Night." (Photo by Tom Hanley)

Nilsson took some mighty swigs of alcohol during the sessions but performed masterfully. Years later he called it "the best album I've ever been associated with." (Photo by Tom Hanley)

At the age of seventy-three, with less than a year to live, Jenkins routinely joked about becoming the first human being to beat Lou Gehrig's disease. He sent his friends this card with the inscription, "How's THAT for a recovery?"

Chapter 13

All Manner of Debauchery

I QUIT THE NEWSPAPER BUSINESS OUTRIGHT in 1972. I had a drunk for a boss, at a little hometown paper in Southern California, and the gig wasn't measuring up to expectations. To give you some idea, one Tuesday night he went out for cocktails and he got back on Friday. The creative hours worked splendidly for him, but not for a twenty-three-year-old novice struggling to lay out the paper. I once filled his neglected column space with a cucumber-sized mug shot of Nolan Ryan.

The highway sounded so much better. I had spent the summer of 1971 cruising around Europe in a light-blue Volkswagen van with my best friend, Jack Pritchett, and now we were sprucing up the rig for an extended trip north—Oregon, Washington, Canada, wherever we pleased, without time limits or restraints of any kind.

We were regrouping in Malibu in the spring of 1973, pondering Mexico or perhaps the East Coast, when some interesting options arrived. I got an offer from the *San Francisco Chronicle*, a personal favorite during my collegiate days in Berkeley, and my father hooked up with singer Harry Nilsson for a recording session in London— all expenses paid, my mother and me included. I told the *Chronicle* I was interested but wouldn't make up my mind until I returned from London—if I came back at all.

It was one of those life-changing episodes. I had the time of my life, tasting the rock-star's life with Nilsson and Derek Taylor, the former Beatles press agent who was producing the album for RCA records. I hooked up with the *Chronicle* that April, for the rest of time. And my buddy Jack, a pre-law student at USC, took the time to ponder an alternative career. Some thirty years later, he's probably the most respected realtor in Malibu, surveying life from a gorgeous mansion in the canyons of Mulholland Drive.

It was a miracle that my dad ever hooked up with Nilsson. Gor was Tchaikovsky, Count Basie, Bessie Smith, Dixieland. Nilsson was "Me and My Arrow," "Everybody's Talkin'," and "Coconut." Few artists summed up the rock-and-roll Seventies better than Nilsson, from his stylish clothes to his rail-thin frame to his wild, jet-setting lifestyle, much of it shared with John Lennon. Gor was 6 a.m. wakeup call, five hours of studious writing, eighteen holes of golf and a quiet dinner. But one afternoon I saw a Nilsson album, "The Point," on the piano of my dad's studio, and I wouldn't have been more shocked if it were Jethro Tull. Ol' Gor—the "museum piece," as Johnny Mandel called him—didn't allow much modern music through the door.

Heaven knows I tried. The studio, a separate building from the house, was my sanctuary on warm summer nights. Jack and I would spend hours out there, a couple of shady characters rolling joints in the shadow of Gor's gold records, laughing hysterically and listening to Traffic or Stephen Stills or the Sons of Champlin. Every now and then he'd pop in, unexpectedly, but Gor was cool. He knew that marijuana was synonymous with our generation, that it didn't mean we were hopeless, that we'd spent months in Europe with enough sense to stay out of trouble. He'd open the door, give us a little wink, then tend to his business quickly so we could resume ours. But there was never a time when my music struck his fancy. I couldn't convince him that Smokey Robinson changed everything with his vocal on "Shop Around"; that there was sublime clarity to "Up On the Roof" and the Impressions' "I'm So Proud"; that a satisfied man walks the neighborhood with "Lickin' Stick" or "Papa Don't Take No Mess" spinning through his head. I couldn't explain to him Hendrix, the Stax horns, Otis Redding or the haunting chords of Steely Dan's "Deacon Blues." There wasn't time for Loading Zone or the Womack brothers singing "It's All Over Now," and I had to hide my extreme crush on the Ronettes, whose music to this day sends a pulsating surge through my soul. I tried Chicago, Cold Blood and what I figured was my ace in the hole, Tower of Power, with Greg Adams's horn arrangements, the down-home lyrics of Mimi Castillo and Steve Kupka and the astonishing combination of drummer Dave Garibaldi and bassist Rocco Prestia—but nothing worked. Nothing until Harry Nilsson, for crying out loud, and that was a wild-hair idea from some other continent.

It was all Derek Taylor's idea, an inspired brainstorm from one of Great Britain's most eclectic heroes. Nilsson called him "Ronald Colman on acid," which was to suggest a handsome, distinguished character with a gleam in his eye and a little something up his sleeve. That was Derek Taylor. He had the looks, good humor and classy British charm of David Niven, but beneath the elegance was a thoroughly saturated product of the Sixties, throwing extravagant, drug-sodden parties and keeping it all together with his unassailable wit and good taste. A product of the Beatles' native Liverpool, Derek hooked up with the band early (1963) as a ghostwriter and assistant to press agent Brian Epstein. That became a difficult relationship, partly because Epstein was gay and fancied the young Derek ("although he never laid a hand on me") and primarily because the two had some heated disagreements. Taylor left the band in 1965 to start a publicity agency in Los Angeles, where he ably represented the Beach Boys, Buffalo Springfield, the Byrds and the Beau Brummels, among other groups. ("I actually became a Hollywood character," he said, "which is easy if you're a murderer or a twat or know a line of Keats.") But he returned to England in 1968, the year after

Epstein's death, to run the press offices at the new Apple company, which housed the Beatles at the height of their powers.

As British author Philip Norman wrote years later in *Rolling Stone,* Taylor hardly looked the part: "He looked as if he'd have felt happier dancing the tango in a Busby Berkeley musical. Only the glass of Scotch and Coke at his elbow and the draggled hand-rolled cigarette hinted at more up-to-date pursuits." Taylor's gifts were his words, said Norman, "and he poured them forth in a soft and slightly wheezy Northern England voice that by turns would be sad, angry, elegiac, mischievously funny or breathtakingly indiscreet."

Armed with pre-rolled joints, the ever-present Scotch and an occasional tab of acid, Derek handled the Beatles' affairs with magnificent skill and flair. There couldn't have been a man more perfectly suited to the task. Surrounded by four secretaries and an unerring sense of optimism, he presided over a kaleidoscopic swirl of madness: Hare Krishnas, the Maharishi Mahesh Yogi, strangers in the hallway, homeless families on the floor, preposterously ornate clothing, George's drug bust, John's drug bust, Ken Kesey's poetry readings, the relentless media, even the Hell's Angels (George invited them to England during a weak moment in San Francisco; they not only accepted but set up camp in an Apple office). "It was like an Altman film," Derek recalled in the massive *Beatles Anthology.* "I would arrive and find the Hell's Angels sitting around on the floor doing those physical things they did—a lot of scratching and farting and generally being awful."

Through it all, somehow, came the Beatles' "White Album," "Yellow Submarine," "Let It Be," "Abbey Road," and a fresh challenge with every sunrise. When it became evident that the shocking nude photographs of John and Yoko Ono would be seen around the world, Derek found a passage in the Book of Genesis in which "the man and his wife were naked and not ashamed" and used it to disarm the press. "One day," Norman wrote, "the ground-floor receptionist rang Derek with the news that Adolf Hitler was downstairs, waiting to see him. Taylor shrank back into his wicker-chair throne and sighed, 'Oh, Christ, not that asshole again … OK, send him up.'"

Taylor had moved on to Warner, Elektra and Atlantic Records in London when Nilsson, a trusted friend and running mate, approached him with the idea of recording some old standards. It was a novel idea at the time, merging a contemporary artist with a venerable arranger-conductor who had intimate familiarity with "Always," "Lazy Moon," "As Time Goes By," and other songs they intended to record. "I spotted Gordon Jenkins when I was sixteen years old [1948]," Taylor wrote in *Fifty Years Adrift*, a superbly told life story. "It was the North of England, an outing on the sea, unbelievably sunny weather for a summer's day. One of us had a portable wind-up gramophone and another had a canvas bag full of 78s. The gramophone played 'Again,' by Gordon Jenkins and his orchestra, a song of infinite beauty which I hear in my head even now. [Singing] *'Again … this couldn't happen again.'* Such an arrangement! America's Number One Recording Artist, they called him. So in some bizarre way, I'd wanted to work with him since I was in my teens, dreaming of great escapes. I had sort of a childhood anxiety about meeting a great man—like meeting Churchill."

Nelson Riddle was "almost too obvious," Derek told me. "Wonderful stuff, but I was intensely political at the time, raging against the absurdities of Watergate and Richard Nixon, and somehow I didn't feel that Riddle was a Democrat. It was the way he carried himself; he walked like a Republican [laughter]. Billy May? The music was too tough, too brassy. Wasn't gentle enough. Don Costa we were certain was a Republican."

In Jenkins, Taylor found a sixty-three-year-old man who signed his letters "Peace" and was willing to embrace a musical generation quite foreign to him. "There also was a wittiness about Gordon that we couldn't find in his contemporaries. I knew a lot of people wouldn't recognize the name, and I liked that, too, even though his body of work—my God, from the Weavers to Sinatra, that's an incredibly good cross-section. The thing with the Weavers was most impressive to me, because it wasn't a very mainstream notion that he should work with such highly political people. There's no way you can see Don Costa or a hundred other arrangers working with *any* of those lefties. I don't think Gordon necessarily lined up with them politically, it's just that he had no boundaries in his work. We felt that would make him most sympathetic to what we were trying to do. And of course, we were absolutely right. We were dead-on."

Later, as he viewed the arrangements, Derek marveled at my father's "trusted old fountain pen, with a beautifully realized sinistral lean to match his left-handedness. His correspondence with me began to gather pace: He had a lovely way with a letter, mixing wry comments and cosmic asides with more businesslike descriptions of time and place. I marveled anew at our brilliance in acquiring his services. He said he would need some forty musicians. The drummer must be 'youngish, jazz-oriented,' the guitarist 'not pushy but *there*.' And 'no cousins in the fiddles,' he said. Like, don't choose any family or friends."

Nilsson knew of my father, said Derek, "because Harry knows everything." Unlikely as it seemed for a man in his early thirties, Nilsson remembered "Manhattan Tower" from his Brooklyn childhood, fleeing to the basement to play his uncle's record collection. "I was fascinated by that record," he said. [Dramatically] *'Then one day, love walked into my tower. . . .'* It was a man reaching the pinnacle of life, not to mention the excesses, and he had this tower suite in the Ritz Hotel. It wasn't a conventional album at all, it was more like Broadway. I saw Gordon Jenkins as a brother of Gershwin; the music had that touch. Such soul . . . it just penetrated. Plus, other than the Beatles, he's the only guy who ever had five of the top ten records—as a writer, conductor and arranger. That's quite a mouthful. So we had a few of my albums sent to him."

True to form, Gor had never heard "Without You" (a Grammy-winning single), the theme from "Midnight Cowboy" or anything else Nilsson had recorded. Nor did he know that Harry was one of the great triple-threat masters of indulgence: alcohol, marijuana and cocaine, relentlessly, day and night. Just as well—Gor addressed the albums "Aerial Ballet," "The Point," and "Nilsson Schmilsson" with a completely open mind, and something clicked (knowing my father's sense of humor, I'm sure he was floored by Harry's immortal verse, "You're breakin' my heart, you're tearin' it apart, so fuck you"). It took him only a few hours to make the decision—let's go.

"Technically, he didn't have much of a voice," Gor said, "but he had good pitch and feeling, and he was willing to work. This is a guy who was terrified of performing live and never did it once. Never stood in front of a conductor, either. But he was passionately interested in this thing. He spent many hours rehearsing with my old piano player, Charlie LaVere, just to get the intervals and the phrasing down."

Taylor: "Harry did that very quietly on his own. The thing is, your basic Harry, without any of the stimulants or whatever, is a very diligent, hard-working, mathematical man from the bank [his former job], working on elaborate computer-type schemes that will all fit together. The madness part makes him exotic and exciting, but what got him to Charlie LaVere was his desire to make the books balance, so that when he stood in front of Gordon, he wouldn't look like a fool."

It was arranged that Gor would fly to London for a meeting, just to verify the spiritual connections in the wind. "I think the whole reason for that visit was Harry wanting to make sure I laughed at Derek's jokes," Gor said. "He didn't want anybody in that studio that didn't think Derek Taylor was brilliant. And hell, he *was* brilliant. Everything he said broke me up. I almost fell out of the car on the way to his office. But the whole thing was in great style. Limousines, television cameras at the airport, kitchen in the apartment, refrigerator full of whiskey, Steinway grand piano in the living room—and this was for the *meeting*. So I had no fault with either one of those cats."

My mother and I arrived to a similarly luxurious setting, in the heart of Mayfair. I'd wake up to the sports section of the London *Times*, offering a brand of sportswriting that was at once literate, bold, witty and eccentric. We traveled by limousine for the daily recording sessions at Wembley, an area best known for its massive soccer stadium. I had the evenings free, and I'll never forget one after-hours walk through the elegant streets of London. I had gone down to Ronnie Scott's to hear one of my idols, jazz trumpeter Freddie Hubbard, and I was a few blocks from our flat when I turned a corner and collided awkwardly with O.J. Simpson. Must have been two or three in the morning.

"O.J.," I announced.

"That's right."

"Man, you did a number on my Cal team a couple years ago," I said, fumbling for conversation. "Nobody's gonna believe I ran into you here. What are you doing?"

"Aw, I don't know," he said. "Just walkin'."

We stayed sixteen days in London, two themes prevailing: class and decadence. Derek had assembled a thirty-nine-piece orchestra with the finest musicians in London, most of them symphonic players from the Philharmonic. My father's name was golden among these wonderful, craggy-faced men; they knew his work intimately. "That's the reason they were there," Nilsson said. "A lot of them said to Gordon, 'I was there for Judy [Garland, on the London dates in 1957].' They looked at him like they were about to embark on a great, magical thing." They reminded me so much of the players from my dad's recording sessions at home: trustworthy and self-deprecating, professional to the core. Harry and Derek were both stunned to discover that after a single take—the band's first look at the music with the "Recording" light on—they had what amounted to a finished product.

"They booked the studio for nine dates and we were finished in eight," Gor said later. "I told 'em I could do it in two, if necessary, and they didn't believe it. Derek and Harry just stared at me. They were used to, you know, 'You play an F chord and I'll hum.'"

"The first day," said my dad's longtime accountant, Harold Plant, "one of the hangers-on said to Gordon, 'I don't understand what's going on here. Everybody's going to record at one time? How do you know what it's going to sound like?' That sums up a lot of rock musicians today. They have to lay down endless tracks, individually, and hear every known variation. If you told them Beethoven was stone deaf when he composed his Ninth Symphony, they wouldn't believe you. And the idea of knocking off four or five tunes in a couple of hours, that's incredible to them."

Taylor: "I'm sorry to say I was involved in numerous cocaine-riddled recording sessions over the years. I'm not speaking of the Beatles' dates, which I rarely attended, but of many other bands. They're not entertaining. They are intensely boring, disorganized and self-indulgent. And that cocaine freeze, that look of anxiety, the point where none of the conversation makes a bit of sense— just frightful. I used to say smile, and the world smiles with you. Grind, and you grind alone."

Nilsson: "Yeah, I probably did ten or eleven of those albums, where you get a bunch of coke and spend months in the studio. To go in with Gordon Jenkins is frightening, a singular experience. You work with him once if you're lucky."

Harry, to his everlasting credit, was a beacon of high performance. Make no mistake, he snuck in a few cocaine blasts and drank with a fervor, routinely dropping out of sight for a swig of brandy or whiskey. But he kept it together—for just about the last time in his career, as it turned out. Nilsson's lifestyle was bringing him down, slowly, to a bitter conclusion, but he sang like an angel for Gordon, particularly on "This Is All I Ask." For the combination of vocals and arrangement, it's one of the better versions this side of Sinatra's.

"I had heard some horrible stories about his various habits, and the havoc wreaked thereof," Gor said. "I'm no stranger to that kind of behavior, as you might imagine. I've known guys who can pull it off, even if they're drunk on their ass, and Harry certainly goes into that category. I kept waiting him for him to fall down, but he didn't. He's an original, this guy. He's not like other people."

Because Nilsson had never worked with a conductor, especially one with a gift for following a singer's tempo, he found himself in conversations like this:

Harry: "What are you gonna do at the end there?"

Gor: "We'll find out then. How do I know what you're gonna do? You've got it backwards."

"But you're slowing down."

"I'm slowing down because *you* slowed down."

"You mean, I can do whatever I want to at the end?"

"Yeah, that's what I do. I get paid quite a bit of money for following you."

"Wow. Cool. That's the best thing I ever heard."

Disc jockey Sandy Singer, a devotee of my father's work, saw some videotape of the Nilsson sessions. "Do you remember the shots from the 'September of My Years' dates with Sinatra, those expressive eyes as Frank looks to Gordon for the approval he wants? I saw that same thing in Nilsson as he watched Gordy for his cue. I have to believe that every singer who ever worked with Gordon fell in love with the man."

The original song list was a bit heavy-handed. Gor promptly

dispatched "Hey Jude," "Auld Lang Syne," and "Let's Not Be Beastly to the Germans" to their proper resting place. "We almost did 'Smoke Gets In Your Eyes,'" said Nilsson, "but I didn't like the line, 'So I laughed and gaily chaffed.' That shouldn't be allowed in any song at any time. There is no such thing as 'gaily chaffing.'"

A final, crucial element was the presence of engineer Phil McDonald, at the time just twenty-seven but already a veteran of several recording masterpieces, including "Abbey Road." Gor raved about McDonald for years afterward, saying he could hardly recall a more competent ally. "We got the sense that we were all the same age," said Derek. "Phil was in his twenties, Harry in his thirties, I was in my forties, the orchestra in their fifties, and Gordon in his sixties. And the whole place was bedazzled. No one has ever forgotten those sessions."

I was amazed to hear how they ranked on the list of Taylor's accomplishments. "I can tell you the three great moments in my life," he said. "One was the Beatles at the Hollywood Bowl for the first time, in 1964, because everything was as wonderful as I'd hoped it would be. The second was the first song of the 1967 Monterey Pop Festival [which he helped organize], a song by the Association, because the sound was right and everything was perfect and you knew the festival was on. The third—and everyone felt it in the studio—was when Gordon Jenkins tapped the podium [knocks the table four times] to begin the first session. There were no journalists hanging around, trying to get the same tired story about a rock star trying to self-destruct. Even though it was an entirely new experience for me, producing this massive orchestra, nobody gave me any trouble. About the only thing that wasn't absolutely first-rate was the food. We had to find what they call a steak house in England, where you get your food on oval plates. I don't know why, but as soon as you see an oval plate, you know it's going to be mass-produced English cooking, without a chef in sight."

Nilsson sort of adopted me for a few days. Darn nice of him, I thought, because he was centuries older in the ways of the world. We walked many miles through London on crisp, sunny afternoons, buoyed by his crackling sense of humor. He changed my view of world sport, forever, by introducing me to the Premiership of British soccer. I was used to artificial turf, ludicrous national-anthem singers, silly halftime shows and the rest of the nonsense that accompanies American sport. Now I was at Stamford Bridge, watching Chelsea play Arsenal: forty-five minutes of continuous action, an intermission featuring nothing but cigarette smoke and earnest conversation, then forty-five minutes to the conclusion. Because it was Harry, we had the very best seats with striking female attendants bringing us Scotch with no ice. But I would have savored it from the rafters. Scrappy laborers broke into song without cue, thousands of them, belting out themes handed down through the decades. People swayed rhythmically in the standing-room sections, passing down the poor unconscious souls who had either keeled over or been punched in the nose. Great charismatic figures came to life on the pitch, players I soon began following through television and the tabloids. I was hooked for life. Not so much in the States, where the passion and quality are so sadly lacking, but on many subsequent trips to Europe, where I could plug back into the most riveting spectacle on earth.

The title of the album, "A Little Touch of Schmilsson in the Night," was Derek's idea. As he explained it, "I knew a bit of Shakespeare and the phrase, 'A little touch of Harry in the night.' King Henry the Fifth, Act Three, scene seven. It's the night before the Battle of Agincourt, the British going to war undermanned against the French, and this was a reassurance, a little squeeze on the shoulder." ("It was either two mad soldiers waiting to kill a king," said Nilsson, "or two homosexuals in a ditch.")

The final stroke of ingenuity came from Stanley Dorfman, a

BBC producer who had become enchanted by the recordings. Assembling a crew in great haste, he asked Jenkins, Nilsson and the orchestra to duplicate the album for the benefit of British television.

"They showed up and we did the whole thing in a single day," Gor said. "It was the best-run TV show I've ever seen. I never did see Dorfman or anybody else. They never bothered us, barged in or tried to ruin it with 'improvements.' It was just in and out, and let's go home. You could never get away with that in America. Too many idiots."

The video aired several times in England, to rousing cheers, and I dispatched copies to my friends; it is by far the lengthiest documentation of my father's work. As for the album, it had longevity, if not instant appeal. It won some esoteric awards, achieved gold-record status in Australia and got rave reviews, including this from Arthur Schmidt in *Rolling Stone:* "Jenkins generally allows his singer a good deal of space, often with the subtlest percussion backing, punctuating the sentences with whatever seems right, and his taste is flawless. He builds walls of sound that would make Phil Spector blush or steal, probably not in that order. In the words of the song that opens and closes the album, moonlight and love songs are never out of date."

Stephanie Salter, who wrote a charming column in the old *San Francisco Examiner,* was enraptured by the album. Playing it at home—generally in the context of cocktails and romance—she found herself blissfully swept away. Not long after Nilsson's death, she wrote that "only one obituary even mentioned what I consider Nilsson's major contribution to society: 'A Little Touch of Schmilsson in the Night,' one of the most bizarre but delightful albums ever created. Keep in mind, it was made way before Barbra Streisand and Barry Gibb married Broadway to bubble-gum rock. Before Linda Ronstadt ("What's New") dreamed of singing in front of Nelson Riddle's big band. Before it occurred to Willie Nelson that he, too, had a right to Irving Berlin and Hoagy Carmichael. In other words, before the term 'cross-over' even existed in music." She said Gor's willingness to take on such a risk "bordered on valor" and that "Nilsson's desire to make an album of beautiful, old standards turned out to be genius."

There is no one left to speak for that album. Nilsson died of heart failure at fifty-two—terribly early, tragically on time—and Taylor passed away in 1997, at the age of sixty-five, after a long illness. I had maintained a steady correspondence with Derek over the years, calling myself Fielding Mellish (after an old Woody Allen character) while he answered as Dirk O'Brandy. I saw him for the last time during the 1990 Wimbledon, using a free afternoon to conduct a lengthy interview at his home in Suffolk. He lived in a magnificently rustic setting near the Mill at Brudon, dating back to the eleventh century. He and his wife, Joan, had produced six children, and Derek had long since gone sober—at least from the drinking and cocaine (I assumed he smoked the well-timed joint, although the subject never came up). Knowing I had developed a fancy for European soccer, he unveiled some old highlight videos from his beloved Liverpool. The film showed crowds going berserk, players floating excitedly around the pitch, and I saw tears in Derek's eyes as he relived some of the finest moments of his life. For some, I'd imagine, this would amount to wading through a stranger's stamp collection. I couldn't have been more entranced.

The Nilsson album seemed to be right up front in his mind— "So refreshing not to be talking about those other people [the Beatles]," he said—and more significant than ever. "I consider it my most important and lasting collaboration," he said. "Everyone agreed it was magic, even Sinatra, who told me it was wonderful in a conversation I had with him. I really think it's one of the great albums of popular music, one of the top five. There are many in the top five. Probably hundreds, you get the idea. Take the top five human beings, for instance. You've got to include Tommy Lasorda and Shakespeare [laughter], then Walt Whitman, and for heaven's sake, you're already out of room. But Gordon and Harry were meant for each other. There was a line from Churchill, 'My whole life has been a preparation for this moment,' and that's how I feel about it.

"There's an extremely wonderful atmosphere inside the record," he went on. "It certainly doesn't feel like an album done in England in the afternoon. It's like 'Sergeant Pepper'—not of this world, really. It was England and it feels like 'The Wizard of Oz.'"

If there was a single experience that guided Derek toward sobriety, it was a trip to New York in May 1973, a month after the recording sessions. "Harry, Phil [McDonald] and I went there for a minimal but crucial overdub, because Harry was not completely happy with a word he had sung in 'This Is All I Ask.' We stayed at the Algonquin and drank heavily, careening around New York like men demented, but we had the time and RCA's money and we were really throwing it around. Don't forget, in the slipstream of the Sixties, we believed that our duty in life was to show everyone a good time, and Harry and I were both full-time members of the Extravagant Club. The word in question was 'sing,' as in, 'as long as there's a song to sing.' That one word cost about $20,000 in drinking time."

One night, around 3 a.m., the very wasted pair decided they needed to find a piano and some privacy—right then. "We'd been drinking for days without sleep, with an enormous bag of cocaine, and we wound up in the lobby of the RCA building, knowing there was a piano on the ninth floor. 'It's me, it's me!' Harry shouted as we burst in, pointing to all these photos and gold records on the wall. Harry had it wired: He knew the piano had a double stool on it and a space between the two cushions [to lay out the coke]. So we're tinkling away when suddenly the elevator doors opened and about fifteen cops appeared. [Menacingly] 'OK, guys, what's going on here?' I got the coke off the stool and just rammed it inside that piano *any* old how. The cops took us downstairs, and it was looking good, because they recognized Nilsson and he's talking 'em up, telling how he kept the whole fucking RCA Corporation in business. But the coke was still up there. I said, 'I know this sounds fussy, but I left some cigarettes upstairs, and they're an English brand, and if you don't mind I'll just fetch them real quick.' But when I got back upstairs, the coke was gone. The cops had it. There cannot be a worse feeling in the world, sensing that your life is about to be ruined.

"We were nearly in very big trouble," Derek said. "What a glorious development that the cops were corrupt."

As we left it that day, the story was off the record. Months later he relented, by mail, saying what the hell and it was true and a ghastly sign of the times. "After your train drew out," he added, "that lizard-lidded chap you met took me back to his moated 15th-century mansion and after being served by pale, trembling, female hands, I went water-divining with a strong green twig. By God, it works, Mellish. I have lived a long and fruitful life but never divined water before."

I had no idea what he meant, but it was so deliciously Derek. "He was a beautiful man," Paul McCartney said upon Taylor's death. "It's a time for tears. Words may come later."

I saw Nilsson just once after the record dates, in the spring of 1988. We set up an interview at Mason's, one of those pretentious power-lunch spots in West Los Angeles, and I was stunned by the sight of him. For one thing, I looked right past Nilsson as he walked in. This man was large, almost bloated—easily twice the size of the old Harry. His thin, movie-star's face had become almost comically round. And he was accompanied by Peter Langan, who I later discovered was a London restauranteur and one of the great roaring drunks of the British Isles. Langan was, indeed, bombed. With Harry I couldn't be sure, but that was nothing new; he stood upright and made perfect sense.

The scene became even more surreal. Just across the way sat Brian Wilson, the once-massive Beach Boy, looking amazingly fit and trim at the age of forty-six. I had the stock image of Brian: drugged-out, grotesquely overweight, barely able to think, pee or bend over. Now he was looking like the sturdy anchor of UCLA's mile-relay team. "One of the Beach Men," cracked Harry. "And look who he's with." It was Eugene Landy, Wilson's psychotherapist and personal manager, the man who had orchestrated his come-back from oblivion. All seemed well with Brian, from his tropical shirt to his animated conversation, with one big exception: He was talking out of the side of his mouth, involuntarily, like the Bill Murray character in "Caddyshack" ("You know, the pool or the pond. The pond's fine"). And I was thinking, this is like one of those old movies: "Tartagula: Land of the Giant Turtles. Where nothing is as it seems." I fully expected to see a twenty-foot chihuahua come to take my order, and a little tiny Wilt Chamberlain at the reception desk.

"My God," said Nilsson, getting a full load of Brian Wilson. "We look like the reverse of one another."

"I wouldn't say he looks so good," Langan barged in. "He looks rather ill to me."

Nilsson was well beyond the fast lane when I knew him in London—he was more like a NASCAR driver, blowing by ordinary revelers—and he obviously hadn't slowed down much. He had become John Lennon's constant companion in the mid-Seventies, after John's estrangement from Yoko, and they often enlisted Ringo and Keith Moon as drinking partners in a full-on rage. "You know, that still haunts me," Nilsson told an interviewer not long before his death. "People still think I'm a rowdy bum from the Seventies who happened to get drunk with John Lennon, that's all."

I knew better. I knew he had sung in front of my father for a solid week without getting shamed out of the room. "I'll remember all of it," he said. "It's God-like, the best album I've ever been associated with. I'll hold it up against anybody's—show me what you got. It neutralizes all the other shit, the drinking and drugging and hanging out and doing silly albums. I know Gordon felt that way, too. He actually told Derek and me one time, 'Beats the shit out of Sinatra.' I don't know if he'd say that publicly, but hell, he's dead, he's not going to refute anything I just said [laughter].

"Do you remember the cufflinks?" he said. "I think that's my best memory. You know how the guys in that band loved Gordon. Worshipped him. At the very end, after the last downbeat of the last tune, one of 'em stood up ... I can still see his face. 'Maestro Mr. Jenkins,' he said, 'On be-hoff of the players and myself, as a token of our appreciation and esteem, we'd like to present you with these.' They were gold cufflinks fashioned from two ha'pennies. Now Gordon, hey, he was a pretty tough guy. But they gave him this little velvet box, he looked inside, snapped it closed, then walked over to a corner of the control room. Tears just streaming down his face. It was so sad, and so beautiful. Even Derek had a little mist, and of course the orchestra. When Gordon walked back in, they applauded him on the backs of their instruments. It was one of those moments you wait for in your lifetime. All the things you've ever done, now comes the reward. That moment, that day."

Hesitantly, I asked Harry about the state of his singing career. "That's sort of like asking Fred Astaire how he dances when he's sixty-five," he said. "It's more the soul than the sound. Hell, I'm a baritone now. I was hopin' to get hoarse like Ray Charles, because the choir-boy thing is gone. I knew it then. I told both Derek and Gordon, this is the last of it. That incredible, flexible, rubber-band-like voice—I just barely snuck in that album under the gun. Years later, on a given night [dreamily], some of it comes back. If I take a really hot, good shower...."

He was forty-seven years old, his voice shot, his career essentially over. He wasn't long for this world, just five more years, and I could only imagine the flow of indulgence that brought him to that state. But eventually, the subject had to come up. Cocaine. The fun of it then, the hell of it now. We talked about nights gone overboard, and the pitiful days after. How it destroyed lives all around us, and how we had the good sense to put it down. Yes, we agreed, it was a thing of the past, a wretched and evil thing, generally the enemy of all mankind, and what a treat to be drug-free as we approach middle age.

"So," he said. "You want some?"

Chapter 14

On Songwriting

"Beautiful girls, walk a little slower when you walk by me."
—*the high point*

DID YOU EVER TRY TO WRITE A SONG? Not some three-chord mess, but something truly lyrical and melodic? Bloody murder, is what it is. It takes a gift, imagination, consummate skill and, at times, a little luck. In my father's words, this is how an ordinary afternoon in 1956 turned into the best song he ever wrote:

"I was back in New York having lunch with a couple of music-publisher friends, and one of them says, sort of as a joke, 'Gordon, we're not doing anything today. Why don't you go home and write us a hit.' The kind of stuff you hear from publishers all the time. I said, all right, meet me around five o'clock, we'll have a drink, and I'll have a hit for you. Everybody had a good laugh and I was on my way.

"The story is so incredible that I sometimes hesitate to tell it. I'm walking down the street, right around 52nd and 5th, where they're tearing a building down and putting a new one up. And on the fence, one of those barriers where you can't see in, one of the construction guys has written, 'Pretty girls, slow down when you walk by here.' Well, I want to tell you, that was like a cartoon when the light goes on in someone's head. I thought to myself, 'Oh, my God—where's the piano?' So I went straight to the office of one of those publishers, re-wrote the phrase, wrote most of the song, then went back to my apartment and finished it. I called the guys and said, 'I've got that song we talked about.' I didn't have a title, but I had the song."

> (Intro)
> *As I approach the prime of my life*
> *I find I have the time of my life*
> *Learning to enjoy at my leisure*
> *All the simple pleasures*
> *And so I happily concede*
> *This is all I ask*
> *This is all I need*
> (Verse)
> *Beautiful girls, walk a little slower*
> *When you walk by me.*
> *Lingering sunsets, stay a little longer*
> *With the lonely sea.*
> *Children everywhere*
> *When you shoot at badmen, shoot at me.*
> *Take me to that strange, enchanted land*
> *Grownups seldom understand.*
> *Wandering rainbows, leave a bit of color*
> *For my heart to own.*
> *Stars in the sky, make my wish come true*
> *Before the night has flown.*
> *And let the music play*
> *As long as there's a song to sing*
> *And I will stay younger than spring.*

That was "This Is All I Ask," a song that didn't have an official title for more than a year. It sort of sat around my dad's piano, a hidden gem, with no hint of anyone's recording it. "For a while I didn't have a title *or* a finish," he said. "But jeez, this guy's got my song written down on a fence for me. I don't even know who to thank. Somewhere in New York there's a pipefitter that I owe a bundle to. I guess it proves how lucky you can be sometimes. It also proves that I'll steal from anybody. Anything that is not nailed down.

"It took me two years to get the song recorded, with Nat Cole [on their album, "The Very Thought of You"], but I still thought it was good. Later on it started selling, and everybody recorded it." Tony Bennett, Burl Ives, Arthur Godfrey and Perry Como were just a few to cut singles; Clark Terry did a jazz instrumental version, and Ben Webster did the same with a very pure saxophone solo. Harry Nilsson uncorked a beauty on "A Little Touch of Schmilsson in the Night," and Frank Sinatra notched the definitive version, for all time, on "September of My Years."

"I don't look for a hit or try to write hits," Gor once said in an interview. "Never did. I don't care what the market is, or what the last song that sold was. I try to write it as well as I can. If it's a hit, fine. I always thought that if you write well enough, somebody will buy it, and I've lived pretty good. 'This Is All I Ask' is my favorite song. It was never on the charts, but there must be two hundred recordings of it."

I was having a delightful conversation with comedian Alan King, over the phone in the summer of 1993, when he suddenly broke into song: "*Walk a little slower when you walk by me . . .* Oh, my God, nothing that's ever been written is more poignant. That's the twilight song for all time. Gordon and Frank were absolutely at the cusp when they recorded that. My favorite single line: *When you shoot at badmen, shoot at me.* Hey, this is *it,* man! I'm in the back of my car having a martini right now, going over the Triboro Bridge and talking about Gordon! Whoo-hoo!"

That song is a powerful statement from a quiet, often reclusive man. In the words of his onetime New York roommate, George Lee, "I loved that somebody put him up to it; that was his style all the way. He was the type of man that if he had a recording session or a TV show, something important, he'd wait until a day or two before, then write non-stop until he had it. He couldn't do any work before the deadline. He just loved that kind of pressure. He would get on a train—say, bound for Chicago, and drink pretty good, and just write. By the time the train arrived, he was done. Or he'd go up to Boston, five hours up and another five back, and there's ten hours with nobody bothering him.

"He had to have a certain genius to have gone as far as he did as a musician," said Lee. "Don't forget, he did everything on his own. Nobody ever taught him anything. I think he surprised everybody when it came to writing lyrics. He wasn't that verbal, and here are these great words coming out of him. I wish he had written more, but he'd get so tied up in arranging...."

While Johnny Mandel had some critical remarks about my dad's limitations as an arranger and conductor, he nevertheless referred to Gor as "my hero." That stemmed entirely from the songwriting angle. "I was just amazed by the amount of work he could put out," Mandel said. "He would just spit out songs and lyrics, and everything was good, and he did it so incredibly fast. He was a very natural songwriter, and he was one of the guys I admired tremendously when I started doing those things."

The notion hadn't occurred to me, but several sources rated Gor with the all-time quadruple-threat artists: writer, arranger, conductor, performer. The latter might have been his weakest link, although he was a crowd-pleasing, extroverted sort when he conducted his favorite artists and he had that distinctive piano style on many of his own sessions, both live and in the studio.

"I think you should throw in orchestration—taking an arrangement and giving it the proper treatment—as a fifth category," said conductor Bud Dant. "Gordon was a master of them all. And when it came to conducting a record date, he was *past* master. He was the epitome. Who else can you say all that about? Johnny Green wrote two songs in his life—'Body and Soul' and 'Out of Nowhere.' Shit, no, he had nowhere near the talent Gordon had; you can't even talk about them in the same breath. Nelson Riddle and Billy May were great arrangers, but they weren't much for writing. Nelson wrote one hit, some Latin tune, and he hated it."

"Oh, he ranks with the highest," said publisher Sam Weiss. "Name me an orchestra leader or conductor who donated as much as he did. A lot of big names had their name on music, and you wondered why. Jimmy Dorsey, for example. He put his name on songs for no good reason. If Gordy's name was on it, it's because he had something to do with it."

"Let me put it this way," said songwriter Floyd Huddleson. "How many people could do a killer arrangement for Frank Sinatra, then turn around and do the same thing for Louis Armstrong, and then one for the Weavers? That's hard to do. You've got to have an understanding of those people."

Gor might have sensed there was a bit of fairy dust involved when the very first song he ever had published, "Blue Prelude" (lyrics by Joe Bishop), became a hit in 1933; and when a song he composed the following year, "Goodbye," became Benny Goodman's closing theme. Songwriter Johnny Mercer spent a lot of time drinking and writing with Gor, and with my father handling the music, they churned out "P.S. I Love You," "When a Woman Loves a Man" and "You Have Taken My Heart."

"I met Johnny in the Brill building in New York, where people used to come in and write," Gor said. "We'd hang around there in the afternoons, just sit at the piano and fool around. On 'P.S. I Love You,' he just walked in with the lyric and said, 'Write me a tune for that.' I did, and we sold it in an instant. It's not a particularly good melody, I don't think; it's very derivative. But it's been a hit three times."

The fastest reaction he ever got on a song was in 1947 with "You Have Taken My Heart." As Gor tells it, "Johnny and I were holed up in a hotel room in Kansas City, trying to finish that song, and the room faced one of those indoor tennis courts. One floor down, the hotel switchboard operators also faced those courts. I guess one of the girls was listening intently, and she called us up. She said, 'Listen, if you've got a completed copy of that tune, you've made at least one sale. I'm crazy about that song. I've got to play it at home tonight.'"

For novice songwriters, Gor offered one piece of advice: "Write a novelty number. They have about fifty times better chance of making money than the other tunes. You'll have to convince some publisher that your opus is worth a $25,000 gamble, but then, every songwriter has to do that. I'm not terribly fond of novelty numbers, but one of 'em helped support my kids for years."

It came about in 1943, when Gor was living in the San Fernando Valley, then a remote patch of farmland considered to be continents away from Hollywood and downtown Los Angeles. He lived on Longridge in Van Nuys (in an area later claimed by Sherman Oaks, just west of Coldwater Canyon), his phone number was simply HI 8781, and he was viewed as an outright lunatic for dropping so drastically off the map. "I bought a real nice house out there for $14,500," he said. "If I'd had just a little money that I wasn't drinking up or spending, I could have bought a big chunk of the Valley and become a multi-millionaire. But it was just empty lots back then, a ghost town, it was too far out. I had orange and lemon trees in my back yard. I had friends who rode horses to get around. Nobody thought anything would ever happen out there. About the only thing I remember in my neighborhood was a liquor store—which was all I needed."

"The Valley in the 1940s was nothing," said drummer Nick Fatool. "Just chicken farms and cabbage patches."

"Yeah, that was the real Valley," said Billy May. "Before it became the Tijuana it is today."

Popular magazines of the time showed celebrities living boldly in the Valley with their goats and cows. A wartime article in *Overture*, the membership magazine of the L.A. musicians' union, claimed that "at present, city planners are trying to keep most Valley land for agriculture."

That didn't work out so well—thanks in part to ol' Gor.

> *Oh, I'm packin' my grip*
> *And I'm leavin' today*
> *'Cause I'm taking a trip*
> *California way.*
> *I'm gonna settle down and never more roam*
> *And make the San Fernando Valley my home.*
> *I'll forget my sins*
> *I'll be makin' new friends*
> *Where the West begins*
> *And the sunset ends.*
> *'Cause I decided where yours truly should be*
> *And it's the San Fernando Valley for me.*

Bing Crosby recorded "San Fernando Valley" in May 1944, and it shot to No. 1 on the *Billboard* charts for five weeks, helping fuel a surge of immigration to the region. The local Chamber of Commerce awarded Gor a key to the city for putting it on the map. All of which made him rather embarrassed—about the migration *and* the song.

"The way I heard it," said singer Mack MacLean, "Gordy was in a strong frame of mind to visit New York. Just had to get there. But his business manager said they didn't have the money to make it happen right then. So Gordon wrote 'San Fernando Valley' in, like, twenty minutes. Took it to the publisher, who forwarded him three or four grand, and he was off to New York. That's the kind of guy Gordon was. Somebody said he could write a song while he was eating breakfast."

"Al Jolson was furious I didn't give it to him," Gor said. "But it wasn't right for him at all. It was a nice, light song, and it didn't take any particular talent to sing it. I know Roy Rogers and Gene Autry both sang it; there had to be a hundred records made of the thing, because in those days everybody sang the same songs. And it was kind of scary how the Valley took off right then. I heard it myself in New York. Cab driver asked me where I was from, and he said, 'Soon as I get a couple dollars, I'm goin' out to that San Fernando Valley.' I said, 'Why do you want to go there?' He said, 'Heard this song on the radio.' And the strange thing is that in the lyrics, I never said anything good about the Valley. It could be a sewer. I just said I wanted to go. But people heard the overall effect and *they* wanted to go. I'm sure the Valley would have been developed just the same, but the song didn't hurt it any."

"Artistically," he said, "it was one of the worst songs I ever wrote. Just a rotten song, really terrible. And I thought that at the time. But I didn't notice it so much, because they kept mailing me money. You don't see as clearly when they're mailing you money."

Nobody appreciated that story more than Mandel, who drew a remarkable comparison from his own career. "When I started writing songs, writing with Mercer and Paul Francis Webster, both of them told me, 'Don't ever throw anything away. You don't know what's gonna happen to it.' And it's true. When I did 'M.A.S.H.' with Robert Altman, we had to have something for the Last Supper scene, sort of a dead space when they're walking around dropping things in a casket. Altman thought it would be a great place for a stupid song, and believe me, I wrote the stupidest song I could think of. And it became the theme ["Suicide is Painless"]. It took on a life of its own. It turned out to be my biggest copyright. I would have thrown it away, and the damn thing's been played two million times."

I don't think I heard "San Fernando Valley" until I was in my twenties; the song was never mentioned around the house, nor could a single copy be found. That wasn't my dad's gig, writing novelty records. He was much more inspired by original material, something fresh and different, and that's what he tried to create in his own music. He once told an interviewer that the first time he saw "Oklahoma" on Broadway, he was literally "shaking" from excitement. "It was such a new way to do a musical, to open with one person on stage, instead of a big chorus singing 'Hello, how ya doin,' and then launch into a bunch of great songs, just one after another. It was *so* much better than anything that had ever been around. When I sensed it was going to end, I involuntarily stood up, with the music still going on. Like, 'No! I don't want you to quit.' Then I sat down again. Felt like a dummy."

As the years passed, there was no telling what he might write. In the jazzy, energetic "Tropicana Holiday" he wrote in 1958 for owner Monte Proser at the Tropicana Hotel in Vegas, there's a momentary pause for "I Live Alone," about a lovesick girl singing her heart out. In 1955, he wrote all original material for an album called "Almanac," each of the twelve songs built around a theme for that month of the year. Straying far from the sound his fans and fellow musicians were used to hearing, he threw some big-time changeups with rapturous, bright material, all completely fresh, evocative and innovative. The year starts big, has a dandy spring, moves slowly through the summer humidity, starts to get melancholy around fall and, true to my dad's musical character, becomes terribly somber at the end. After the Sinatra body of work, it's the album I play most often, and I keep waiting for certain songs to be discovered for modern-day use. (Count Basie used the sweet, moody "August Heat" in his live act for a spell.)

Jenkins's most original composition might have been the theme album "Seven Dreams," a complete seven-part show written especially for home enjoyment. Like "Manhattan Tower," the piece has a narrator, soloists and chorus, but it is infinitely wider in scope. The 51-minute album reached the No. 8 slot on *Billboard* in January 1954 and then disappeared, and while there were constant rumors about its being developed into a Broadway show or film, nothing ever happened. The album is nearly fifty years old now, stashed and buried, alive mostly in the memories of senior citizens who thrilled to the piece in their youth. The theme song, recurring throughout the album, is one of the loveliest, most touching melodies he ever wrote.

"That album was a really rare thing for me," he said, "because it was one of the few times where I wrote something without having a commitment to someone. It wasn't a job, it was something I just felt like doing. And I gave it the proper time. Took me two years. They had a terrible time in those days getting it all on the record, and I couldn't get it played. Nobody would play 51 minutes. I got it played once, by the disc jockeys in each town the first time around, but that was about it."

"Seven Dreams" is a dramatic projection of every man's dreams: the fantasies, the flights of fancy, the total confusion, the nightmares. Each episode starts with the loud ringing of an alarm clock, the morning wake-up call, snapping the narrator out of his latest journey. There's a college professor teaching students to fly; a pink houseboat where inhabitants step outside to feed the angels; a caretaker singing, "I'll die among the living, but I live among the dead" (the reference to "a child who died on Christmas Day" is Rowan Jenkins, the promising little brother who died before Gordon was born); and a man in desperate flight, being chased by unknown demons.

The narrator is Bill Lee, who had one of the richest speaking and singing voices of his or any other era, and most of Lee's words hold up splendidly. Stuck in a dreadful cocktail party, he laments, "Modern society's alcoholic refuge for the insecure. As I looked wearily around the room, I felt a cold, gray cloud of boredom settling on me. I got the impression that every dull acquaintance of a lifetime was gathered in that stuffy room. As I started the uneven battle of Man vs. Martini, I saw an old high-school buddy approaching. One of the depressingly cheerful boys."

In a scathing indictment of politicians—something I heard from Gor my entire life around the dinner table—the second dream finds the narrator walking through the cars of a cross-country train when he encounters a blustery candidate and some interested parties.

"Are you for or against the farmers?" someone asks.

"On the contrary," says the politician, "if a foreclosing policy is maintained as to an equitable percent of parity, a munificent bounty should evade the tillers of our soil, negating the marketing aspects of crop rotation, as outlined in form 77B."

"What is your stand on foreign policy?"

"I'm glad you asked me that. I view with alarm the iconoclastic tendency toward isolationistic totalitarianism, promulgated by selfish benefactors solely bent upon stifling the vital accord incumbent upon any vacillation of the vested interests."

The narrator walked on, and the train began to slow down. "As it lumbered to a stop, I stepped off for a breath of middle-western air," said Lee. "As I lit a cigarette, I heard a voice from a shack across the way."

It was my mother's voice. The former Beverly Mahr, now Mrs. Jenkins, was singin' the lonesome, low-down blues, just as she'd done since her teenage years in Oklahoma. The song was called

"Crescent City Blues," and somewhere, Johnny Cash was listening. In 1955, his "Folsom Prison Blues" was a shameless ripoff of my dad's lyrics. The complete song is on the left, with crucial Cash passages alongside:

I hear the train a-comin'	*I hear the train a-comin'*
It's rollin' round the bend	*It's rollin' round the bend*
And I ain't been kissed, lord	*And I ain't seen the sunshine*
Since I don't know when	*Since I don't know when*
The boys in Crescent City	
Don't seem to know I'm here	
That lonesome whistle seems to tell me	
Oooh-oooh, Sue, disappear	
When I was just a baby	*When I was just a baby*
My mama told me, Sue	*My mama told me, Son*
When you're grown up	
I want that you should go and see and do	
But I'm stuck in Crescent City	
Just watchin' life mosey by	
When I hear that whistle blowin'	*When I hear that whistle blowin'*
I hang my head and cry	*I hang my head and cry*
I see the rich folks eatin'	*I bet there's rich folks eatin'*
In that fancy dinin' car	*In a fancy dinin' car*
They're probably havin' pheasant breast	
And eastern caviar	
Now I ain't cryin' envy	
And I ain't cryin' mean	
It's just that they get to see things	
That I've never seen	
If I owned that lonesome whistle	*Well, if they freed me from this prison*
If that railroad train was mine	*If that railroad train was mine*
I bet I'd find a man	*I bet I'd move it on*

A little farther down the line	*A little farther down the line*
Far from Crescent City	*Far from Folsom Prison*
Is where I'd like to stay	*That's where I want to stay*
And I'd let that lonesome whistle	*And I'd let that lonesome whistle*
Blow my blues away.	*Blow my blues away.*

Being Johnny Cash, in all his magnificence, he apparently thought nobody would notice. And for nearly fifteen years, nobody did. But when Cash sang "Folsom Prison Blues" on a national TV show in 1969, people noticed it all over hell. "I'm watching Cash one night, singing this big hit record of his and it's the biggest theft I ever heard," said Bruce Hudson. "It was unbelievable, the guts it took to do that. I called Gordon and said, 'What the hell is this?'" Not to worry. Gordon had already brought it to the attention of his agent, Harold Plant, who promptly filed a lawsuit.

"Shortly before the trial was beginning," Plant told me, "Cash's personal manager asked if we could meet. He wondered if I had any 'material' that could substantiate our claim. They were acting like they didn't know what we were talking about. So I had Gordon make a short tape of his song, and right behind that, Cash's song. And I played it for the guy. Dead silence. He never said another word, except, 'We'll call you back.'"

(Harold told me that under the terms of the settlement, he would not be allowed to disclose anything publicly. I found out years later it amounted to $75,000.)

"Seven Dreams" is not easily capsulized, and I've barely scratched the surface here, but it ends with "The Girl on the Rock," where the narrator encounters a beautiful woman who promises to love and care for him in a land where they will stay forever young—but if he leaves, he can never return. The man sings out his reservations but slowly starts to relent, and in the end he accepts. The dreamer stays in his dreams. The morning alarm rings one last time, this time without a response, and the woman cries out, "Let it ring. Let it ring!"

Much like "Manhattan Tower," the album sailed past a legion of skeptics who couldn't have cared less. But for those who indulged, "Seven Dreams" was a rich experience. I was researching a magazine piece on big-wave surfing in Hawaii when I came across Ricky Grigg, who had gone to my high school (Santa Monica) before earning his fame as both an athlete and oceanographer. To my astonishment, in a 1999 issue of *The Surfer's Path*, he specifically mentioned my father and the album.

"I used to dream of flying—being a bird, or being able to fly— and in 'Seven Dreams' one of the dreams was flying," he said. "The man talked about the liberation and the beauty of it, and it just hit me hard, because I've always believed that once in a while in life, you fly. You have an emotional flight."

Not long thereafter, I sent Grigg a copy of "Seven Dreams," which he had regrettably lost over the years. He wrote back: "Wow! It hit me all over again. Tears, the works. 'Seven Dreams' is hauntingly beautiful, from the magnificence of the angels to the girl on the rock, to the contrarian view of polite society, the mockery of convention, the church, mediocrity, the drudgery of conforming to a life among the dead, and back to the dream of Mary, a land on a distant shore, a true glorification of idealism and romance. In fact, I've never awakened from that seventh dream. Let me thank your father for that. My God, he was way ahead of his time. 'Seven Dreams' is truly precious to me. It affected my life, helping me choose a life in the islands and live the dream."

The "September of My Years" album (with Sinatra) made a huge, Grammy-winning impact on the music business in 1965, but it was hardly representative of my dad's workload. Things slowed to a halt after that, and while he had more than enough money to get by, he yearned for the days when two dozen great singers were readily available. "Who am I going to record with?" he said in July 1977. "There's nobody around of any interest to me. You can't go from Sinatra or Nat Cole to ... who? There are no singers. I'd love to work with Jack Jones, he's a great singer, but nobody will hire him. I would only go in a legitimate vein. I wouldn't go with any electronic gear or synthesizers. I don't understand them, and I'm not fond of the results. I know it's an old-fashioned view, but it always struck me as a cop-out for people who couldn't write a good enough melody for a legitimate instrument. They were forced to make it louder, electrify it, and commercialize on it. That's always been against my policy.

"I'm only retired because nobody calls that I'm interested in working with. Somebody asked me to work with Vicki Carr. Well, I can't do anything for Vicki Carr. There's nothing I can do to further her. She's not good enough. After you've worked with Judy and Frank and Nat, it's awfully hard to get your interest up for Vicki Carr. Streisand, I'd love to work with. She wrote me a letter a long time ago and said she'd love to do it. It never happened, for some reason. They always say how tough she is to work with—well, leave me at her [laughter]. That doesn't bother me. I worked with Sinatra and Al Jolson and Bea Lillie, and they don't get any tougher than that."

When it came to critics of rock 'n' roll, Gor was a hard-liner for the ages. He couldn't stand more than three or four bars at a time, and true to his museum-piece reputation, he found no exceptions. I had quite a few entries in my collection but *never* let my dad hear any samples. There was no point to it. He called the Beatles "the greatest put-on of all time" and said, "Kids just buy what they hear. If they hear junk, they buy junk. I heard a little girl come into a record store and ask for the No. 1 record. She didn't even care what it was. There's nothin' I can do to compete with that. That's another world entirely."

A big problem, he said in the 1978 interview with Chuck Cecil, was that "you need editors. If I was ever in doubt about a word or a phrase, I'd ask Beverly and she'd tell me; she didn't hold back. That's the trouble in the business today, there are no editors. Some kid writes a song, and nobody's around to tell him it's awful. He just goes ahead and makes the record. And if his last record was a hit, nobody's gonna mention that it's a bad song. There's nobody to set a level of anything. I don't object to people making money, but I hate to see kids coming up where that's their primary aim—or to be seen with their shirt off, you know, to attract the girls and get laid later on.

"I've had a bunch of kids come down to the studio, and I'm not gonna tell 'em they're lousy songwriters. They're eighteen years old, and I'm a hundred to them. But they know I did pretty well, and they're sort of curious as to what I think. So I don't say anything. I just look at 'em. And a whole bunch of 'em said the same thing: 'Well, it's not any worse than the Beatles.' And to me, that's a terrible thing to say. I wouldn't be caught dead saying my song wasn't any worse than something. They make a lot of money real fast, but through the years, when that particular act dies out, they have no place to go. They can't play their instruments well enough to play in my band or Percy Faith's band. They get old, they're not cute any more, and they're not musicians. You hand 'em a real good song, and they don't know those chords, and they're not interested in knowing 'em, because they're making a lot of money with the three that they do know.

"I'm not sure a great song like 'Night and Day' would even get recorded today, because the people that run the record companies are idiots. All they want is the latest copy of the latest rock and roll hit. A song that good . . . I doubt if they'd hear it all the way through. They'd stop in the middle and say, 'What else you got?'"

Cecil: "I hope you don't mind if I use this stuff on the air, Gordon.

A lot of people are afraid they're going to offend someone."

"I hope I have," Gor said. "I hope I've offended all the people who have made rotten records, all the people who give false impressions. I'd be tickled to death to offend them. See, you can't live forever in a world of Andy Warhol and Jacqueline Susann, junk writers. There have to be some talented people coming through the ranks someplace. In years past, people like Harold Arlen, Richard Rodgers, Cole Porter, Jerome Kern didn't write the same kind of songs as each other. Nobody would intentionally copy anyone else, whereas today, that's all that goes on. You have that kind of hit record for a while until somebody has another kind of hit. In those days, you wouldn't be caught dead copying anybody, because people would tell you to your face. It was no good, against the rules."

My father's rule was that no new music would be played in his studio unless it met his own high standards of competence—so damn little was played. That was fine with him. He and my mother spent hours listening to opera, the symphony and especially old blues records, such a big part of their upbringing. One day, they got an idea: Why not round up some of the great Dixieland players and have them back up Beverly on an album of blues songs? The result was a self-produced album called "My Wife the Blues Singer," featuring a cast of legends: Matty Matlock on clarinet, Walt Yoder on bass, Ray Sherman (one of Woody Herman's original guys) on piano, Al Hendrickson on guitar, Nick Fatool on drums, Moe Schneider on trombone and the electrifying Eddie Miller on tenor sax. "All those cats were fine, fine blues boys," said Mike Dutton, who produced some of Gor's NBC radio material in the Forties. "And they played great for Beverly."

Gor sketched out some arrangements, but mostly they were sessions of spontaneity, letting the boys play as they felt. They knew the numbers by heart, the likes of "It's A Low-Down Dirty Shame" and Sonny Boy Williamson's "Western Union Man," and Gor contributed a new one he'd just written, an inspired little number called "Daylight Savings Blues." A few passages:

Well, say, this here ol' daylight savins
Has really got me in a spin
Because the way my man's savin' daylight
Is a natural sin
He leaves the house in daylight
And it's daylight when he comes in.

He says he's savin' daylight
That's why he sleeps all day
He may be storin' up vim and vigor
But precious little comes my way

Yeah, this here ol' daylight savins
Can drive a poor girl mad
If they'd only start savin' nighttime
I'd see a little more o' dad.

It seemed that Gor could compose in any vein, any musical genre, and make it truly authentic. In 1968, when the rock era swirled in tandem with marijuana and kids were tripping out to Hendrix and the Jefferson Airplane, Gor went into the studio for "Soul of a People," his all-instrumental arrangements of traditional Jewish melodies. It was an expensive, first-class project with a huge fiddle section full of wonderful players, and a highly moving experience for everyone involved. Unbeknownst to the orchestra, Gor played a little trick just prior to the recording.

"You get a hundred fiddle players, and ninety-nine of 'em are Jewish," said bass player Mike Rubin. "They've known these songs since they were kids, but there was this one that a few guys had trouble remembering. Eventually, they all agreed they'd heard it.

'Oh, yeah, I remember my mother singing that.' Or, 'Sure, I know that one.' Turned out they were all wrong. Gordon needed one extra tune and he had composed that thing himself, like two weeks before."

The most discouraging part of my research was the simple passage of time, more than ten years, knowing that many of my father's golden-years admirers were dying: the ones who bought his hit records on Decca in the 1950s, the "Manhattan Tower" fans, the ones who embraced his albums of pure romance—all-instrumental collections with titles like "Stolen Hours" and "Night Dreams." It's nice to think that so many people embellished special nights with his music in the background, but for the most part, those days are long gone.

"My God, you wanna talk about romance?" Alan King told me. "How about the population explosion? This is a guy responsible for that. He was great for what we used to call crotch dancing. You know how many people got laid to your father's music?"

(So let's see: He ruined the music business with the Weavers, he almost single-handedly caused a rush of immigration to the San Fernando Valley, and he was a big part of the population boom. Kind of an interesting triple crown he put together.)

Still, there are some traditional hearts out there. There's no need to make a big deal out of his fan letters, but one of them, from a budding songwriter named Tom Murray, really stood out:

"Sometimes, when I am alone, listening to your music, the sheer beauty of it makes me feel such emotion that I weep and feel the pain of such overwhelming beauty. You may laugh and think me a very foolish person, but I will risk that to tell you I admire you greatly. Through your music I have come to know you very well. I think of you every day, for your music comes into my mind each day. It will live forever, there is no doubt of that. And perhaps, your greatest recognition is yet to come. I sit here listening, spellbound, the violins pleading, cutting to the very heart, evoking such emotion, knowing that a great artist has made his message very clear."

If you put together a list of Jenkins's best songs—and somebody had to do it, since it would never occur to him—it would go something like this:

P.S. I Love You
Blue Prelude
Goodbye
Blue Evening
You Have Taken My Heart
Homesick, That's All
This Is All I Ask
Married I Can Always Get
New York's My Home
The Red Balloon
That's All There Is
When a Woman Loves a Man
I Live Alone
But I Loved Her
I Thought About Marie

Armed with that list, I went to see Sammy Cahn. I wanted to know what one of the all-time great lyricists thought of Gordon Jenkins, and this would be a departure from my countless forays into San Fernando Valley suburbia to interview his old partners in the band and chorus. Sammy Cahn lived on stately Canon Road in the heart of Beverly Hills. Walking down the street, through a sea of mansions, I saw two dozen Japanese tourists on one side of the road and an immense black woman, obviously someone's maid, making her way to work on the other side. It was 1988. Mr. Cahn, then seventy-five, had about five years to live. The walls of his office were lined with Oscars, commendations, awards and photos. Sammy with Peter Lawford, Sammy with Sinatra, Sammy with Aristotle and Zeus. This is the man who wrote "I Should Care," "It's Magic," "Love and Marriage," "All the Way," "High Hopes," "The Second Time Around"—hell, he wrote everything. Every single song, Sammy Cahn wrote. It was quite a privilege to be there.

"I thought Gordon was a very rare talent, and he did it with both words and music," said Mr. Cahn, "and when he thought he needed some words, he went to the best guys. If he didn't think he could do it, he was smart enough to know that Johnny Mercer could.

"It's a curious thing about songwriting. If you spend a lifetime writing songs, and at the end of that lifetime you can point to six songs people will know [snapping his fingers], you have done an incredibly good job. Well, why don't we just look, shall we? Let's look in the book of Who Wrote What."

That was Cahn's title—I like his better—for a comprehensive history of popular songs and writers. "I've got six right here," he said, perusing the Jenkins section. "'Goodbye,' 'P.S. I Love You' and 'Blue Prelude,' no question. 'This Is All I Ask,' absolutely. All of 'Manhattan Tower,' that was really something people talked about, and in particular 'Married I Can Always Get'—terrific song. And everyone knows 'San Fernando Valley.' So that's six right there. Listen, I had the pleasure [as president of the organization] of inducting him into the Songwriters Hall of Fame. It gave me great personal satisfaction to do that.

"It sounds clichéd and trite, but he was one of the nice, nice men. To me, those were the great men, standing in front of an orchestra and painting that sound. They're beyond my ... I'm in awe of them. Gordon Jenkins, my God, he was very special. I don't say this self-servingly, but anyone who's been around Sinatra, there's a distinction. It's a very important mark. Wherever you go in the world, where ladies and gentlemen meet in black ties and gowns, those are the sounds you will hear. I have that theory. Therefore you'll hear Gordon, and Sammy Cahn, all the people whose lives have been most touched by Sinatra. It's the single most incredible career in all of show business."

I asked Cahn who he thought would be in Gor's class as a multiple-threat musician. "There's only one guy, Johnny Green," he said. "Would you like to talk to him? He's right over on Bedford Drive. Let's call him."

Within two or three minutes, it was done. I could hear Cahn say, "I'll send him over," to end the conversation. "There you go," he told me. "Two for the price of one."

The scene could not have been more different. Cahn was vital and energetic, looking as if he could have sat down at the piano and cranked out a gem right on the spot. Green, about to turn eighty, was emaciated, withered, looking spent and forlorn after months of serious respiratory problems. He had less than a year to live. Surely the accolades were somewhere, the Oscars he won for his collaborations on "An American in Paris," "West Side Story," and "Oliver," maybe some choice mementos from all those years of songwriting and conducting. But I was shown into a small, mostly empty room, where Green sat alone.

About the time I started wondering to myself, "Just how long has this cat been around?" he said, "I first came into prominence when I played for the engagement reception of Mary Todd and Abraham Lincoln," and there wasn't a hint of levity in his face. But the mention of Gordon Jenkins—anything that brought his own career into focus, I discovered—brought him to life. I opened with the four-threat thing and let him roll.

"There aren't too many. I was one. Your father, of course. George Gershwin was another, and Harold Arlen, to some extent. Johnny Mercer in a different way, because he was a singer when he first came up, with the Whiteman band. There weren't too many of us. Today, Hank Mancini. Big, big man. Big talent. Orchestrates and arranges brilliantly, conducts adequately, and is a hell of a composer. There's also Marvin Hamlisch. Arranging? [Shrugs] Ipsy-pipsy. But a very effective writer-performer-pianist. And Billy May: brilliant arranger, very good trumpet player. As my late grandmother used to say, comparisons are odious. Gordon Jenkins and the guys I've been mentioning are the same kind of fellas.

"If I wanted to sound like Noel Coward," he went on, "I would say there was great 'civility' between Gordon and myself. We were never close friends, which I regretted, and we were very competitive. People would say, 'What do you think of Johnny Green?' And you'd hear, 'Well, he's very talented, but he's no Gordon Jenkins.' Or, 'Johnny Green, he isn't.' And when that's going on, it's hard to be friendly. People were constantly comparing us. We were both first-rate arrangers and wrote beautifully for the orchestra; I mean no conceit. Hank Mancini is of that same cloth today, while [Burt] Bacharach and Hamlisch are not.

"I think Gordon wished sometimes that he had received more serious acclaim than he did. In that regard I think he may have been somewhat envious of me, in extended forms. [Not true: Near the end, at a time when he was unable to speak, my father wrote on a notepad, "I am probably one of the few men alive who never envied anyone—ever."] Because I was so frequently compared with George, as the younger Gershwin in the making, and that didn't happen with your father. But they were damn effective pieces that he wrote —'Seven Dreams,' the extended works—and mighty good to listen to."

As for style, "With a Gordon Jenkins record, nobody had to tell you or show you the label. You knew who it was. He had an approach to string writing that, while not as immediately accessible as David Rose's, was highly distinctive. I think the guy most influenced by your dad's string writing was Nelson Riddle, which I don't think you'll hear many people say. And he had a very special approach to swing.

When he swung melody, you could say, 'That's Gordon Jenkins.'

"Emotion? Oh, God, yes. He was a sentimental slob. I used to say, any time they're looking for a sentimental slob, if they can't get you, they're gonna get me. Much more than Nelson."

Green paused and took some long, difficult breaths. "I'm glad you didn't ask me about certain people," he said, "because I'd cut 'em at the knees and the neck. Amateurs wearing professional suits. I loathe them."

"What do you think of the business today?" I asked.

"In a word?" he said.

"Sure."

He made the sound of an especially crisp fart.

The conversation strayed away from Jenkins at this point, which was entirely Green's doing, and it was wonderful. "It's great to be innovative in music and to have something to *say* with it," he said. "That's the thing. Cole Porter never went near a piano until he had a melodic line to play. I remember having lunch with Cole, thousands of years ago at the Waldorf Towers. I adored him. I idolized him. And I was assigned to arrange some songs from 'Jubilee.' And I said, 'Cole, I'd like to come and hear the composer play me the songs.'

"He mentioned that he had picked me specifically for the task, and he said, 'Here's where I think I'm gonna lose you. There's no verse, no chorus, just one unit, and it's eighty-four bars long.' I said, 'Why should you lose me?' He said, 'Well, everybody's gonna say I'm crazy.' And I said, 'Some idiot publishers, maybe, but no. Everybody isn't. Don't change a note.'

"So he sat down at the piano. And he played, *Da-da-da-dee . . . da-da-dummm. . . .* 'Begin the Beguine.' I cried then, and I cry now. One hundred percent diatonic. One thousand percent original. And one million percent beautiful. Oh, the whole concept of that lyric. The deep, deep analysis of the human psyche in that lyric. No, I said, don't let them. Make them play. See that *life?* The human inability to make up one's mind, in eighty-four bars? No wonder the guy's immortal."

A stunning, fortyish blonde woman, Johnny's wife, walked in and reminded him that it was time for lunch.

"You heard what she said," he told me. "That I have to have some lunch. And I am not well. You gonna make me vomit before I have lunch?"

I answered his thin smile with one of my own.

"All right, enough of you," he said. "Go. God bless you."

I was left with a final glimpse of a man whose music had thrilled Americans for decades on end, a very sick man whose body was saying farewell as his mind played on. It was a troubling sight, one I knew a little too well.

Chapter 15

All Is Lost, or Not

I T's A CRAZY WIND THAT BLOWS through Southern California in autumn, bone dry and Caribbean warm. It's a time for shorts, sunglasses and halter tops, while the rest of the country shivers, and everything's fine until it isn't. The winds blow hard out of the mountains, carrying with them an arsonist's perversion. He bides his time until it really starts to howl, and then he strikes, armed with a book of matches, an erection and a grudge. One flick of the wrist, and he sets the whole world on fire.

We survived the big one in 1956, despite strong rumors to the contrary. It was Christmas night, and the fire rushed over the Malibu hills with satanic intent. I was eight years old, dreaming of cookies and elves and sparkling new bicycles when I awoke to shouting and a bright-orange sky. The winds were so fierce, great clumps of fire passed over our heads like bullets. The smoke was blinding, the heat a punishing assault on the eyes and face, and as half-dressed people snatched their most precious belongings, leaving fresh Christmas gifts behind, there was a scattershot stampede of deer, coyotes, rabbits and horses fleeing the mountains for sea level.

Our evacuation led us some forty miles to the San Fernando Valley, where we camped out at my uncle's house. The following morning, after a full day of brushfires that blackened some eight thousand acres, we read in a local newspaper that "the beachfront home of bandleader Gordon Jenkins" was among those destroyed.

Imagine our surprise when we drove back to the beach and found it still standing.

That little miracle bought us twenty-two years. We had some scares and evacuations, but always with the belief that the ocean would somehow save us. Then came the fearsome blaze of October 23, 1978, a crisis that did not discriminate. I was watching network-news footage from my home in Northern California when the phone call came from Jerry Pritchett, one of our neighbors on Broad Beach Road and a trusted family friend.

"Your parents are OK," he told me. "The house didn't make it."

All investigations pointed to an arsonist in Agoura, some twelve miles inland. He casually lit the match in mid-morning and within an hour, a hundred acres were in flames. The winds were in vintage form, all hot and bothered, and in the words of the L.A. County Fire Inspector, "It moved at such a tremendous rate of speed, toward the ocean, it was unbelievable." Nearly two hundred Malibu houses went down, including Neil Young's place on Sea Level Drive and the two oldest, most tradition-rich establishments on Broad Beach: ours and Lucien Ballard's, the stylish three-story mansion near Trancas Point.

I got to the scene about two days later, numb and in complete denial. The news was so impossibly bad, it felt somehow unreal. As I approached our driveway, everything seemed in order. The houses on either side of us were unblemished—not even the hint of trouble. My dad's studio had been miraculously spared, along with the garage, and our thick pine trees and bougainvillea obscured the horror. It wasn't until I opened our streetside gate that I saw the lonesome brick chimney—all that remained of our cherished Cape Cod house. It seemed important to sift through the ashes, to find some remnant of the last thirty years, perhaps to bring a smile or two. But I couldn't get past the books. Some of them hadn't burned all the way through and the pages, while blackened and brittle, were partially readable. My heart broke right in two.

There's always the maddening notion that the place could have been saved. With a little more attention from the L.A. County Fire Department, all we needed was one heroic fellow with a power hose. But all of Malibu was chaos that day; history showed that oceanfront homes were somewhere down the priority list. And it didn't take much, just a windswept ball of flame latching onto a dry, gray-shingled home that couldn't have been more vulnerable. They say it took less than a half-hour to go down.

We forever savored the fact that Gor's career had, in essence, been preserved. The studio housed all of his instruments, sheet music and recording equipment, along with some awards and gold records that had survived his indifference. But so much was gone: paintings, photographs, countless reels of edited 16-millimeter home movies, the little downstairs bedroom where I had grown up, high-school yearbooks, thousands of baseball cards from the Fifties and Sixties (scary to think what they'd be worth today), the picture windows, the sunporch.

A preposterous scene unfolded on the day after that fire, matching our fate with the intensely blind ignorance of people in a crisis. As Gordon and Beverly made the left turn off Highway 1, preparing to face the wreckage, they were stopped by a California Highway Patrolman.

"Sorry, sir, only residents can pass this point," he said.

"I am a resident," said Gor. "Or, at least, I was. My house burned to the ground."

The cop checked his license, then waved them through with a cheery "Have a nice day."

Have a *what?*

That story got a lot of mileage—all the way back to New York, where Thomas Middleton based an entire *Saturday Review* article on that loathsome, ubiquitous phrase. As he wrote, "The Jenkinses got about two hundred feet down the road before the 'have a nice day' sank all the way in and their gales of laughter burst out. Surely, no other phrase could have made them laugh all the way to the ashes of their home. That mindless pleasantry brightened a dark day."

Yeah, "Have a nice day," my ass. There ought to be a jail sentence for a crack like that. But anger wasn't the appropriate reaction in our family, nor was bitterness or uncontrollable sobbing. My father simply wouldn't allow it. If you couldn't keep your head up after October 23, 1978, he didn't want you around. One of the many casualties that day was his massive, well-stocked workshop, and that was particularly troubling news for Scott Pritchett, the younger brother of my best friend, Jack. Scott was a budding carpenter and had a special relationship with Gor inside that shop.

"I loved taking things apart and putting them together," Scott told me later. "Instead of spending time with my friends, I'd go down to Gor's shop. It was like Mecca. I thought to myself, 'He's got everything here. The guy's a wizard.' He had a sign that read, 'Quiet please, a genius is working' [laughter], and he said to me once, 'The shop is a man's retreat. And never let it be clean.'

"On the day of the fire, I was up in Ojai on a remodeling job, the first day I'd ever worked out of Malibu," Scott said. "I walked out and the whole sky was black. I called Dad's office, and whoever picked up the phone, I don't know. All I heard was, 'Oh my God, it's coming over the highway!' and then the line went dead.

"By the next day, I was delirious. I'd been up twenty hours, driving all over Malibu, barfing, not eating, heat burns on my face. I finally got down to your place to face the truth of it all, and I stumbled on Gor, just walking around the ruins. I had no idea what to say to him. I just mumbled something like, 'God, I'm so sorry.'

"And do you know what he said? 'Well, at least I don't have to re-pipe.' And we both started laughing like crazy. That was Gor. That's the line I'll remember the rest of my life."

It wasn't long before heavy depression set in. Each day brought a stiffer realization that virtually everything was gone. My parents took a rental home about a mile down the road on Broad Beach, but when the so-called "friend" raised their rent by a full $1,000 per month, they bailed out to Woodland Hills—not terribly far inland, but a veritable Nebraska once you've lived on the beach. They struggled mightily with the notion of rebuilding, often giving up hope; even a handsome insurance payment offered little relief. That's about the time Frank Sinatra stepped in, sending a check for $25,000 without the slightest provocation from anyone in the family. ("Yeah, well, listen," he told me, "you gotta be there for your buddies. Otherwise you're not a buddy.") That was a stroke of generosity, friendship and musical connection, a pure lightning bolt of revival. By the summer of 1981, after a maze of work permits and coastal commissions and nearly three years after the fire, we had a new, two-story house on our Broad Beach lot.

It was a lovely place, fully modern but in step with the traditional beach-house feel we'd enjoyed for so many years. And for the rest of my parents' lives, it housed a living hell. I had the luxury of some lengthy summertime visits with my wife, Martha, including some especially precious times with our newborn daughter, Molly, in the late Nineties. But I don't really remember the house that way. I remember the scent of tragedy, a procession of full-time nurses, a body in decline and a once-sharp mind deteriorating into vacancy. It was the place where I watched my parents die, slowly and with no chance of recovery.

It started in the most innocent way: an odd slurring of my father's speech. He had lost control of his tongue, somehow, and found it difficult to swallow. "What the hell's wrong with Gordon?" one of his friends asked another. "I talked to him around eight this morning, and he sounded like he was drunk."

That's how it begins with Lou Gehrig's disease, or Amyotrophic

Lateral Sclerosis (ALS)—something curiously minor: numbness in a finger, perhaps some twitching in the forearm, ailments you might associate with arthritis or fatigue. Whatever it might be, the process has begun, irrevocably. One by one, each of the body's muscles becomes useless, felled by the atrophy of motor-neuron degeneration. The disease generally strikes the aged, it comes without pain or brain damage, and it runs its course within two or three years. (David Niven, Rita Hayworth, Arlene Francis, E.B. White, Charlie Mingus and Catfish Hunter all died from it.) By the end, the ALS victim is a lifeless blob, fully paralyzed with his intelligence completely intact. What a strange, perverse way to go. Friends and family force their way into upbeat moods as they watch it happen, knowing there isn't a damn thing anyone can do.

Before the diagnosis, we figured it was just a really bad break, something that would naturally repair itself in time. There were difficulties on the set of "The First Deadly Sin," the 1980 Sinatra film for which Gor wrote the soundtrack; musicians had a hard time understanding him and couldn't figure out what was wrong. But in typical Jenkins family fashion, the whole thing was worth a good laugh or two.

"One night we were all at dinner," said Floyd Huddleston, "I think it was Nick Fatool and Sarge Weiss, my wife and I, Gordon and Beverly, and it was right about the time he started having trouble talking. Sarge said something about how great Gordy looked. And Bev said, 'Oh, yeah, he's in great shape. Only trouble is, he don't talk worth a shit.' And Gordon just fell down. He started laughing so hard, he had to get up and leave the table."

In my mother's case, the curse was Alzheimer's, an ailment quite difficult to trace or diagnose. It eventually took her down in December 1996, but Marguerite Stevens felt that in an undeniable way, the fire had left her vulnerable. "I really think that was the beginning of it all," she said. "It affected Beverly more than anybody knew.

She was the type of person where everything was always OK, and she wanted it to be that way with everybody, but that fire really broke her. Because she lost absolutely everything. She had her albums and her piano in the sunporch, and of course, all of her clothes and belongings in the other rooms. The first time I saw her after the fire, she was upstairs in their rented place, all curled up; I'd never seen her that way. Finally she turned to me and said, 'OK, get in the car, girl, I want to show you something.' And she took me down to the old house. We sat there on the studio steps, just staring at the rubble. I said, 'Beverly, I don't think I can look at this.' She said, 'Well, I have to look at it, and so can you.' So we sat there and had a little cry. 'I just hate the house we're in,' she said. She was completely devastated."

Not long after my mother's death, I came across some memoirs she'd written in the first week of November 1978, only days after the fire. She entitled the entry "Death of a Romantic," and at the very end she wrote, "All my life, I loved to dance to records. Someone once told me that when I stopped doing that, I'd be dead.

"I haven't danced in November."

As a little kid, you never dream of your house burning down or other catastrophes, like your parents getting in a terrible auto wreck. You figure those things happen to other people. But this was a whole new era for my family—after what my father called "a sixty-eight-year run of unblemished good luck"—and I was about to get another dagger to the throat. I was spending the night at Jack Pritchett's place in November 1981 when the phone rang at about 3 a.m.

That's the worst kind of call. Nothing can be good at that hour. It was someone from the police department, telling us that Mr. and Mrs. Gordon Jenkins had been seriously injured in a car crash, and we could find both of them in the Intensive Care Unit of Woodland Hills Hospital.

I couldn't have been in better company. Jack's one of those high-focus, get-it-done types, a kid who was both a quarterback and Student Body President in high school, a mantle of leadership he wears to this day. With Jack at the wheel, I was able to tremble and agonize on my own good time. I felt stronger, better equipped to deal with what loomed as the most terrifying experience imaginable.

The news turned out to be even worse than we'd heard. My uncle, Pete Barnum, had been in the car with his wife, Julia, Beverly's sister and singing partner in the old New York radio days. Both in their seventies, they had driven through hours of heavy rainstorms to get to Southern California from their home in Camano Island, Washington, an irritating and exhausting trip that made them wonder if the whole thing was worthwhile. But they'd all had a nice evening at the San Fernando Valley home of Bob Scott and his delightful wife, Gitchy, yet another standout from that Kay Thompson vocal chorus in the late 1930s.

There was a thick fog in the Malibu hills as they drove home that night, my dad at the wheel, Pete in the passenger seat, the two women in back. They were crawling along in a red Honda Accord on Kanan Road, a new and decidedly dangerous road connecting Malibu with the Valley. A series of mountain tunnels was only partially completed at the time, forcing drivers into one-lane, oncoming-traffic situations instead of separate passages for each direction.

The tunnel gave my dad a bit of respite, a chance to drive at normal speed, but he wasn't counting on Michael LaJoie, a raging idiot heading his way. The twenty-seven-year-old LaJoie had a brand-new Porsche and he was trying to impress his girlfriend with some fancy driving in the fog. There's a fairly sharp turn heading into the tunnel from the west (another bit of poor planning), and LaJoie couldn't handle it. The exact path of his car was difficult to determine, but it had spun 180 degrees and was traveling backwards, at some 30 mph, when it entered the tunnel. My father was trapped; nowhere to run. The passenger side of the Porsche slammed into the Honda with a sickening crash. And then there was silence.

I was visited months later by a twenty-six-year-old Malibu surfer, Kirby Cottler, who had been the first driver on the scene. He'd been hesitant to contact me but felt I should know. He described a man walking aimlessly about the tunnel, dazed and bleeding profusely from the face: my father. He saw Pete Barnum, a massive figure of some three hundred pounds, lying dead on the street. The sisters were still in the car, badly injured and unable to move. Cottler described the scene so vividly, I suddenly had a riveting mental picture—one I'll never be able to shake.

I found it discouraging that the Barnums' story got so little play. Pete was one of the underground gems of Hollywood, an award-winning writer and producer on (among other projects) the Stan Freberg show that so brilliantly displayed the talents of Daws Butler, Peter Leeds, June Foray, bandleader Billy May and Freberg himself; many have called it the greatest comedy show ever produced on radio. As for Julia, that night haunted her physically and emotionally until her death in 1998. The entire right side of her body was crushed by the impact, and at her age she was hardly equipped to regain her strength. She moved slowly, reluctantly, and there was bitterness in her conversation. I always got the terrible feeling she was just playing out the string.

When Jack and I arrived at the hospital, there was a man shifting nervously about the waiting room. We walked quickly past and never saw him again, but we later learned it was LaJoie, a good-time guy who had just put his girlfriend and my parents in the hospital (Clare Smurda had serious injuries but, as far as we know, recovered). Big Mike couldn't have been more spry, of course; not a single bruise or scratch. He was later charged with vehicular manslaughter, but the whole episode had a frightening absence of justice.

We sort of tiptoed into ICU, fearing the worst. And there they were, Beverly and Gordon, propped back at a 45-degree angle, both of them just covered in bandages. My father had collapsed lungs, a badly broken jaw and a number of cuts and bruises. My mother was banged up everywhere, but primarily she had absorbed a brutal concussion, a blow that transformed her into a decidedly different person for the rest of her life: distant, troubled, forgetful, not so quick to smile. "Everyone always said that Beverly was the only survivor who came out OK from that accident," said Marguerite Stevens. "Well, she was like a little crushed bird. She was more psychologically damaged than any of 'em. She would fake things and pretend everything was OK, but I knew it wasn't."

For my father, that awful morning triggered a two-and-a-half-year run that defined the human spirit at its very best. He already had ALS, adding now a shattered jaw, and by the time they unwired it six weeks later, his failing tongue was completely dead. He never spoke another word. But you weren't hearing any sad stories from Gordon. Not from the start. When I walked into that room, shattered beyond words, I saw a little gleam in his eye. It was a look that suggested, "Where are the dancing girls?" or "I've got OJ if you've got the vodka." You could save your pity for Gordon Jenkins, forever.

Without the power of speech, he began writing, relentlessly. The forever-quiet man couldn't wait to tell people how he was feeling, about anything. He had his pen and his yellow legal pads, and those became the tools of his existence, a way to make himself and everyone else feel better. "After they got him home, I think I was the first person Beverly allowed in to see him," said Milt Gabler, Gor's old partner from the hit-making days at Decca Records. "He didn't want to be seen in bed, so they put him on a couch and propped him up with pillows. I was intending to give him some sort of pep talk, but I didn't have to. He was writing stuff that had me laughing out loud. So sad ... my God, what can happen to a great man."

For Sinatra, who had only recently completed the "Trilogy" project with my father, Billy May and Don Costa, it was a time of great regret. He had always been good about mentioning Gor or Nelson Riddle or whoever did the best arrangements for his concert material; now he was putting in special words for Jenkins, resting quite uncomfortably after the accident. "Frank has been great through all of my recent problems," Gor wrote on one of his legal-pad specials. "Calls all the time. You will hear a lot of people rap him, but I won't be one of them."

About a year after the accident, the Sinatra office sent me a typewritten letter Gor had written. It began with an enthusiastic "Francis Albert!!!" and read, in part, "I heard from Clark Dennis, who saw one of your shows, and he said you were most kind in your references to me. In our business, a kind word from you is more important than the front page of *The New York Times*.

"So there I was in the hospital, weighing a snappy 122, tubes all over the place and a cock-catheter to pee through. And I thought, what the hell, I might not make it too long, the way things are going. I've had a great life, maybe the greatest. If I'm taken out of the game now, so what? I wrote the introduction to 'Laura.'

"It's all behind me, thank the Lord, and we finally got a settlement [some $175,000] from the cat who hit me. He was tried for manslaughter, given a long probation and a light sentence, but I never felt the bitterness that the rest of the family did. I really don't feel that he had much to do with it. I've always been a fatalist, and I believe that when it's your turn, they stop by and get you.

"When I was seventeen, I had a head-on collision in which seven people were cut up pretty good, and they wouldn't even let me look at the car, it was such a mess. I had maybe a skinned knee . . . it just wasn't my turn. Vincente Minnelli's secretary was looking for me in New York, in 1936, and called a saloon. The thing was, I had never been in that bar before in my life. Something told me where to go, and told her where to call. I got my first conducting job as a result.

"To say that I should get a heavier car [than a Honda] is to look forward to more trouble; that's living in fear. You might as well say, 'Don't go over to the Scotts' place for dinner again, you might crash on the way home.' I don't know what I'll buy, but big or small, I'll be tootling along Kanan Road, same as before, with no fear."

He closed the letter: "It's nice that you're concerned about me. I like that part." And in typical Gor fashion, he attached a little bonus at the end:

"Ethnic joke: A Czechoslovakian went to the eye doctor.

"Doc: Can you read the bottom line?

"Czech: What do you mean, read it—I *know* him."

There were elements of mercy to it all. Gor was able to walk, and use his hands, until the final weeks of his life. He could write, arrange, play the piano and work the recording equipment in a studio/control room he had cleverly built inside the new house. But he became almost comically disabled as some really crucial body parts took leave. At one point he had eight tubes burrowing into his body for food, medication and nourishment: one each in his nose, mouth, stomach, arm and throat, two in his lungs, "and one down below," he wrote, "for simple toidy." He had spectacularly messy accidents with his bowel movements—completely beyond his control, after all—and for a man who savored those meat-and-potato feasts, there was no authentic food. Ever. Just 79,000 cans of something called Sustacal, sent into his body through tubes.

It seemed that our house had become the province of nurses, and most of our friends were terribly reluctant to come visit. Invariably, they'd start up a conversation with Beverly while Gor sat there in silence, grinning at the absurdity of it all, waiting to weigh in with a written comment. "The timing is worse than a bad comedian," he wrote. "By the time people read what I say, they've moved on to something else." But some of his notes became legendary. I didn't realize it at the time, but people kept them like souvenirs—

an especially fine development after he'd passed away, because they came back my way.

A few examples:

"I never told you—back in 1977 I went to a fortune teller. She looked into the crystal ball and said, 'Your house is going to burn down, your tongue will go bad, preventing you from eating or talking, you will be hit by a car and spend most of a year flat on your back, and you will wear a brace around your neck.' I said, 'You're full of shit,' and left."

"I was signing albums once in a record store, and a gorgeous, stacked fifteen-year-old said, 'How 'bout a kiss instead?' I said, 'Honey, I can't kiss you in front of all these people.' Said she, 'There's a room in the back.'"

"I can handle not talking, not swallowing, and dying, but diarrhea is really the shits."

"When I was still in the hospital, my son Bruce was walking me around. Some guy was staring at me, my tubes and all, really annoying, and Bruce said, 'Why don't you go over and speak to him?' I went right over and said, 'Fuck you.' He said, 'I'm fine. How are you feeling?' That's when I knew I had a speech problem."

(After learning that Bruce Hudson was planning a European vacation) "It saddens me that you would rather go to Italy than listen to me talk."

"I have a wonderful nurse, Berniece, and it turns out her twenty-year-old daughter is a giant fan of mine. When she, her mother, Beverly and the doctor were all in the room, I was dying to get up, make a slow pirouette and say, 'Look, everybody, I have shitted in my pants.' Of course, not being able to talk might take some edge off the gag."

(To Milt Gabler) "Here's a way you can help me. I've been looking for 'Evil Man Blues' by Hot Lips Page, with a great vocal by Teddy Bunn. Also, 'Mean Old Bed Bug Blues' by Billy Banks. I've been looking for these records for thirty years."

"Did you know that Dick Eckels's daughter is a reed player, too? The first date she played, he sent me a note: 'I'm too nervous to come down, but don't worry about her. She's as ready as a drunk in the Hi-Ho Motel.'"

(Waiting impatiently for a lab technician to take a blood sample) "I lose my getaway car in three minutes, so if you'll just show me where the money is, I'll be on my way."

"A nurse came by and asked me, 'What's in your mouth?' I pointed to a box of Kleenex and she said, 'Is there something wrong with you?' This has to be one of the top three stupid questions ever asked in a hospital room. I said, 'No, they're delicious—especially with sauerkraut.' The poor girl didn't know whether to shave or go east."

(When a nurse asked if he'd 'made peace with your God yet'): "I didn't know we were fightin'."

"The doctors all say no one has beat ALS. I gaze dreamily out the window and murmur, 'Until now.' I have no intention of losing to a disease I can't even spell. I have decided not to die, and you will get a detailed letter explaining why."

He wrote that last one to Bruce Hudson, and he delivered splendidly. Everyone kept marveling at how he never complained; that's because he had no intention of losing. I relayed the following letter to Sinatra in the months leading up to our interview, and he told me, "You've captured the whole Gordon Jenkins thing, right there." It was written on December 27, 1983, about five months before he died, and it read like this:

"There is a very dull feeling that I get, listening to men who spent a lot of years and money telling me at length what they *don't* know. I always feel like I should give them a little pat and say, 'That's OK, Doc, I didn't know it, either.' What they don't know is what causes ALS and how to cure it. They sort of tell you in a nice way that it's fatal, give you that horrible half-smile and leave, before I can get to my pad and write, 'Fatal for those other people, maybe, but *not me.*'

"I have a good, sound reason why this disease is not going to kill me. I just plain and simple don't want to go. I have left many a party early, but not this one. I've always thought of death as a beginning, not an end, and while it might be fun to beat you all there, and kind of get things ready, I want the years with Beverly more.

"Any musician who has ever seen me conduct a really hard dramatic show can verify this: I sort of screw both feet onto the podium, take a tight grip on the baton and say to myself, 'OK, you sonsabitches, let's get it on the road. I am Gordon Jenkins, and I am the best there is at what I do.' I won't say I never made a mistake. If someone is stupid enough to point one out, I would simply say, 'Oh, *that,*' and sidle towards the bar (I held the fast-sidle record at NBC for years).

"I was told I couldn't sell folk music. I did. I was told that orchestrations for a Broadway show had to play the melody. I said no, they were wrong, and they were. The cat with the scythe had a good shot at me in a tunnel on Kanan Road. He didn't take me then, and he's not going to get me now.

"So skip the obituaries, but keep an eye on the medical journals. That's where you'll see my name, because I am going to win. You can bet your ass."

It was through such determination that "Geritol Jazz" was born, a big-band miracle through the magic of over-dubbing, right there in our home studio. Gor played the piano, bass and electric-guitar parts and keyed a digital drum machine to the proper style and pace. Bruce Hudson played five trumpet parts and Wayne Songer, who went all the way back to the first Louis Armstrong date (1949) with my father, handled three sax parts and two clarinet. They played old standards with a solid Count Basie influence, dubbing and mixing and adjusting until they felt they had it right. Occasionally my dad would mix in some applause, from a sound-effects record, to make it sound like an audience was going crazy. They had no intention of selling the recordings or even exposing them in any way; they were just three old geezers, well into their seventies, going out in style.

"I hadn't seen the horn in five years, but I picked it up pretty good," Hudson told me. "Gordon had picked up a little computer where he could type in his comments from the control room, and we could read 'em on a TV screen in the studio. We never, ever discussed Gordon's illness; hell, he was too busy cranking out our arrangements. He'd see the list, ask what key, sit down and play it. Didn't make any difference to him. Wayne was an absolute genius, and always had been. He could play thirty-two consecutive bars of ad-lib, and have it like a story. If you said, 'Let's do it again,' he'd do it completely different. Wouldn't be one thing he'd done the first time. He worked for Phil Harris a long time, played for years on the Jack Benny show, always knocking everybody out."

At one point, when Hudson had left for his European vacation, Gor took a playful stab at the reality of his situation. He pretended that he had died—something about a doctor ogling a nurse's breasts and making a faulty incision—and was off to "the harp farm," as he called it. So he sat down to write Hudson and tell him all about it:

"It's not bad at all up here. For one thing, I've got a lot more friends than where I formerly was. Charlie [LaVere] and I go around and listen to impromptu concerts with Louis, Big Sid Catlett, Jack Jenney, Bix, Bunny, you wouldn't believe it.

"I've spent a lot of time with Charlie Griffard [his lead trumpet player for years]. He asked me who had been playing first for me, and when I said Bruce Hudson, it got quite a laugh. When I told him you were also on second, third, fourth and fifth, he started backing away, looking frantically for a sedative. He finally said, 'OK, Bruce Hudson, but what if you want a real high note?' I filled him in further, but I don't think he's really convinced. He just wanders around muttering, 'Bruce Hudson ... Bruce *Hudson?*'

"They have no factories up here, hence no recording equipment. However, the guys generally gather out in a beautiful forest and play. I'm not sure how it's done, but you can go out to the same place later, sit down and hear the whole thing again. See, there are no instruments here, either. Louis just fingers the air, or Jack moves his hand like there's a slide in it, and you hear the sounds perfectly. I mean, you haven't died until you hear Pee Wee Russell squeak with no clarinet in his hand.

"Same sort of thing with golf. What you do, you stand on the tee, no club or ball, and *wish* where you want your drive to go. Like on earth, it doesn't always get there, but they put a little glow on it, so it's easy to find. When I asked the pro about the course, he told me, 'The closest a golf club came to here was when Bob Spink five-putted number six at Las Posas.'"

In closing, he told Hudson, "Can't wait for you to get here. I can see you now, leaning against a tree, empty-handed, practicing long tones. Keep a good eye on Beverly for me, and if you can hurry her up here in a non-painful way, I wouldn't mind."

If only it could have happened that way. Gor put a defiantly personal stamp on certain death, battling it with flair and good humor. "Even at the very end, his eyes were glistening," said Nick Perito. "He still had that look. Three days before he died, we had some guys in the control room trying to fix some problems they'd had with overdubbing. I tried to help out and they're like, 'No, we know all about it.' Gordon grabbed his pad and wrote, 'I'll give you 8 to 5 they fuck it up.' And sure enough, they did. They completely erased a track."

I had come to the house for the final days, vague as the time period seemed, and managed to time it right. The last time I saw him, he was lying down on his bed upstairs, graced by the afternoon sun, stripped of everything but his mind. I held his hand as we talked, and at one point I felt just the slightest movement of his finger, a farewell of sorts. "I feel like I'm running out of life," he had written just hours before, and he left us that first of May 1984. Something startled me at around 3 a.m. in my downstairs bedroom, and I watched two men carry his body out of the house on a stretcher. I did not get up. All the preparations had been made well in advance. I eased back down and went about the business of not sleeping.

My mother's life effectively ended that night—and she had twelve years to live. She got an occasional smile out of the notes he'd left behind, but she couldn't play Gordon's music; too painful. She was more fond of "Nostalgia Rides Again," the lively series of cassettes he made of blues records from the 1920s and 1930s. That was her whole upbringing, those records, and they took her back to a time when she was youthful and lovely and singing her heart out.

Beverly was losing her mind, quite literally, and the scene was sort of wacky for a while. She'd call up phrases from a half-century back, like "I'll put in with ya," "Hip-Hoo, Home Brew" or "And now, a word from Charles Martin," stuff that completely baffled me but sounded pretty good. Even when things got grim—she once wandered into the living room, dropped a great big turd on my easy chair and left it there, inside her diaper—we tried to laugh and forget about it. She certainly did.

"I thought I had Alzheimer's," sportswriter Jim Murray (a long-time friend of the family) told me in 1991, "because I kept losing stuff, couldn't find my car keys, that sort of thing. The doctor told me, 'You're not close. Alzheimer's is when you can't remember what the keys are for.'"

Somebody suggested that she take a long trip to Hawaii with her equally broken sister, Julia, to get away from it all. And they did, taking a place near Waikiki for three solid months. She sent the occasional upbeat postcard, and I really felt we'd see a change when she got back home. When we got back from the airport that night, Beverly went upstairs, looked into my father's empty bedroom and came back out, in complete shock. "He's still not here," she said, and in my mind I heard one of those low-register, horror-film chords banged angrily on the piano, a dissonant reminder that something—everything—was terribly wrong. I got severe chills right then; I get them now. If there was any doubt about the tenor of that house, for the rest of time, it was thoroughly removed that night.

"I kept calling her," Kay Thompson said, "but I felt she'd lost everything when she lost Gordon. It was a hovering thought, from the sound of her voice. She wasn't really saying anything."

By around 1990 we had to deal with a disturbing remake of her countenance, her personality, anything that ever mattered before. She could identify only a few faces—I was glad to be one of them—and had lost all sense of tact and diplomacy. Loyal friends wanted badly to see her, to reminisce about Gordon, to get that heady rush of ocean breeze, warm sand and salt air, but they just couldn't bring themselves to go. They could not see Beverly that way, so completely absent.

There was no way it could get any worse, but it did. Over her last two years, she didn't recognize a soul, including me. I'd look into her face and get an absolute blank wall, someone who appeared to have been staring into nothingness for months. I spent long nights talking about it with Jack Pritchett, who had been entrusted as the caretaker of my parents' estate. One heartbreaking day—March 18, 1996—came the inevitable move, something we could barely acknowledge in our hearts, yet had to address as the most sensible solution. We moved her to a rest home, a truly beautiful and first-rate place overlooking the blue Pacific on Point Dume. I'll never forget the excruciating agony of wheeling her past her rose garden one last time, not knowing what she might be thinking, and a truly startling thing that happened that day. Someone turned on her trusty radio in the new digs, and as if by magic, it was playing "September of My Years."

"That's Gordon and Frank Sinatra," my mother said. She hadn't spoken a word in months.

She wasn't far from the end. It came quietly that December, without any pain or fuss. There was a cremation and I took the same path I'd followed in Gor's passing, swimming the ashes out beyond the Trancas breakers and tossing them to the wind. And there was a wonderful day not long thereafter at a fashionable Malibu restaurant, where we commandeered the main room and had a thoroughly modern-day ceremony, some sixty friends sharing beverages and their favorite Beverly stories. I'll never forget that day because I was in charge, the master of ceremonies, and I'm the worst public speaker of all time. I choke up from outright terror on my way to the podium, leaving myself with just enough breath for "Ugh" or a helpless gasping sound. But something happened that day; it was as if my mom's hospitable, diplomatic spirit descended into my soul. I was Alan Ludden, the life of the party, not a word out of place. Only the best things seemed relevant right then, and while it was a gut-wrenching experience to eventually sell the house and release a fifty-year Malibu connection, I heeded the words of Chris Finnegan, a dear friend who told me, "Change is good, no matter how old you are. You'll get over it. Life will be better."

That's how my father always looked at things. He told jokes when his house burned down. He was certain he'd be the first to beat ALS. In the wake of a shattering car crash, he rounded up two fellow codgers and created a full-scale band within the confines of his house. Sadness may have been his theme, but he never actively shared it. Life was far too good, too exciting, too rich in possibilities. Through his influence, I've always thought that a tremendous, life-changing development could happen at any moment. And in a crazy way, I feel that Gordon Jenkins still looks after me.

On the 15th of May 1998, the night after Sinatra died, I was in New York on assignment, heading to a downtown restaurant to meet Steve Fainaru, the noted author and journalist and a close friend for many years. Following an old custom, I jumped out of the cab about four blocks early to catch a little atmosphere. Suddenly, at the corner of Perhaps and Who Knows, I heard Sinatra and my father in "It Was a Very Good Year." Not faintly, but with amazing volume and clarity. I felt as if I'd stepped into a nightclub and they were performing it right on stage.

My destination was straight ahead, but with no real say in the matter, I instinctively turned right. *"When I was seventeen . . . it was a very good year. . . ."* Where the hell was it coming from? The more I approached the middle of the block, the more powerful and resonant it became. Finally I looked up, about three floors' worth, and saw that someone had rigged some very professional-looking speakers from an apartment sound system. It was a farewell tribute, filling the New York air with Sinatra and (as I imagined it) lasting the whole day and night.

I lingered there, frozen and transported. It took me several minutes to compose myself and get back in real time. But that's the thing: It *was* reality. The past was present and the musical dead were alive, the sound as fresh as the moment it was recorded. Above all else, that's my inheritance. He's right around the corner.

FRANK SINATRA

February 8, 1988

Mr. Bruce Jenkins
30746 Broad Beach Road
Malibu, Calif. 90265

Dear Bruce,

Thank you very much for sending me
your nice note and the beautiful
words written by your Dad...It was
painful for me to read - it brought
back so many warm and wonderful
memories of him and for that,I thank
you for sharing it with me.

Take care of yourself, Bruce, and
please give your Mom my love...we'll
talk soon.

Warmest regards,

Francis Albert

Selected Discography

The Complete Works with Frank Sinatra

WHERE ARE YOU?
Reprise, April 10, 29 and May 1, 1957

Where Are You?
The Night We Called It a Day
I Cover the Waterfront
Maybe You'll Be There
Laura
Lonely Town
Autumn Leaves
I'm a Fool to Want You
I Think of You
Where Is the One?
There's No You
Baby, Won't You Please Come Home?

A JOLLY CHRISTMAS FROM FRANK SINATRA
Capitol, July 10, 16–17, 1957

Jingle Bells
The Christmas Song
Mistletoe and Holly
I'll Be Home for Christmas
The Christmas Waltz
Have Yourself a Merry Little Christmas
The First Noel
Hark! The Herald Angels Sing
O Little Town of Bethlehem

Adeste Fidelis
It Came Upon a Midnight Clear
Silent Night

NO ONE CARES
Capitol, March 24–26 and May 14, 1959

When No One Cares
A Cottage for Sale
Stormy Weather
Where Do You Go?
A Ghost of a Chance
Here's That Rainy Day
I Can't Get Started
Why Try to Change Me Now?
Just Friends
I'll Never Smile Again
None But the Lonely Heart
(added on CD, 1991)
The One I Love Belongs to Somebody Else
This Was My Love*
I Could Have Told You*
You Forgot All the Words*
*Nelson Riddle arrangements

ALL ALONE
Reprise, January 15–17, 1962

All Alone
The Girl Next Door
Are You Lonesome Tonight?
Charmaine
What'll I Do?

When I Lost You
Oh, How I Miss You Tonight
Indiscreet
Remember
Together
The Song Is Ended
Come Waltz with Me (released later on CD)

SEPTEMBER OF MY YEARS
Reprise, April 13–14, 22 and May 27, 1965

The September of My Years
How Old Am I?
Don't Wait Too Long
It Gets Lonely Early
This Is All I Ask
Last Night When We Were Young
The Man in the Looking Glass
It Was a Very Good Year
When the Wind Was Green
Hello, Young Lovers
I See It Now
Once Upon a Time
September Song

SINATRA '65
Reprise, 1965
Compilation includes Jenkins's arrangement and conducting on
"Tell Her (You Love Her Each Day)"

SINATRA, A MAN AND HIS MUSIC
(NBC Television, November 24, 1965, shared the conducting with
Nelson Riddle)

A MAN AND HIS MUSIC, PART II
(NBC Television, December 7, 1966, shared conducting with Riddle)

THE WORLD WE KNEW
Reprise, 1967
(Jenkins arranged and conducted "Born Free," "You Are There" and "This Is My Love")

OL' BLUE EYES IS BACK
Reprise, dates in June and August 1973

> You Will Be My Music
> You're So Right
> Winners*
> Nobody Wins
> Send in the Clowns
> Dream Away*
> Let Me Try Again*
> There Used to Be a Ballpark
> Noah
> *Jenkins conducting, Don Costa arrangement

SOME NICE THINGS I'VE MISSED
Reprise, 1974
(Jenkins arranged and conducted "The Summer Knows" and "If")

TRILOGY: PAST, PRESENT AND FUTURE
Reprise, December 17–18, 1979
(Jenkins arranged and conducted "The Future")

> What Time Does the Next Miracle Leave?
> World War None

Song Without Words
The Future
I've Been There
Before the Music Ends

THE FIRST DEADLY SIN
(Film, 1980, with Sinatra and Faye Dunaway; wrote musical score)

SHE SHOT ME DOWN
Reprise, 1981, dates in April, July, August and September
(Arranged by Jenkins, Don Costa and Nelson Riddle)

Good Thing Going
Hey Look, No Crying
Thanks for the Memory*
A Long Night*
Bang, Bang*
Monday Morning Quarterback*
South—To a Warmer Place*
But I Loved Her*
The Gal That Got Away/It Never Entered My
   Mind
*Jenkins arrangements and conducting

I SING THE SONGS
Reprise (Italy), 1982
Compilation used Jenkins arrangements of "Empty Tables" and
"The Hurt Doesn't Go Away," from 1973, and "The Saddest Thing
of All," 1975

THE COMPLETE REPRISE STUDIO RECORDINGS
1995
    Compilation used Jenkins arrangements of "Walk Away," 1973, and "Everything Happens To Me" and "Just As Though You Were Here," 1974

With Louis Armstrong

SATCHMO IN STYLE
Verve, 2001 release (original Decca LP: May 1959)
    From the Jenkins-Armstrong recording sessions of 1949, 1951, 1952 and 1954
    Among the personnel: Billy Butterfield and Yank Lawson, trumpets; Red Ballard, trombone; Eddie Miller, tenor sax; Milt Yaner, alto sax; Charlie LaVere, piano; Carl Kress, guitar; Cozy Cole and Nick Fatool, drums; Velma Middleton, vocal

    Blueberry Hill
    It's All in the Game
    Jeannine (I Dream of Lilac Time)
    Chloe
    Indian Love Call
    Listen to the Mockin' Bird
    That Lucky Old Sun
    The Whiffenpoof Song
    Trees
    Bye and Bye
    Spooks
    When It's Sleepy Time Down South
    You're Just in Love
    If
    I Want a Big Butter and Egg Man

With Nat Cole

LOVE IS THE THING
Capitol, 1957

> When I Fall in Love
> Stardust
> Stay as Sweet as You Are
> Where Can I Go Without You?
> Maybe It's Because I Love You Too Much
> Love Letters
> Ain't Misbehavin'
> I Thought About Marie
> At Last
> It's All in the Game
> When Sunny Gets Blue
> Love Is the Thing

THE VERY THOUGHT OF YOU
Capitol, 1958

> The Very Thought of You
> But Beautiful
> Impossible
> I Wish I Knew the Way to Your Heart
> I Found a Million-Dollar Baby
> Magnificent Obsession
> My Heart Tells Me
> Paradise
> This Is All I Ask
> Cherie, I Love You
> Making Believe You're Here
> Cherchez la Femme
> For All We Know

The More I See You
Don't Blame Me*
There Is No Greater Love*
*added for CD release

WHERE DID EVERYONE GO?
Capitol, 1963

Where Did Everyone Go?
Say It Isn't So
If Love Ain't There
When the World Was Young
Am I Blue?
Someone to Tell It To
The End of a Love Affair
I Keep Going Back to Joe's
Laughing on the Outside
No, I Don't Want Her
Spring Is Here
That's All There Is

NAT KING COLE/GORDON JENKINS: SPIRITUALS
With the First Church of Deliverance Choir
Capitol, 1959

Every Time I Feel the Spirit
I Want to Be Ready
Sweet Hour of Prayer
Ain't Gonna Study War No More
I Found the Answer
Standin' in the Need of Prayer
Oh Mary Don't You Weep
Go Down Moses

Nobody Knows the Trouble I've Seen
In the Sweet By and By
I Couldn't Hear Nobody Pray
Steal Away

With Judy Garland

ALONE
Capitol, 1957

By Myself
Little Girl Blue
Me and My Shadow
Among My Souvenirs
I Got a Right to Sing the Blues
I Get the Blues When it Rains
Mean to Me
How About Me
Just a Memory
Blue Prelude
Happy New Year
Then You've Never Been Blue

THE LETTER
Capitol, 1959

Beautiful Trouble
Love in the Village
Charlie's Blues (vocal: Charlie LaVere)
The Worst Kind of Man
That's All There Is (There Isn't Any More)
Love in Central Park
The Red Balloon
The Fight

At the Stroke of Midnight
Come Back

GORDON JENKINS'S COMPOSITIONS

(Selected List)

Blue Prelude (words)
P.S. I Love You (music)
Goodbye
You Have Taken My Heart (music)
When a Woman Loves a Man (music)
Blue Evening (words)
San Fernando Valley
This Is All I Ask
Homesick, That's All
Daylight Savings Blues
By Nightfall
How Old Am I?
I Thought About Marie
The Red Balloon
I Live Alone
Trilogy ("The Future")
Happy New Year
That's All There Is
In the Heat of the Day
I Know What Let's Do
Herman's Tune
Crescent City Blues
I Feel Like a New Man
But I Loved Her

MANHATTAN TOWER
(Complete version, Capitol LP, 1956)

> Magical City
> Happiness Cocktail
> I'm Learnin' My Latin
> Once Upon a Dream
> Never Leave Me
> This Close to the Dawn
> Repeat After Me
> The Magic Fire
> Married I Can Always Get
> The Statue of Liberty
> The Party
> New York's My Home

SEVEN DREAMS
(Decca, 1954)

> The Professor
> The Conductor
> The Caretaker
> The Cocktail Party
> The Pink Houseboat
> The Nightmare
> The Girl on the Rock

Acknowledgments

I ONCE KNEW A MAN NAMED BUS. His full name was Harold Saidt, a genial Philadelphia sportswriter who doubled as a nightclub singer, and he loved my father's music. On the few occasions we'd meet, Bus would break into a few bars of *This Is All I Ask* ("Beautiful girls ... walk a little slower ..."), and that was our connection. Over the years, as the completion of this project seemed little more than a rumor, it was the sort of thing that kept me going.

Scott Price, known as S.L. to his *Sports Illustrated* readers, was a pillar of conviction. He absolutely insisted that I finish the book, and that it would be published. Over cocktails in the taverns of London, New York and Miami, he engaged me in spirited conversation about the music that truly matters.

Heartfelt thanks to Richard Grossinger, Kathy Glass, Julie Brand, Mark Ouimet, Paula Morrison, Debbie Matsumoto and the rest of the staff at North Atlantic Books/Frog Ltd., for their kindness and understanding.

Thanks, also:

To my oldest girls, Angelica and Haleanna, who have genuine musical talent in my father's tradition, and to their mother, Dawn, who raised them so well.

To Jack Pritchett, for all of the good days in Malibu and a lifetime's worth of friendship, and to all of the Pritchetts, who lived just down the way on Broad Beach Road.

To Lon Porter, a friend since the beginning of time, for giving the book its most incisive editing.

To Rich, Rob, Marguerite and Bob Stevens, who dug my dad's music to the bone.

To Cal and Adele, and Carmen, and the Ulyates, and Leslie and

Phoebe, who knew the pleasures of the Jenkins home before it burned down.

To Susan, Gordon Jr. and Page Jenkins, who always resisted the temptation to bop me on top of the head.

To Steve Flink and Joel Drucker, for the inspiration and the Altoids.

To Steve LaVere, son of Charlie, for inviting me into the halls of his record collection.

To Sandy Singer, the nationally syndicated disc jockey and a student of my father's career, for his constant support, advice and reference material.

To Joe Shea, one of the great newspaper editors and an even better man, for giving the book his attention.

To radio personalities Fred Hall, Bill Stewart, Wink Martindale, Chuck Cecil and Pete Smith, for taking the time to interview my father. Those tapes bring his voice to life.

To Lyle Spencer, Bill Madden, Steve Kupka, Bud Geracie, Roger Angell, Jake Whidbee, Andrew Dimas, Gary Radnich, Tom Stantonelli, Brian Murphy, Eric Colby, Michael Crapser, Mark and Steve Fainaru, Scott and Judge Murphy, Florence Stanton, Don Olivet, Ron Bergman, Bruce Schoenfeld, John Gaines, Chris Hummel, Michael Wallace, Ed O'Brien, Andrew Blauner and Chris Unruh, for contributions of all kinds.

And most of all to Martha, my beloved wife of eleven years, and our beautiful daughter, Molly. Every man should be so lucky.

Index